Total English

Pearson Education Limited
Edinburgh Gate
Harlow
Essex CM20 2JE
England
and Associated Companies throughout the world.

www.pearsonelt.com

© Pearson Education Limited 2012

First published 2012
Third impression 2012

ISBN: 978-1-4082-6719-6
Book with Active Book and MyEnglishLab pack

Set in MetaPlusBook-Roman
Printed in Slovakia by Neografia

Acknowledgements

The publishers and authors would like to thank the following people and institutions for their feedback and comments during the development of the material:

Reporters

Serpil Acar M.E.V. Özel Basınköy High School, Istanbul, Turkey; Victoria Bordera Lorono, EOI de San Fernando de Henares, Madrid, Spain; Dennis Delany, Excel College, Manchester, UK; Lily Evans, Folkuniversitet, Stockholm, Sweden; Yolanda González Molano, Escuelas Oficiales de Idiomas de Madrid, Spain; Luis Alfredo Grasso, Centro Universitario de Idiomas, Argentina; Pawel Dominik Madej, The School of Foreign Languages, Warsaw University, Poland; Antonio Mota Cosano, EOI Arganda del Rey, Madrid, Spain; Sanjay Nanwani, Universidad Externado de Colombia, Bogotá, Colombia; Maria Pophristova, Warsaw School of Social Science and Humanities, Poland; Maria Josep Porta de Lafuente, Escola Oficial d'Idiomes de Figueres, Spain; Maria Angels Sanz Borell, Spain

We are grateful to the following for permission to reproduce copyright material:

Logos

Logo 8.1 from Slow Movement logo, http://www.slowmovement. com/, © Copyright 2010 Footprint Choices. All rights reserved; Company details and logo in Writing Bank 1, www.couchsurfing.org copyright © CouchSurfing International, Inc, "CouchSurfing" and "CouchSurfer" are registered and unregistered service marks of CouchSurfing International, Inc. – a Non-Profit Organization.

In some instances we have been unable to trace the owners of copyright material, and we would appreciate any information that would enable us to do so.

Photo acknowledgements

The publisher would like to thank the following for their kind permission to reproduce their photographs:
(Key: b-bottom; c-centre; l-left; r-right; t-top)

Alamy Images: Ahmad Faizal Yahya 12tl, irishphoto 106tl, Robert Slade / Manor Photography 120tr; Axiom Photographic Agency Ltd: Jenny Acheson 39bl, Steve J Benbow 99tc; Corbis: BRENDAN MCDERMID / Reuters 32tl, Edward Bock 9bl, epa / Jens Kalaene 56tl, Flirt / George Shelley 49, Gary Houlder 119cl, Lawrence Manning 19cl, Michael Prince 50bl, Mike Hutchings 62tr, moodboard plus 19t, Neville Elder 30-31tc, OLIVER BERG 50r, People Avenue / Stephane Cardinale 34br, Sven Hagolani 102tc, Vera Berger 16tl; Deborah Metcalfe, Blue Eye FX Productions; Deborah Metcalfe, Blue Eye FX Productions; Deborah Metcalfe, Blue Eye FX Productions: 40; Don Campbell Inc: 24cr; Electronic Arts Inc: 64tr; Mary Evans Picture Library: 110bc, 110br; www.eyevinearchive. com: Joel Anderson 70tr, 70cr; Getty Images: B Busco 10tc (C), Blend Images / Hill Street Studios 10br, Briony Campbell 50cr, Bruce Laurance 134cl, Cavan Images, LLC 142tr, Chris Williams 31, Clive Mason 79bl, Colin Hawkins 76tr, Daly and Newton 93cr, David Lees 138bl, DK Stock / Marc Rochon 9tl, DreamPictures 109cl, Evan Agostini 116c, flashfilm 89cl, Francis Hammond 119tl, Frans Lemmens 99t, Gerard Fritz 81cl, Ghislain & Marie David de Lossy 79cl, Giantstep Inc, Giantstep Inc, Giantstep Inc 14b, Greg Trott 125t, Haywood Magee 55br, isifa 19tl, Jim Franco 135cr, Joe Robbins 109t, John Robbins 73tr, Juan Silva 69cl, Jupiterimages 106cr, Karen Moskowitz 75tl, Michael Dunning 99, Paul Chesley 106tr, Paul Conrath 10b, Paul Natkin / WireImage 136cl, Ron Krisel 143tl, Sami Sarkis 52cr, Steve Raymer 9t, Steven Puetzer 8bc/5, Taxi 96tr, TORSTEN BLACKWOOD 90tc, Vincent Besnault 130cr, Vincent Besnault, Vincent Besnault, Vincent Besnault 130cr, White Packert 72tl, Yellow Dog Productions 76cr, 102t (C); Ronald Grant Archive: 105t, 105bl; iStockphoto: FotografiaBasica 14cl, FotografiaBasica 14cl, jsemeniuk 137br, milosluz 137bl, P.Wei 102tl; Kobal Collection Ltd: 20TH CENTURY FOX 105br, COLUMBIA / DANJAQ / EON 21bl; Lebrecht Music and Arts Photo Library: 24tc; Leo Dickinson: 40cl; Lonely Planet Images: Alfredo Maiquez 66c/2, Frans Lemmens 39tc; Pearson Education Ltd: 79tl, 99cl; Photolibrary.com: 4x5 Coll-Francisco Cruz - 8bl/6, 66tr/3, adp Photostudios GmbH 119t, Amit Somvanshi, Amit Somvanshi, Amit Somvanshi, Amit Somvanshi 82tr, Chad Ehlers 66cr/4, 138cl, Daniel Hurst 29t, Daniel Vega 140, Dennis Hardley 66cl/1, Digital Vision 9cl, Dominic Dibbs 29bl, Dr Wilfried Bahnmüller 8tr/3, Fancy 49t, Ferebee Brandon 8tc/2, Gavin Hellier 144tr, Imagesource 102 (B), 102br, Imagesource 102 (B), 102br, James McCormick 42cr, John Warburton-Lee 59bl, Larry Dale Gordon 60t, Mike Kemp 76br, Monica & Michael Sweet 135tr, moodboard moodboard 19b, North Wind Picture Archives 24tr, Ralph Kerpa 29tl, Rene Mattes 29cl, Robert Glenn 109bl, Ted Wilcox 39tl, Werner Bachmeier 119bl; Plainpicture Ltd: clack 14, Jim Erickson 89t; Reuters: Dylan Martinez 84tc, Luis Galdamez 133br, Mario Anzuoni 22tr, Mike Segar 79tc; Rex Features: c.W.Disney / Everett 34bc, c.Warner Br / Everett , c.Warner Br / Everett / Rex Features, , 114tr, Camilla Morandi 129cr, Giuliano Bevilacqua 116tl, Image Source 50cl, 86tc, Image Source 50cl, 86tc, Juergen Hasenkop 56t, Maggie Hardie 116tc, Neale Haynes 40tr, Sipa Press 56cr, Sipa Press 54tr, 54cr, Stewart Cook 136cr; Science Photo Library Ltd: 89tl; The Advertising Archives: Image courtesy of The Advertising Archives 109tl; TopFoto: The Granger Collection 110otr

Cover images: *Front*: Photolibrary.com: George Hammerstein

All other images © Pearson Education

Every effort has been made to trace the copyright holders and we apologise in advance for any unintentional omissions. We would be pleased to insert the appropriate acknowledgement in any subsequent edition of this publication.

Illustrated by Ian Mitchell, Jode Thompson and Kveta (All from *Three in a box*).

NEW

Total English

PRE-INTERMEDIATE

Students' Book with ActiveBook and MyEnglishLab
plus Vocabulary Trainer

eBOOK & LMS   VOCAB TRAINER

Araminta Crace
with Richard Acklam

A2-B1

Contents

Contents

Contents

Contents

Do you know...?

1 Do you know grammar terms? Complete the table with the words in **bold** from sentences 1–10.

a)	pronoun	*They* (sentence 2)
b)	countable noun	
c)	comparative adjective	
d)	possessive pronoun	
e)	modal verb	
f)	auxiliary verb	
g)	contraction	
h)	uncountable noun	
i)	article	
j)	Present Perfect	

1 She is **a** doctor.
2 ~~They~~ are very generous.
3 This book is **yours**.
4 **Does** she eat meat?
5 You **can** smoke outside.
6 Keith **has written** four novels.
7 How much **water** do you drink every day?
8 Could you give this **pen** to him?
9 This watch is **cheaper than** the last one.
10 **He's** quite late.

2 **a** Do you know parts of speech? Complete the table with the words from the box.

> at   beautiful   carefully   cinema   down
> factory   give up   green   happy   listen
> look after   quickly   sister   ~~write~~

1 noun	
2 verb	*write*
3 phrasal verb	
4 adjective	
5 adverb	
6 preposition	

b Complete the sentences with words from the box above.

1 My _____ is nearly three years older than me.
2 We stayed in a really _____ hotel.
3 Please don't look _____ me like that!
4 Please _____ to me very carefully.
5 I ran as _____ as I could.
6 I've decided to _____ chocolate in the New Year.

3 Do you know pronunciation terms? Look at the words in the box and answer the questions about each word.

> chocolate   cinema   sister   factory

1 How many syllables are there?
2 Where is the main stress?

4 Match the topic words with the pictures. What other vocabulary do you know related to these topics? Make a list.

> food   work   ~~travel~~   money   music   home

travel

5 Do you know classroom language? Match the questions (1–8) with the replies (a–h).

1 What does 'charity' mean? ☐ *f*
2 How do you spell 'exercise'? ☐
3 Can you say that again, please? ☐
4 What page is that on? ☐
5 Could you speak up a bit, please? ☐
6 What's the answer to number 5? ☐
7 What's our homework? ☐
8 How do you pronounce the eighth and eleventh words in line 5 of the text on page 10? ☐

a Page 18, at the end of Unit 1.
b Do exercises 3, 4 and 5 on page 64.
c I don't know. We should ask Mario. He's good at grammar.
d /ˈkwaɪət/ and /kwaɪt/
e E–X–E–R–C–I–S–E
f It's an organisation that helps people.
g Of course. It is quite noisy in here.
h Sure, no problem. All of it or just the last part?

24 hours

Lead-in

1 Work in pairs and discuss the questions.

1 What is your favourite time of day/day of the week? Why?
2 Which time of day/day of the week do you dislike the most? Why?

2 Make verb phrases with the words from A and B. Which phrases can you see in the photos? Which phrases are not in the photos?

meet some friends

A

> chat   check   do (x2)   get up   go (x4)   have (x4)   listen   make
> ~~meet~~   read   stay   take   watch

B

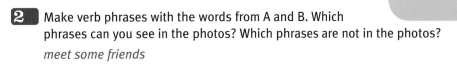

> to bed late   breakfast/lunch/dinner   a bus/train   early   your emails
> in for the evening   some exercise   a family meal   ~~some friends~~   a lie-in
> a magazine/newspaper   a nap   nothing   on the phone   to the radio
> shopping   for a swim   a take-away   TV/a DVD   for a walk

3 **a** Look at the verb phrases from exercise 2 again.

Write **D** next to the things you do every day.
Write **W** next to the things you only do at the weekend.
Write **S** next to the things you sometimes do.
Write **N** next to the things you never do.

b In pairs, compare your answers. Do you do the same things?

A 3   B ☐   C ☐   D ☐

Reading

1 **a** Match the photos (A–D) with the descriptions (1–4).

1 You are a 'party animal'. You like going out late and dancing. You like spending your free time with friends.

2 You are a 'workaholic'. You spend most of your time working and you aren't interested in other things. You don't go out much.

3 You are a 'couch potato'. You like staying in and eating junk food. You spend a lot of time watching television.

4 You are a 'culture vulture'. You like reading and learning new things. You spend your free time at museums and art galleries.

b Read the text. Is each person a 'party animal', a 'workaholic', a 'couch potato' or a 'culture vulture'?

2 Complete the sentences with *Marek*, *Lola* or *Henry*.

Henry doesn't like getting up early at the weekend.

1 _____ likes having a lot to eat for breakfast.

2 _____ doesn't usually have breakfast at home on Saturdays.

3 _____ likes checking his emails during breakfast.

4 _____ likes art and music.

5 _____ likes relaxing in the park.

6 _____ spends a lot of time at work.

7 _____ likes going for a walk on Sundays.

8 _____ likes watching TV on Sundays.

3 Choose someone in your family or one of your friends. Is his/her typical weekend like Marek, Lola or Henry's? Why/Why not?

What do you like doing at the weekend?

I like getting up early on Saturdays – usually at about 7:00 a.m. I have coffee and toast for breakfast and, at the same time, I turn my computer on. I like checking my emails regularly because I get so many of them. I have a very busy job, so I sometimes go to work on Saturdays. The office is quiet and I quite like working on my own. On Sundays, I like going ice skating and I sometimes go bowling with some friends in the new place not far from the centre of Krakow. But I do some work in the afternoons, too. My job is really interesting, so I don't mind working a lot. My girlfriend says I work all the time – but I prefer working to doing nothing!
Marek Kowalczyk, Krakow, Poland

I can't stand doing nothing, so I get up early on Saturdays. I really like having breakfast in a café, so I take a bus into town at about 9:00 a.m. I'm quite keen on art, so after breakfast I often go to an exhibition with some friends. I do different things on Saturday evenings. I don't like staying out late or going clubbing, but I love going to a concert or to the theatre. Actually, my favourite evening is going to a musical with friends. On Sundays, I go for a walk. Sometimes, I go on a guided walk around a different part of my city. I like learning about the history of Barcelona – it's a really interesting city.
Lola Gutierrez, Barcelona, Spain

I don't like getting up early at the weekends, so I usually have a lie-in – sometimes until about 10:30 a.m.! I absolutely love having a big breakfast on Saturdays. I don't have many hobbies and I really hate the gym or doing exercise, but I sometimes go to a park in the afternoon. There are some nice parks in Manchester and I like meeting friends and just lying on the grass and doing nothing. I'm not very keen on going out on Saturday evenings. Sometimes I go to the cinema – but mostly I stay in, watch a DVD at home and have a take-away pizza. Sundays are similar to Saturdays for me – I like relaxing, getting up late and watching TV a lot.
Henry Rogers, Manchester, UK

Vocabulary | going out

4 Make verb phrases with the words from A and B. Look at the text from exercise 1b to help you.

go ice skating

A

> go   go on   go to

B

> bowling   the cinema   clubbing   a concert
> an exhibition   a guided walk/tour   ~~ice skating~~
> a musical   the theatre

5 Which activities from exercise 4 do you do in a typical weekend?

Grammar | likes and dislikes

6 Complete the Active grammar box. Check your answers with the text from exercise 1b.

Active grammar

☺☺☺ *I absolutely love having a big breakfast on Saturdays.*

1   ☺☺ *I _____ having breakfast in a café.*
    ☺ *I quite like working on my own.*

2   ☺ *I _____ art.*

3   ☹ *I _____ working a lot.*

4   ☹ *I _____ going out on Saturday evenings.*
    ☹ *I don't like getting up early at the weekends.*

5   ☹☹ *I _____ the gym.*
    ☹☹ *I can't stand doing nothing.*

After all the verb phrases, we use a verb in the -*ing* form or a noun.

---

see Reference page 17

7 Write complete sentences using the prompts. Don't forget to change the verb if necessary.

☺ bowling *I'm quite keen on bowling.*

1   ☺ musicals
2   ☹☹ my job
3   ☺☺ guided tours
4   ☹ go ice skating
5   ☺ do nothing
6   ☺ coffee
7   ☹☹ chat on the phone in English
8   ☺☺☺ go clubbing

Pronunciation | sentence stress

8 a 🔊 1.2 When we speak, we stress particular types of words. Listen to two sentences and <u>underline</u> six words in each sentence which are stressed.

1   I <u>really</u> like watching television and I absolutely love going to the cinema.

2   He quite likes going for a walk, but he really hates going to the gym.

b Tick (✓) the types of words which are stressed in exercise 8a.

a   content words, e.g. nouns and main verbs   ☐

b   non-content words, e.g. prepositions and pronouns   ☐

9 Make the sentences from exercise 7 true for you. Work in pairs and tell each other your sentences. Use appropriate sentence stress.

see Pronunciation bank page 148

Speaking

10 Work in pairs and follow the instructions.

Student A: ask your partner the questions below. Make a note of his/her answers. Then answer your partner's questions.

Student B: answer your partner's questions. Then ask your partner the questions on page 129. Make a note of his/her answers.

A: *What are your main hobbies and interests?*

B: *I absolutely love playing the guitar. I'm in a band and we practise every Tuesday.*

How do you like spending your free time?

1   What are your main hobbies/interests?

2   Do you like musicals? Why/Why not?

3   What three things do you like doing on your birthday? Why?

4   What three kinds of sport or exercise do you like? Why?

5   What three things do you like doing with your family? Why?

6   Do you like going to art exhibitions? Why/Why not?

7   What three things don't you like doing? Why?

11 Which description from exercise 1a best describes your partner? Do you agree with your partner's description of you? Why/Why not?

Grammar Present Simple; adverbs of frequency

Can do talk about how often you do things

Listening

1 **a** Look at the photos of Valentino Rossi. What job do you think he does?

b 🔵 1.3 Listen to the first part of a dialogue. Check your answer to exercise 1a and complete the fact file.

2 **a** What do you think Rossi does ...

1 on a race day?

2 on a normal day (when he doesn't go to a race)?

Use the ideas from the box to help you.

> go out in the evening
> go to bed early/late
> go to the gym
> get up early/late
> talk to his family/friends

b 🔵 1.4 Listen to the second part of the dialogue and check your ideas.

3 Listen to the second part of the dialogue again and answer the questions.

1 What time does Rossi get up on race days?

2 What time does Rossi get up on normal days?

3 Does he chat to his family in the morning?

4 What time does he go to the gym?

5 What three things does he do in the afternoon when he doesn't go to a race?

6 What does he do in the evening?

7 What time does he usually go to bed?

8 Does he go to bed early before a race day?

4 Work in pairs and discuss the questions.

1 Rossi says that his normal life is like being on holiday. Do you agree?

2 Would you like to have his lifestyle? Why/Why not?

Fact file

Name:	Valentino Rossi
Date of birth:	16 February 1979
Nationality:	
Job:	
Number of world championships:	

Vocabulary | describing your day and lifestyle

5 Complete the sentences about Rossi with the adjectives from the box. Use the notes in brackets to help you.

> boring   busy   ~~exciting~~   fun   lazy   relaxing   stressful
> unusual

Rossi's life is very _exciting_ ! (It makes him happy and interested.)

1 My life is really _____ ! (It is not interesting.)

2 His race days are very _____ . (There are a lot of things to do.)

3 His race days are _____ . (They make him worry a lot.)

4 'Normal' days for Rossi are _____ . (They make him calm and happy.)

5 He has quite a _____ lifestyle. (There is a lot of time to do nothing.)

6 His evenings are _____ . (There are a lot of enjoyable things to do.)

7 For a sportsman, his routine is _____ . (It isn't what most sportspeople do.)

6 Work in pairs and discuss the questions. Give details.

1 Do you think you have a stressful lifestyle?

2 Do you know anyone with an unusual daily routine?

3 Do you prefer lazy or very busy weekends?

4 What do you do for a relaxing evening?

5 What exciting things do you like doing?

Grammar | Present Simple; adverbs of frequency

7 **a** Look at part A of the Active grammar box.

1 Complete the rule with *habits* (things you often do) or *events* (things you do just once).

2 Complete the table with *do, does, don't* or *doesn't*. Check your answers with audioscript 1.4 on page 150.

b Look at part B of the Active grammar box and choose the correct words in *italics*.

Active grammar

Ⓐ We use the Present Simple to talk about _____ .

➕ *He goes to bed at two or three in the morning.*

➖ *I _____ chat to anyone in the mornings.*

❓ *What time _____ he get up?*
How often _____ you go to the gym?

Ⓑ We use adverbs of frequency to say how often we do something.

always, usually, often, sometimes, not often, hardly ever, never
100% ————————————————➤ *0%*

1 With regular verbs (positive and negative), adverbs of frequency generally come *before/after* the main verb.
I never get up late. I don't usually have breakfast.

2 With the verb *to be*, the adverb of frequency generally comes *before/after* the verb. *He's always quiet in the mornings.*

3 Longer adverb phrases generally come at the *beginning/end* of the sentence. *I go to the gym about once a week.*

---

see Reference page 17

8 Find the mistakes in each question and each answer and correct them.

1 **A:** Does you get up early? *Do you get up early?*
B: Yes, I do. I get up always early because I start work at 8:30.

2 **A:** Do your brother go to the gym?
B: Yes, he do. He usually goes to the gym three times a week.

3 **A:** You go clubbing at the weekends?
B: No, I not. I hardly ever go clubbing.

4 **A:** Your sister does go out after work?
B: No, she doesn't. But she phones sometimes her friends.

Pronunciation | *do/does*

9 🌐 1.5 We can say *do/does* in different ways. Listen and repeat.

1 **A:** Do you get up early? **B:** Yes, I do.
/də/ weak pronunciation   /duː/ strong pronunciation

2 **A:** Does your brother go to the gym? **B:** Yes, he does.
/dəz/ weak pronunciation   /dʌz/ strong pronunciation

see Pronunciation bank page 148

Speaking

10 **a** 🌐 1.6 Listen to two people talking about their habits. Which topics from the box do they mention?

> breakfast/lunch/dinner
> exercise/sport   getting up
> going out   going to bed
> school/work   watching TV

b Listen again and look at the How to... box. Number the phrases in the order you hear them.

How to... respond to information

Respond with surprise	*Do you?!*	☐
	Six o'clock!	1
	Are you serious?!	☐
Respond saying you are the same	*Really? Me too!*	☐
	Yes, that's the same as me!	☐
Respond saying you are different	*Really? I don't.*	☐

---

11 **a** Prepare to ask another student about his/her habits and how often he/she does things. Write five questions. Use the ideas from exercise 10.

b In pairs, ask and answer your questions. Use the phrases from the How to... box when you respond.

A: *What time do you usually go to bed?*

B: *I often go to bed at 10:00 p.m.*

A: *Really? I don't. That's very early! I never go to bed before midnight.*

Reading

1 In groups, discuss the questions.

1 How often do you use social networking sites, e.g. Facebook, Twitter and MSN?

2 How often do you buy things online or bid for things on eBay?

2 Read the text quickly. What two things is Joe looking at on eBay?

3 Read the text again and answer the questions.

1 Why does Joe want to buy a guitar?

2 Who is teaching him the guitar?

3 What is the price of the guitar at 10:47?

4 Where is Joe at the moment?

5 At 11:44, what is Joe's decision about his top price?

6 How much does Joe pay for the guitar?

4 Work in groups.

1 Look at what Debbie writes at 12:38. Do you agree with her? Why/Why not?

2 Think of one good thing and one bad thing about social networking sites. Discuss your ideas with your classmates.

Joe Duley

Wall   **Info**   **Photos**

Write something ...

Attach   **Share**

Joe Duley is looking at a fantastic guitar on eBay now. I really want to buy it!
14 September at 09:24 · Comment · Like

5 people like this

Rick Ferrell You don't need one. You don't play the guitar. Save your money!
09:41

Joe Duley I'm having guitar lessons at the moment – so I do need one.
10:04

Paula Schaffer Really? I can't believe it ... you're not musical at all! Why are you learning the guitar?
10:15

Joe Duley Hey! Give me a chance! I am musical! I love music! I listen to music every day! Ha ha! Anyway, I've got a lot of work these days ... . I'm working all the time and I want to do something relaxing at the end of the day.
10:26

Paula Schaffer Where are you having lessons?
10:30

Joe Duley I'm having lessons from someone I work with. I have a lesson every Thursday evening and it's great – but I need a guitar to practise on at home.
10:32

Rick Ferrell How much is it?
10:33

Joe Duley There is a bid for €50 now ... but lots of people are interested. Every time I look at the computer, the price goes up!
10:47

Rick Ferrell €50!! Don't do it! Are you bidding for it now?
11:01

Joe Duley I'm at work so it's a bit difficult. Right now, I'm doing two things at once ... . I'm writing a report and trying to buy a guitar – so I'm not writing a very good report! It's mad ... but there's one hour, twenty minutes left for the bidding.
11:15

Joe Duley OK ... I'm making my first bid now – €55. I know it's a lot of money ... but my decision is that €70 is my top price. So I'm OK at the moment.
11:44

Joe Duley Latest update: someone else is bidding €70! It's all happening very quickly now.
12:05

Paula Schaffer That's your top price so you can stop now.
12:14

Joe Duley There's five minutes left ... and I'm bidding €95 now ...
12:30

Rick Ferrell What?!
12:32

Joe Duley I got it! I got it! €150 isn't bad and it's a really exciting way of shopping.
12:35

Debbie Kirwan €150? Are you serious? I don't think shopping on eBay is exciting. You don't see what you're buying and you don't know how much you're paying. You're crazy! Good luck with the lessons, Joe!
12:38

Joe Duley There's a pair of ice skates here for €20 ... . What about ice skating? That's a relaxing thing to do.
13:06

Write a comment ...

Grammar | Present Continuous: now and around now

5 **a** Complete the Active grammar box with the headings.

1 Actions happening at this moment (Present Continuous)

2 Temporary actions happening 'around now' but not only at this moment (Present Continuous)

b Look at the text from exercise 2 again. Find more examples for each heading in the Active grammar box.

Active grammar

A _____

I'm having guitar lessons at the moment.
Why are you learning the guitar?

B _____

Joe Duley is looking at a fantastic guitar on eBay.
I'm not writing a very good report.
Are you bidding for it now?

We use the Present Simple ...
- with state verbs (e.g. *be, know, like, love*).
  I know it's a lot of money.
- to talk about habits and things you often do.
  I listen to music every day!

see Reference page 17

6 Complete the sentences with the Present Simple or Present Continuous form of the verbs in brackets.

1 I *'m doing* (do) a Spanish evening class this term. I _____ (go) once a week.

2 I never _____ (buy) things on eBay. I _____ (not like) paying for things online.

3 A: What _____ (usually/do) in the summer holidays?
   B: I _____ (go) to Sicily every summer.

4 She _____ (not/study) at university this year. She _____ (travel) for six months.

5 A: _____ (you/know) how to speak French?
   B: Yes, I _____ (learn) it at the moment.

6 A: What _____ (do) these days?
   B: I _____ (work) in a restaurant until the end of June.

Vocabulary | time phrases

7 Match the phrases from the box with the underlined phrases in the sentences.

> 24 hours a day ~~at the moment~~
> at the same time each time

Anyway, I've got a lot of work <u>these days</u>.
at the moment

1 I'm working <u>all the time</u> and I want to do something relaxing sometimes.

2 <u>Every time</u> I look at the computer, the price goes up!

3 Right now, I'm doing two things <u>at once</u>.

8 Choose the correct words in *italics*.

I'm buying a lot of things online *each time/these days*.

1 I'm listening to some music and writing an essay *at the same time/every time*.

2 *24 hours a day/Every time* I check my emails, I've got ten more messages.

3 I like multi-tasking – I'm good at doing two things *each time/at once*.

4 I play computer games *all the time/at the same time* when I'm at home.

5 *Each time/All the time* I look at Facebook, I write a comment on someone's wall.

6 I'm chatting on MSN to three people *every time/at the moment*.

7 It is very tempting to have your mobile on *24 hours a day/at once*.

9 Work in pairs. Ask and answer the questions.

1 What are you studying at the moment?

2 Do you like doing your homework and listening to music at the same time?

3 Do you answer your phone every time it rings?

4 Do you like having your mobile phone on all the time?

5 Do you think you are good at doing more than two things at once?

Speaking

10 **a** Write down an example of: a city, a job, a hobby, a foreign language and a musical instrument.

b Imagine you meet an old friend. The last time you saw him/her was six years ago. Use your notes from exercise 10a and talk about your life now.

My life is very different now. I'm living in Bilbao and I'm not doing the same job ...

1 Communication

1 Work in groups and discuss the questions.

1 What are three common reasons for learning a language?

2 What do a lot of people find easy/difficult about learning a language?

2 a 🔘 1.7 Listen to two people, Stig and Tessie, talking about learning a language. Answer the questions.

1 What language is he/she learning and why?

2 What is he/she good at?

3 What does he/she find difficult?

4 What does he/she most want to improve?

b Listen again and look at the phrases in the How to... box. Which phrases does Stig say? Which does Tessie say? Write *S* or *T*.

3 In pairs, ask and answer the questions. Use the language from the How to... box.

1 Why are you learning English?

2 What do you think you are good at?

3 What do you find difficult about learning English?

4 What do you want to work on?

4 Look at the Lifelong learning box. How often do you do each of the tips? Write one more tip on how to improve each aspect of your English.

How to... talk about your learning needs

Say what you are good at	*I'm quite good at* speaking. ☑ S
	My listening's not bad. ☐
	I'm quite good at understanding what people say. ☐
	I'm pretty good at reading. ☐
Say what is difficult for you	*The most difficult thing is learning to read and write.* ☐
	I'm finding it (rather) difficult to express myself. ☐
	I'm not very good at speaking fluently.
Say what you want to work on	*I really want to improve* my reading and writing. ☐
	I would really like to improve my speaking skills. ☐
	Communication is the most important thing. ☐

Improving your English

❗ There are a lot of ways to improve your English. For example:

- **Speaking:** chat on the phone to your classmates
- **Listening:** listen to an English language radio station
- **Reading:** read your favourite magazine in English
- **Writing:** send emails to your classmates
- **Vocabulary:** write new vocabulary in a notebook
- **Grammar:** do revision exercises on the Active Book

Lifelong learning

5 Work in groups and discuss your ideas from exercise 4. Make a note of the three best learning tips you hear.

Likes and dislikes

We can talk about our likes and dislikes using the following phrases. After all the verb phrases, we use a verb in the *-ing* form or a noun.

☺☺☺ I *absolutely love* playing tennis.

☺☺ I *really like* coffee.

☺ I *quite like* going to the cinema.

☺ I'm *quite keen on* horror films.

☺ I *don't mind* swimming.

☹ I'm *not very keen on* computer games.

☹ I *don't like* classical music.

☹☹ I *really hate* getting up early.

☹☹ I *can't stand* hot weather.

Present Simple

⊕ ⊖	I/You/We/ They	go don't go	to bed early.
	He/She/It	goes doesn't go	
❓	Do	you/we/they get up	early?
	Does	he/she/it get up	
	Yes, I do./No, I don't. Yes, he does./No, he doesn't.		

We use the Present Simple to talk about habits/things we often do. *I call my parents on Sundays.*

contractions: *don't = do not; doesn't = does not*

He/She/It: add *s* to the verb in the affirmative.

Adverbs of frequency

We use adverbs of frequency to say how often we do something. *I usually play the piano in the evenings.*

With regular verbs, adverbs of frequency generally come before the main verb.

He sometimes goes clubbing on Saturdays.

She doesn't usually take the train.

! We use the affirmative with *never* and *hardly ever*, not the negative. *He hardly ever stays in bed late.*

With the verb *to be*, the adverb of frequency generally comes after the verb. *I'm never late.*

With the verb *have got*, the adverb of frequency comes between *have* and *got*. *He's usually got a lot of money.*

Longer adverb phrases generally come at the end of the sentence. *I go to the cinema about once a week.*

Common adverbs of frequency: *always; usually; often; sometimes; hardly ever; never; once a year; twice a week*.

Present Continuous

⊕	I	am	
	He/She/It	is	
	We/You/They	are	working.
⊖	I	am not	
	He/She/It	is not	
	You/We/They	are not	
❓	Am	I	
	Is	he/she/it	having a lie-in?
	Are	you/we/they	
	Yes, I am./No, I'm not. Yes, you are./No, you aren't. Yes, he is./No, he isn't (he's not).		

We use the Present Continuous to talk about actions happening at this moment and temporary actions happening around now. *I'm doing the washing-up now. He's doing a lot of exercise these days.*

State verbs

believe   hate   know   like   love   need   prefer
remember   understand   want

We use the Present Simple (NOT ~~the Present Continuous~~) with state verbs. *I know how to play chess.*

Key vocabulary

Verb–noun phrases about daily routine

chat on the phone   check your emails   do nothing
do some exercise   get up early   go for a swim
go for a walk   go shopping   go to bed late
have a family meal   have a lie-in   have a nap
have a take-away   listen to the radio
make breakfast/lunch/dinner   meet some friends
read a magazine/newspaper   stay in for the evening
take a bus/train   watch TV/a DVD

Going out

go bowling   go clubbing   go ice skating
go on a guided walk/tour   go to a concert
go to a musical   go to an exhibition
go to the cinema   go to the theatre

Describing your day and lifestyle

boring   busy   exciting   fun   lazy   relaxing
stressful   unusual

Time phrases

24 hours a day/all the time   at once/at the same time
at the moment/these days   each time/every time

 Listen to these words.

ACTIVE BOOK

 see Writing bank page 135

1 Each sentence has one word missing. Write the missing word in the correct place. Use the symbols to help you.

☺☺☺ I love the colour pink.
I absolutely love the colour pink.

1 ☺ I'm quite on watching football.

   _____ .

2 ☹☹ I stand science fiction films.

   _____ .

3 ☺☺ I like sending text messages.

   _____ .

4 ☹☹ I really the winter.

   _____ .

5 ☺ I quite pizza.

   _____ .

6 ☺☺☺ I absolutely going to the beach.

   _____ .

7 ☺ I mind getting up early.

   _____ .

8 ☹ I not very keen on dancing.

   _____ .

2 Complete the dialogues with the correct form of the Present Simple.

A: *Do you get up* (you/get up) early?
B: Yes, I do. In the week, (1) _____ (I/usually/get up) at about 6:30.
A: What time (2) _____ (you/start) work?
B: At about 9:00. (3) _____ (I/go to bed) early, too.
A: (4) _____ (you/go to bed) before ten o'clock?
B: No, I don't. (5) _____ (I/usually/watch a DVD) in the evenings.
A: (6) _____ (you/have a snack) before you go to bed?
B: No, I don't. (7) _____ (I/have dinner) late every evening.
A: My brother is a really good swimmer.
B: (8) _____ (he/swim) a lot?
A: Yes, he does. (9) _____ (He/always/get up) very early and (10) _____ (swim) for two hours before breakfast. Then (11) _____ (he/go) back to the swimming pool after work.
B: How often (12) _____ (he/go) out with his friends?
A: Only at weekends. (13) _____ (He/not often/go) out in the week.

3 Complete the dialogues with the Present Continuous form of the verbs from the box.

check ~~do~~ do go have sit walk watch

A: What *are you doing* (you) at the moment?
B: I (1) _____ on a bus with some friends. What about you?
A: I (2) _____ lunch with my family.
A: (3) _____ (Jack) TV?
B: No, he isn't. He (4) _____ his emails.
A: (5) _____ (John) any exercise at the moment?
B: Yes, lots! He (6) _____ to work and he (7) _____ to the gym a lot at the moment.

4 Choose the correct words in *italics*.

I *usually go/am usually going* to work by car.

1 Listen to that man. What language *does he speak/is he speaking*?
2 It *doesn't rain/isn't raining* much in the summer here.
3 You *work/'re working* very hard today.
4 *Do you prefer/Are you preferring* tea or coffee?
5 I *stay/'m staying* at the Savoy Hotel in London for a week.
6 Who's that woman? What *does she want/is she wanting*?
7 *Do you study/Are you studying* French this term?
8 She *works/'s working* in India for three months.

5 Complete each sentence with one word.

Do you *watch* TV every evening?

1 How often do you _____ to an art exhibition?
2 I'm working very hard at the _____ .
3 Do you usually _____ to the radio at work?
4 I don't usually do my homework and listen to music at the _____ time.
5 How often do you _____ a bus to work?
6 He always _____ a lie-in on Sunday mornings.
7 I like going on _____ walks around different cities.
8 Where are you living _____ days?

Music

Lead-in

1 What musical instruments can you see in the photos? What other instruments do you know?

2 **a** 🔊 1.8 Listen to eight extracts of music and write what types of music they are.

> classical   country   folk   heavy metal   hip hop   jazz
> Latin   opera   pop   rap   reggae   rock   soul   techno

b What type(s) of music do you like/dislike?

3 **a** Complete the sentences with the words from the box.

> album   artist   ~~band~~   composer   concert   download
> read music   single

My favourite ___*band*___ is Coldplay. I've got all their music on my iPod.

1 I can't _____ , but I can play by ear.
2 I love the _____ *Sweet Dreams* from Beyoncé's _____
   I Am … Sasha Fierce.
3 I _____ a lot of music from the internet.
4 My favourite _____ is Mariah Carey and my favourite song is *Hero*.
5 I love Mozart's music. He's my favourite _____ .
6 I paid £85 to see a _____ at the Sydney Opera House.

b Make sentences about you. Use the words from exercise 3a and tell your partner.

2.1 Music for 007

Grammar Past Simple

Can do describe personal events in the past

Listening

1 **a** Work in pairs and try to answer the questions about James Bond.

1 Who wrote the James Bond books?
2 What is James Bond's job?
3 Which actor played the first Bond?
4 Which Bond film did Jack White and Alicia Keys sing in?

b 🔵 1.9 Listen to the first part of a radio programme about James Bond films and check your answers.

2 **a** 🔵 1.10 Listen to the second part of the programme. Match the artists (a–f) with the Bond songs.

a Carly Simon   d Duran Duran
b Alicia Keys and Jack White   e Madonna
c Paul McCartney and Wings   f Shirley Bassey

Another Way to Die ⬚b⬚   *Goldfinger* ☐
Diamonds Are Forever ☐   *Moonraker* ☐
A View to a Kill ☐   *Live and Let Die* ☐
Nobody Does It Better ☐   *Die Another Day* ☐

b Listen again and complete the sentences.

1 *Another Way to Die* came out in the year _____ .
2 The first James Bond theme song was _____ .
3 Shirley Bassey sang _____ Bond songs in total.
4 *Diamonds Are Forever* came out in _____ .
5 The only Bond theme song to reach Number One on the Billboard charts is _____ .
6 Paul McCartney and Carly Simon had James Bond hits in the _____ .
7 There was a mixed reaction to the song _____ .

3 In groups, discuss the questions.

1 Do you like James Bond/other spy films? Why/Why not?
2 Do you think it is important for films to have good music? Why/Why not?

Vocabulary | music

4 Complete the sentences with the singular or plural form of the words from the box.

> chorus   duet   flop   hit   lead singer
> lyrics   solo   soundtrack   theme song
> top of the charts

1 *Another Way to Die* is a _____ by Alicia Keys and Jack White.
2 Jack White is the _____ of The White Stripes.
3 All the other Bond songs are _____ – with just one singer.
4 The _____ are really good and have a strong message.
5 The first two Bond films had great _____ .
6 After *Goldfinger*, people expected a great _____ in every film.
7 Many Bond songs got to the _____ .
8 Not all Bond songs were _____ .
9 *Die Another Day* wasn't a complete _____ .
10 It had a really catchy _____ .

5 Work in groups and discuss the questions.

1 Do you know the lyrics of many songs in English? Which ones do you like?
2 Do you ever download film soundtracks? If so, which ones?
3 Which artists are at the top of the charts at the moment?
4 Think of a song you like: is it a solo, a duet or a group? Who is the lead singer? Can you sing the chorus of the song?

Grammar | Past Simple

6 **a** Complete the Active grammar box with the correct Past Simple form of the verbs in brackets.

b Which verbs from the Active grammar box are regular? Which are irregular?

Active grammar

We use the Past Simple for completed actions in the past.

➕ *That song ____ Shirley Bassey's career in 1964.* (start)

She ____ an international star immediately. (become)

People ____ a great theme song in every film. (expect)

➖ *The first two films ____ a theme song.* (not have)

Moonraker ____ a very successful film. (not be)

❓ *How many Bond songs ____ ?* (she/sing)

When ____ the first famous theme song? (be)

---

see Reference page 27 and Irregular verb table page 149

7 Complete the paragraph with the Past Simple form of the verbs in brackets.

Alicia Keys was born on 25 January 1981 and she (1) _____ (grow up) in New York. She (2) _____ (not have) any brothers or sisters and her parents (3) _____ (separate) when she was two. She first (4) _____ (appear) on TV when she was four and she (5) _____ (begin) playing the piano when she was seven. Five years later, she (6) _____ (go) to a Performing Arts School. After leaving school, she (7) _____ (start) at Columbia University, but (8) _____ (not finish) her studies. After four weeks, she (9) _____ (leave) university to become a singer. She (10) _____ (make) her first album when she was twenty, called *Songs in A Minor*.

8 **a** Write complete Past Simple questions about Alicia Keys using the prompts.

where/Alicia Keys/live when she was a child?
Where did Alicia Keys live when she was a child?

1   she/have/any brothers and sisters?
2   when/she/begin playing a musical instrument?
3   what/she/do when she was twelve?
4   how long/she/spend at university?
5   when/she/make her first album?

b Cover the text from exercise 7 and answer the questions.

Speaking

9 Complete the How to... box. Look at audioscript 1.10 on page 150 and use the underlined phrases to help you.

How to... refer to past times

Say when an action happened

---

*I was born **on** 25 January 1981/Monday 1 June.*

She moved to Sicily (1) ____ 1964/February 2004/the summer of 08.

I worked for a record company (2) ____ early seventies/mid eighties/late nineties.

I wanted to become a dancer (3) ____ I left school/I was fifteen.

*He graduated from university **last** year/week/month.*

*I started training to be an architect three months/two years **ago**.*

Link an action to another action

I travelled for a year. After (4) ____ , I decided to go to university.

***After travelling** for a year, I decided to go to university.*

I started travelling. A year (5) ____ , I decided to go to university.

---

10 **a** Write six questions to ask another student about his/her life. Use the prompts.

• when/where born
• where grew up
• what liked/disliked about school
• what job wanted to do
• what hobbies/sports did as teenager
• what did when left school

b In pairs, ask and answer your questions. Use the How to... box to help you.

Grammar	Present Perfect Simple: experience
Can do	talk about personal achievements and experiences

The achievements and ambitions of Shakira – *pop star and business woman*

There is no question that Shakira is one of the most successful pop stars in the world. But, she's certainly not just a pop star. Yes, <u>she's sold</u> over sixty million albums worldwide and she's done many concert tours. But she has also given millions of dollars to charity, especially to those who help children living in poverty. In 1995, when Shakira was only nineteen, <u>she started</u> her own charity, using the money she earned. The Pies Descalzos Foundation (or Barefoot Foundation in English) builds schools which provide education, as well as food and medical support, for poor children all around Colombia.

Reading

1 What is the connection between Shakira and the child in the photo? Read the text and check your ideas.

2 **a** Work in pairs and follow the instructions.
Student A: read the text on page 129 and answer the questions.
Student B: read the text on page 133 and answer the questions.

b Tell your partner about your half of the text.

3 In groups, discuss the questions.

1 What do you think are the two most interesting things about Shakira's story?

2 Do you think pop stars who are rich and famous should do work for charity? Why/Why not?

Grammar | Present Perfect Simple: experience

4 **a** Look at the <u>underlined</u> verb phrases in the text from exercise 1. What are the two tenses? Do we know when each action happened?

b Complete the rules with *Present Perfect Simple* or *Past Simple*.

- We use the _____ to talk about an action or experience at a specific time in the past.
- We use the _____ to talk about an action or experience at some time in the past up until now. The specific time is not important or not known.

5 **a** Complete the Active grammar box.

b Look at the texts about Shakira from exercises 1 and 2a again. Find more examples of the Present Perfect Simple.

Active grammar

Present Perfect Simple: *have/has* + past participle

➕ *I've won a prize for singing.*
She _____ given millions of dollars to charity.

➖ *They haven't sold a lot of records.*
He _____ seen the film.

❓ *Has she started her own company?*
_____ you ever been on TV?

Present Perfect Simple or Past Simple?
I've given a lot of speeches.
I _____ a speech to 150 people last year.

ever (in questions) means at any point up until now: *Have you ever met Shakira?*

never means at no point in the past up until now: *He's never met Shakira.*

see Reference page 27

6 Complete the text with the Present Perfect Simple form of the verbs.

> buy   download   have   learn   not have
> not meet   not pay   ~~see~~

I'm a huge Shakira fan and I'm lucky because my friend, Jason, works for her record company. I *'ve seen* Shakira play in over twenty concerts. Jason (1) _____ dinner with Shakira three times, but I (2) _____ her in person. I (3) _____ for any Shakira CDs because Jason gets free copies for me. I (4) _____ the lyrics of most of Shakira's songs and I (5) _____ some Shakira videos from the internet. My parents (6) _____ a guitar for me, but I (7) _____ any lessons.

7 Complete the dialogues with the correct Present Perfect Simple or Past Simple form of the verbs in brackets.

A: (1) _____ (you ever win) a competition?
B: Yes, I (2) _____ . I (3) _____ (win) a singing competition when I was six.
A: (4) _____ (he ever meet) Shakira?
B: Yes, he (5) _____ . He (6) _____ (meet) her three times.
A: (7) _____ (you ever play) a musical instrument in public?
B: Yes, I (8) _____ . I (9) _____ (be) in a band when I was a teenager.
A: (10) _____ (you ever meet) a famous person?
B: No, I (11) _____ . But I (12) _____ (see) Kylie in concert last year!

Pronunciation | *have/has*

8 🔘 1.11 We can say *have/has* in different ways. Listen and repeat.
1 A: Have you ever won a competition?
      /həv/ weak pronunciation
   B: Yes, I have.
      /hæv/ strong pronunciation
2 A: Has he ever met Shakira?
      /həz/ weak pronunciation
   B: Yes, he has.
      /hæz/ strong pronunciation

see Pronunciation bank page 148

9 Work in pairs and ask and answer the questions from exercise 7. Give answers which are true for you.

Vocabulary | achievements

10 a In pairs, match the verbs from A with the noun phrases from B. Check your answers with the texts from exercises 1 and 2a.

A	B
1 learn	a) an award/a prize/a competition
2 give	b) a good job
3 start	c) an exam (with distinction)
4 win	d) your own company/charity
5 pass	e) a lot of money
6 do	f) a speech to (hundreds of people)
7 earn	g) to speak another language
8 get	h) a lot of work for charity

b Choose the correct words in *italics*.

1 I felt very nervous before I *did/got/gave* a speech to my work colleagues.
2 My sister *won/passed/earned* a prize for singing when we were on holiday.
3 I'd really like to learn to *say/talk/speak* Japanese. I'm sure it's very difficult!
4 When I left school, I *got/earned/won* a really good job as an accountant.
5 She *does/gets/gives* a lot of work for charity in her spare time.
6 The proudest day of my life was when I *did/started/earned* my own company.
7 My cousin *did/won/earned* a lot of money from his clothing business.
8 I felt really good when I *passed/won/got* my piano exam with distinction.

Speaking

11 Choose a topic (1–5) and prepare to talk about it. Make notes.

1 What have you achieved in your life that you are proud of? When did you do it and why?
2 Have you met or heard about anyone who really surprised you? What was surprising?
3 Have you ever performed in public? What did you perform? Did you enjoy it?
4 Have you ever done any work for charity? What did you do and why?
5 How many countries have you visited? What did you like about them?

12 Now work in groups and take turns to talk about your topics for one minute. Find out more details from each speaker by asking him/her three questions in the Past Simple.

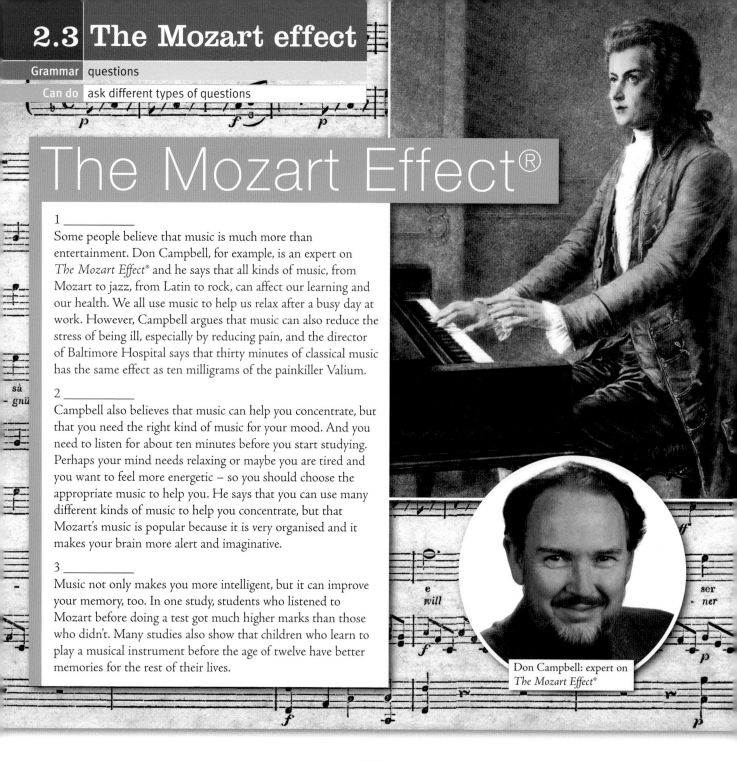

The Mozart Effect®

1 _____

Some people believe that music is much more than entertainment. Don Campbell, for example, is an expert on *The Mozart Effect®* and he says that all kinds of music, from Mozart to jazz, from Latin to rock, can affect our learning and our health. We all use music to help us relax after a busy day at work. However, Campbell argues that music can also reduce the stress of being ill, especially by reducing pain, and the director of Baltimore Hospital says that thirty minutes of classical music has the same effect as ten milligrams of the painkiller Valium.

2 _____

Campbell also believes that music can help you concentrate, but that you need the right kind of music for your mood. And you need to listen for about ten minutes before you start studying. Perhaps your mind needs relaxing or maybe you are tired and you want to feel more energetic – so you should choose the appropriate music to help you. He says that you can use many different kinds of music to help you concentrate, but that Mozart's music is popular because it is very organised and it makes your brain more alert and imaginative.

3 _____

Music not only makes you more intelligent, but it can improve your memory, too. In one study, students who listened to Mozart before doing a test got much higher marks than those who didn't. Many studies also show that children who learn to play a musical instrument before the age of twelve have better memories for the rest of their lives.

Don Campbell: expert on *The Mozart Effect®*

Reading

1 🔘 1.12 Listen to three pieces of music by Mozart. How does each one make you feel? Use the adjectives from the box and your own words.

This piece makes me feel relaxed and calm.

> awake   calm   happy   relaxed   sad
> sleepy   thoughtful

2 Read the text quickly and match the headings (a–c) with the paragraphs (1–3).

a The right music to study better

b Music for stress and pain

c Get a better score and remember more

3 Read the text again. Write true (T), false (F) or not given (NG).

1 Don Campbell loves Mozart's music. ☐

2 People listen to music to relax before work. ☐

3 Listening to music when you are ill is a good idea. ☐

4 Many hospitals use music to help with pain. ☐

5 Listening to music before you study is a bad idea. ☐

6 Only Mozart's music helps you to study. ☐

7 The students listened to Mozart for ten minutes before doing the test. ☐

8 It's a good idea for children to learn to play a musical instrument. ☐

4 Work in pairs and discuss the questions.

1 What music do you listen to when you want to relax?

2 Do you listen to music when you're studying? Why/ Why not?

Listening

5 🔵 1.13 Listen to two people talking about music. Write true (T) or false (F).

1 The article is about *The Mozart Effect®*. ☐

2 The woman doesn't like music that reminds her of old times. ☐

3 She listens to music a lot. ☐

4 She sometimes sings at the same time as listening to music. ☐

6 Listen again and tick (✓) the questions you hear.

1 Can music change how you feel? ☐

2 What music do you find annoying? ☐

3 How often do you listen to music? ☐

4 Have you got an iPod? If not, would you like one? ☐

5 Do you listen to music when you're travelling? ☐

6 What's your favourite type of music? ☐

7 Are you learning a musical instrument at the moment? ☐

8 Did you play any musical instruments when you were a child? ☐

9 When did you last see live music? ☐

10 Have you ever seen a famous artist or band in concert? ☐

7 Listen again and answer the questions you ticked in exercise 6.

Grammar | questions

8 Complete the Active grammar box with *before* or *after*.

Active grammar

There are two main types of questions.

- *Yes/No* questions: *Do you listen to music when you're travelling?*
- *Wh-/How* questions: *What music do you find annoying?*

Make questions by changing the word order.

A With the Present Simple and Past Simple tenses, we put *do/does/did* _____ the subject + infinitive.

How often do you listen to music?

When did you last see live music?

B We put other auxiliary verbs or modal verbs (*can, have, would, be,* etc.) _____ the subject + verb.

Can music change how you feel?

Would you like an iPod?

C When the main verb is *to be*, we put the verb _____ the subject.

What is your favourite type of music?

---

see Reference page 27

9 Find the mistakes in eight of the questions and correct them.

1 What kind of music you like?

2 Do you can play the piano?

3 What music did you listen to ten years ago?

4 Would like to be a professional musician?

5 Has you ever downloaded music from the internet?

6 Who your favourite singer or group?

7 What music you listen to in the mornings?

8 Have you got a radio in your bedroom?

9 Did you took music exams when you were a child?

10 You are listening to music at the moment?

Pronunciation | intonation in questions

10 🔵 1.14 Our tone of voice changes when we ask different types of questions. Listen and repeat the questions. Try to copy the intonation.

Wh- question: What kind of music do you like?

Yes/No question: Can you play the piano?

see Pronunciation bank page 148

Speaking

11 a Prepare to do a survey about music. Write six questions. Use exercises 6 and 9 or your own ideas.

b Ask and answer the questions with your classmates.

2 Communication

Can do explain why you like a piece of music

1 a You're going to listen to a radio programme. Look at the photo. What do you think it's about?

b 🔵 1.15 Listen to the introduction. Were you correct?

2 a 🔵 1.16 Listen to the rest of the programme and complete the table.

Piece of music	Artist
3	
2	
1	

b In pairs, compare your answers.

3 Work in groups and discuss the questions.

1 What do you think about the music that Mark chose?

2 Which piece do you like best? Why?

4 a Complete the sentences from the radio programme with the words from the box.

cry   happy   memories   remember   reminds (x2)

1 It _____ me of when I was at school.

2 It makes me feel so _____ .

3 It's got great _____ for me!

4 When I first heard it, it made me _____ !

5 It _____ me of a great holiday I had.

6 I _____ listening to it when I was on the beach.

b 🔵 1.17 Listen and check your answers.

c Look at the Lifelong learning box. Read the tip and record the other words from exercise 4a.

Recording vocabulary

❗ When you're recording new vocabulary, include the stress, the part of speech, a definition and an example sentence.

remind (verb)

to make you remember someone or something

The smell of coffee reminds me of my grandfather's house.

Lifelong learning

5 Choose your top three pieces of music. For each piece, make a note of the artist and why you like it.

6 a Work in groups of three and take turns to talk about your choices. Use your notes from exercise 5 and the words from exercise 4a.

b Is your taste in music similar to or different from the other students in your group?

26

2 | Reference

Past simple

> **Regular verbs**
>
> ➕ : *I played jazz music all day yesterday.*
> ➖ : *He didn't finish his exams.*
> ❓ : *Why did you wait for so long?*
> : *Did you like the last Coldplay CD?*
> : *Yes, I did./No, I didn't.*

> **Verb *to be***
>
> ➕ : *I/He/She was at home this morning.*
> ➖ : *You/We/They weren't on holiday last week.*
> ❓ : *Was she at school yesterday?*
> : *Were they happy about that?*
> : *Yes, he was./No, he wasn't.*

We use the Past Simple for completed actions in the past.

❗ We use the same form for all pronouns (but *was/were* for the verb *to be*).

We add *-ed* to regular verbs to make the past form.

We use *didn't (did not)* to make the negative.

See Irregular verbs table page 149

Present Perfect Simple: experience

> **Present Perfect Simple: *has/have* + past participle**

➕ ➖ : *I/You/We/They She/He/It*	*have/haven't has/hasn't*	*won a prize.*
❓ : *Have* *Has*	*I/you/we/they ever he/she/it ever*	*heard this song?*
: *Yes, I have./No, I haven't.*		
: *Yes, he has./No, he hasn't.*		

We use the Present Perfect Simple to talk about an action or experience at some point in the past up until now. The specific time is not important or is not known.

❗ We don't use the Present Perfect Simple with past time expressions, e.g. *last night, two weeks ago.*

We use the Past Simple to talk about an action or experience at a specific time in the past.

A: *I've visited eleven countries in my life.*
B: *Have you ever been to Asia?*
A: *Yes, I have. I went to Thailand in 2001.*

ever and *never*

We often use *ever* and *never* with the Present Perfect Simple when we are talking about experience.

ever (in questions) means at any point up until now.
***Have** you **ever broken** your leg?*

never means at no point in the past up until now.
*I**'ve never tried** Japanese food.*

❗ With *never*, we use the verb in the affirmative (NOT in the negative). ~~She **hasn't never been** to Italy.~~

Questions

There are two main types of questions.

Yes/No questions: *Do you like watching football?*
Wh-/How questions: ***What** did you do last weekend?*
The most common *Wh-* question words are:
what, where, when, who, why, which, whose and *how.*
We often put *Wh-* question words together with other words, e.g. *what time, what kind, how much, how many, how often, how long, which one.*

Word order

With the Present Simple and Past Simple tenses, we put *do/does/did* before the subject + infinitive.
***Do you like** computer games?*

We put other modal or auxiliary verbs (*can, have, would, be,* etc.) before the subject + verb.
***Can you play** the piano?*

When the main verb is *to be*, we put the verb before the subject. *Where **were you** yesterday?*

> **Key vocabulary**
>
> **Music**
> classical country folk heavy metal hip hop jazz Latin opera pop rap reggae rock soul techno
> album artist band composer concert download read music single
> chorus duet flop hit lead singer lyrics solo soundtrack theme song top of the charts
>
> **Achievements**
> do a lot of work for charity earn a lot of money get a good job give a speech to (hundreds of people) learn to speak another language pass an exam start your own company/charity win an award/a prize/a competition
>
> Listen to these words.
> ACTIVE BOOK

 see Writing bank page 136

1 Complete the sentences with the Past Simple form of the verbs in brackets.

I _learned_ to play the piano when I was a child.
My father _taught_ me. (learn/teach)

1 He _____ his old computer and _____ a new one. (sell/buy)

2 My grandmother _____ on the pavement and _____ her arm. (fall/break)

3 When I was a child, I _____ in the countryside and _____ to school every day. (live/walk)

4 I was on a special diet last week. I only _____ fruit and I only _____ water. (eat/drink)

5 When we _____ on holiday last year, I _____ a lot of photos. (be/take)

6 I _____ to a concert last night and _____ two really good bands. (go/see)

2 Complete the dialogues with the correct Past Simple form of the verbs from the boxes.

> do   go   not/like   meet   say   think

A: What _did you do_ (you) last weekend?
B: On Friday evening, I (1) _____ my friend Natalia and we (2) _____ to see a film. I (3) _____ it was a really good film, but Natalia (4) _____ it. She (5) _____ it was boring.

> be   hate   like   not/like   live   stop

A: Where (6) _____ (you) born?
B: In Scotland. I (7) _____ in the countryside when I was a child.
A: (8) _____ (you) it?
B: No, I (9) _____ it. I (10) _____ the weather because it never (11) _____ raining!

3 Complete the sentences with the correct Present Perfect Simple form of the verbs in brackets.

Susie _has seen_ the new Bond film five times at the cinema! (see)

1 I _____ of that band. (not hear)

2 _____ a marathon? (you/ever/run)

3 I _____ to Carnival in Brazil twice. (be)

4 _____ your leg? (you/ever/break)

5 She's nervous because she _____ a horse before. (not ride)

6 _____ any climbing before? (you/do)

7 I _____ all over the world. (work)

8 _____ music from the internet? (you/ever/download)

4 Choose the correct words in *italics*.

A: Hello. I'd like to apply for the job of sales assistant.
B: Well, I hope you *had/('ve had)* the right kind of experience. (1) *Did you do/Have you done* this kind of job before?
A: Yes, I (2) *did/have*.
B: Where?
A: Well, I (3) *had/'ve had* some experience in a music shop.
B: Oh, really?
A: Yes, I (4) *worked/'ve worked* there two years ago.
B: (5) *Were you/Have you been* a sales assistant?
A: No, I (6) *wasn't/haven't*. I (7) *was/'ve been* a cleaner.
B: Oh, I'm sorry. We need someone who (8) *had/'s had* experience as a sales assistant.

5 Write complete questions using the prompts.

My favourite drink is ...
What _is your favourite drink_ ?

1 I like eating ... for breakfast.
What _____ ?

2 We usually go to ... for our holidays.
Where _____ ?

3 She played the ... when she was a child.
What _____ ?

4 I bought a ... yesterday.
What _____ ?

5 My mother can ... really well.
What _____ ?

6 I went to see Beyoncé in concert last ...
When _____ ?

7 They were late for school ... last week.
How many times _____ ?

6 Find the mistake in each sentence and correct it.

Who is the ~~main~~ singer of U2? *lead*

1 I find it difficult to understand the letters of English songs.

2 The film had great music. I really want to buy the soundbite.

3 My sister earned lots of prizes for singing when she was young.

4 I never buy CDs from shops. I always read music from the internet.

5 I was nervous about giving a speak to over 200 people.

6 She was pleased when she won her piano exam with distinction.

7 I'd like to listen to more classic music.

3

Lead-in

1 Look at the photos and put the words from the box into three groups: (a) food and drink, (b) people, (c) kitchen equipment. Add more words to each group.

> aubergine   bread   chef   cooker   customer
> mineral water   olive oil   plum   saucepan   waiter/waitress

2 **a** Complete the sentences with the words and phrases from the box.

> allergic   chefs   diets   main course   menu   ~~recipe~~
> traditional dish   vegetarian

1 Do you usually follow a ___*recipe*___ when you cook? Why/Why not? ☐
2 Have you ever been a _____ ? Why/Why not? ☐
3 What is your favourite _____ from your country? ☐
4 Do you usually prefer meat or fish for your _____ ? ☐
5 Do you know any special _____ for people who want to lose weight fast? Do you think they work? ☐
6 Are there any celebrity _____ in your country? ☐
7 Are you _____ to any kinds of food? ☐
8 Do you prefer a _____ to have a lot of different dishes to choose from, or not many? Why? ☐

b 🔊 1.18 Now listen and match the answers (A–H) with the questions from exercise 2a.

3 In pairs, ask and answer the questions from exercise 2a.

Grammar	*be going to*: future plans
Can do	tell a friend about your future plans

Reading

1 Look at the photos and read the first paragraph of the text. Who is Jamie Oliver and what has he achieved?

2 Read the rest of the text. In which areas has Jamie Oliver made a difference to people's lives?

a   training chefs in restaurants ☐

b   working with doctors and hospitals ☐

c   giving food to homeless people ☐

d   working with unemployed people ☐

e   teaching children about good food ☐

3 Read the text again and complete each sentence with one word.

1   When he was young, Jamie Oliver wanted to manage a _____ .

2   When the trainees join the Fifteen programme, they are young and _____ .

3   After Lloyd Hayes left Fifteen, he became a professional _____ .

4   In the Pass It On scheme, each person teaches a _____ to four other people.

5   During the Jamie's School Dinners project, some schools decided to change their _____ .

4 Find the phrases in the text. In pairs, look at the context around each phrase and try to work out the meaning.

1   his passion for   4   success story

2   no previous experience   5   affordable food

3   top-class chefs   6   cooking habits

5 Work in groups and discuss the questions.

1   Which of Jamie's projects (Fifteen, Pass It On or Jamie's School Dinners) do you think is the most interesting? Why?

2   Would you like to learn to be a top-class chef? Why/Why not?

Grammar | *be going to*: future plans

6 **a** Complete the Active grammar box. Check your answers with the last paragraph of the text from exercise 1.

b Find three more examples of *be going to* in the text.

Active grammar

We use *be going to* to talk about future plans and intentions (when the speaker makes the decision before speaking).

➕ : My children _____ to eat their vegetables.

➖ : I _____ to miss it!

❓ : What _____ to do next?

---

see Reference page 37

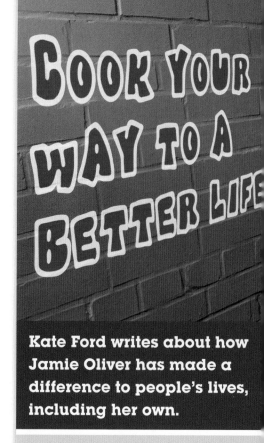

COOK YOUR WAY TO A BETTER LIFE

Kate Ford writes about how Jamie Oliver has made a difference to people's lives, including her own.

1   When he was fourteen, his ambition was to run a pub, just like his dad. But in the last twenty years, celebrity chef Jamie Oliver has achieved far more. With a chain of restaurants, a number of popular television series and best-selling cookery books, Jamie Oliver is a well-known name in every UK household. I'm a huge 'Jamie fan'. I admire his passion for improving the food we eat and helping people change their lives.

2   Jamie's first project, Fifteen, in 2002, aimed to help young people. He took fifteen unemployed young people, with no previous experience of cooking, and trained them to be top-class chefs in his restaurant, also called Fifteen. I remember one trainee, Lloyd Hayes. He left school with no qualifications and started getting into crime. But the project worked and Lloyd got a good job as a chef in a top London restaurant. I heard recently that in the future he is going to teach people to cook professionally. I think it's this kind of success story that makes Jamie and his projects so special.

3   Another special project is Jamie's Ministry of Food which he started in 2008. There are two aims: firstly, to teach people how to cook healthy, affordable food instead of eating fast food; secondly, to set up the Pass It On scheme: encouraging each

7 Write complete sentences using the prompts and the correct form of *be going to*.

1 I/start making my own bread.
2 Rachel/not/use a recipe for her cake.
3 we/have pizza or pasta tonight?
4 they/not/eat fast food anymore.
5 what/you/have for the main course?
6 he/book the restaurant for 8 o'clock.
7 you/try that new dish she made?
8 where/you/do your cookery course?

Speaking

8 Complete the How to... box with the headings (a–d).

a Describe your plans   c Give a time reference
b Give a reason   d Ask someone about their plans

How to... talk about future plans

1	*What are your plans for* the next two years?
	What are you going to do this year?
2	*I want to* work in a restaurant as a chef.
3	*I'm going to* get a job as a waiter *in October*.
4	*I'd like to* speak English better *because I want to* work abroad.
	I'm going to get a place at college *to learn about* hotel management.

Pronunciation | connected speech (1)

9 **a** 🔊 1.19 We usually link words that end in a consonant sound with words that begin with a vowel sound. Listen to the question from the How to... box and notice the linking.

What are your plans for the next two years?

b 🔊 1.20 Look at the sentences from the How to... box again. Mark the linking. Then listen, check and repeat.

see Pronunciation bank page 148

10 **a** What are your plans for the next two years? Think about the topics from the box and make notes.

> education   friends and family   hobbies and sports   home
> travel   work

b Now work in groups and discuss your future plans. Use the How to... box to help you.

person to pass on a recipe they learned to four other people. Those four people then teach four more people, and so on. Thousands of people have changed their cooking habits as a result – and I'm one of them. I've decided I'm not going to eat fast food anymore. I'm going to cook for my friends and take time to eat good food.

It's not only adults, but children, too. Jamie's School Dinners, one of Jamie's best-known projects, tried to improve food in schools and encourage children to eat well. It was difficult to convince some of the children, but in the end, many schools improved their menus. And my children are going to eat their vegetables now! So what's Jamie going to do next? Well, whatever it is, one thing is for sure, I'm not going to miss it!

3.2 Let's celebrate!

Grammar Present Continuous: future arrangements

Can do make arrangements with a friend

Listening

1 In groups, look at the photo and discuss the questions.

   1 Which country can you see?

   2 Which festival are the people celebrating?

2 **a** Prepare to listen to two friends, Tarin (from the US) and Marcos (from Spain), talking about Thanksgiving Day. Label the pictures (A–E) with the types of food from the box.

> apple pie ☐   cranberry sauce ☐   maple syrup ☐
> stuffing ☐   sweet potatoes ☐   turkey ☐

b 🔊 1.21 Now listen to the dialogue and number the words from exercise 2a in the order you hear them.

A

_____ and _____

B

C

_____

D

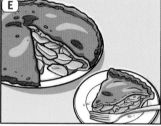

E

_____

3 Listen again and answer the questions.

   1 Where is Tarin planning to have the Thanksgiving meal?

   2 What do people usually do after the meal?

   3 Do people usually buy presents for their family and friends?

   4 What kinds of things do people have with sweet potatoes?

   5 What are the two basic ingredients of stuffing?

   6 Does everyone in the US eat apple pie at Thanksgiving?

   7 What time does Tarin's Thanksgiving meal start?

4 Work in pairs and discuss the questions.

   1 Do you think you would enjoy Tarin's Thanksgiving Day meal? Why/Why not?

   2 Do you think you would enjoy the Macy's Thanksgiving Day Parade? Why/Why not?

Vocabulary | describing food

5 Look at the adjectives for describing food and answer the questions.

> baked   boiled   fresh   fried   grilled
> raw   roast   savoury   spicy   sweet

   1 Which five adjectives describe how food is cooked?

   2 Which three adjectives describe the taste of food?

   3 What is the difference in meaning between *roast* and *baked*?

   4 What is the difference in meaning between *fresh* and *raw*?

6 Find the mistakes in seven of the sentences and correct them.

1 On name days in Spain, people traditionally eat cakes and other spicy things.

2 I go shopping every day to buy fresh vegetables in the market.

3 In Australia, I had boiled sausages and other meat done on the barbecue.

4 I love the smell of the freshly roast bread that my mother makes.

5 For breakfast, I often have fried egg and bacon with toast.

6 I didn't like the grilled chicken because it was in the oven for too long.

7 On Friday nights, we often get a take-away of raw Indian curry.

8 I like pasta which is boiled for a short time and isn't too soft.

9 When I have a snack, I try to have something spicy like nuts or cheese.

10 In Japan, I had delicious boiled fish; it wasn't cooked at all.

7 Work in small groups and discuss the questions.

1 Think about an important celebration in your country (or a country you know about). What different kinds of food do people usually have? How do you cook the food? What else do people do?

2 What kinds of food have you tried from different countries? What did you like? What would you like to try?

Grammar | Present Continuous: future arrangements

8 🔘 1.22 Listen to part of the dialogue from exercise 2b and complete the Active grammar box.

Active grammar

We use the Present Continuous to talk about future arrangements (a time and place are decided).

Present Continuous: *be* + verb + *-ing*

➕   *My brother _____ with friends next week.*

  I _____ a meal at my house to celebrate Thanksgiving.

➖   *I _____ anything.*

❓   *What _____ next Thursday?*

Note: we use *be going to* when we have a plan or intention (but no arrangement about a time or place).

---

see Reference page 37

9 Choose the correct words in *italics*.

1 My parents *are coming/are going to come* for dinner at my house at 6:30 p.m. this evening.

2 She *is celebrating/is going to celebrate* her birthday in a restaurant, but she isn't sure which one.

3 *I'm meeting/I'm going to meet* Anna at the station at five o'clock for the parade.

4 My sister *is taking part/is going to take part* in a cookery competition at school on Friday afternoon.

5 *I'm learning/I'm going to learn* how to cook properly, but I'm not sure what course to do.

6 He *is leaving/is going to leave* tomorrow on the 7:30 train.

Speaking

10 🔘 1.23 Listen to two extracts from the dialogue from exercise 2b and read audioscript 1.23 on page 152. Add one phrase to each section of the How to... box.

How to... make arrangements

Make a suggestion	*Let's go to the Indian restaurant tonight.* (1) _____
Accept or reject	*Great idea!* *Oh! I'm not keen on spicy food.* *I'm busy, I'm afraid. I'm seeing Jo.* (2) _____
Arrange to meet	*Shall we meet at the restaurant at 7:30?* (3) _____
Confirm	*Actually, 8:00 is better for me.* (4) _____

---

11 **a** Prepare to make arrangements with other students to have meals together in the next week. First, make notes about ...

1 a meal you want to cook or a restaurant you want to go to.

2 the day of your meal (in the next seven days).

3 the time you want to have the meal.

b Now, walk around and talk to your classmates. Make as many arrangements as possible.

Reading

1 **a** Look at the photo and read the dictionary definition. Then work in pairs and discuss the questions.

> **ra–ta–tou–ille** /ˌrætəˈtuːi/ (n) a vegetable stew which originates in France; usually made with onions, tomatoes, peppers, aubergines, courgettes, herbs and garlic

1 Why is the film called *Ratatouille*?
2 Who do you think the characters in the picture are?
3 What do you think their relationship is?
4 What do you think the film is about?

b Read the text and check your answers.

2 Read the text again and complete the notes.

1 Name of film: *The film is called 'Ratatouille'.*
2 Time/place: *It's set in …*
3 Main characters: *It's about …*
4 Problem: *The problem is that …*
5 The plan:

3 Think of a film you like. Make notes using the headings from exercise 2. Then work in pairs and describe your films.

Grammar | defining relative clauses

4 Look at the underlined sentences in the text from exercise 1b. Complete the Active grammar box with *where*, *who* and *which*.

> ### Active grammar
>
> Defining relative clauses give essential information to identify the person, thing or place we are talking about.
>
> They come directly after the noun.
>
> A We use _____ for people.
>
> B We use _____ for things.
>
> C We use _____ to say what happens in a place.
>
> We can use *that* instead of *who* or *which* (informal).

see Reference page 37

RATATOUILLE

Remy is the main character in the film *Ratatouille*. He is a rat, but not an ordinary rat. At the beginning of the film, he lives with his family in the countryside in modern-day France. But he is not like the other rats who live in his colony. He has an incredible sense of smell and taste, and his ambition is to learn to cook. His hero is a great chef called Chef Gusteau. Whenever he can, Remy watches Gusteau's old cookery programmes on TV and begins to learn different recipes. Only Remy's brother, Emile, knows about this ambition and Emile loves eating the food which his brother prepares.

One day, the owner of the house where Remy and Emile live tries to kill all the rats. They escape, but Remy becomes separated from his family and travels to Paris alone. By chance, he arrives at the restaurant which Chef Gusteau ran when he was alive. At first, Remy is pleased. But there is a problem: the restaurant had a bad review written by the food critic Anton Ego. The new cook, Chef Skinner, makes boring food and the restaurant is losing more and more customers.

Linguini is the boy who works in the kitchen. He wants to make the food more interesting and help the restaurant to improve, but he doesn't know what to do. Remy watches him and decides to help. While Chef Skinner is asleep, Linguini and Remy become a partnership with the rat sitting inside Linguini's chef hat. He tells Linguini how to cook by pulling on his hair in different ways to control his actions. So, in the end, Remy lives his dream of being a master chef and creating fantastic dishes. His life is good and he even finds Emile again and gives him food from the restaurant. The food critic, Anton Ego, finally comes back to the restaurant. He tastes the food which Remy cooks and gives the restaurant a rave review.

5 **a** Complete the sentences with *who*, *which* or *where*.

1 This is the café _____ I always buy my lunch.
2 She's the woman _____ owns the café.
3 Is that the bag _____ your friend gave you?
4 This is the town _____ I lived as a child.
5 You are the only person _____ noticed my new haircut.
6 Do you have the money _____ I gave you yesterday?
7 Is she the one _____ you don't like?
8 Look at this photo. You can see the village _____ we went on holiday last year.

b In which sentences above can you also use *that*?

6 Look at the Lifelong learning box and read the tip. Then work in pairs and follow the instructions.

Student A: look at page 129.
Student B: look at page 134.

Defining what you mean

! If you don't know the name of something in English, explain what you mean with these phrases.

It's the thing that you use for eating soup. (spoon)

It's the stuff that you eat with turkey at Thanksgiving. (stuffing).

It's the person who runs the kitchen in a restaurant. (chef)

Use *thing* for countable nouns, *stuff* for uncountable nouns and *person* for people.

Lifelong learning

Pronunciation | silent letters

7 **a** Some words in English have silent letters – they are not pronounced. Look at the dictionary definition. How is chocolate pronounced? Which letter is silent?

> **choco‑late** /ˈtʃɒklət/ (n) a sweet hard brown food: *Can I have a piece of chocolate?*

b 🔘 1.24 Circle the silent letters in the words from the box. Then listen, check and repeat.

> calm   comfortable   hour   island   knife
> lamb   receipt   spaghetti   vegetable
> Wednesday   yoghurt

8 🔘 1.25 Work in pairs. Listen and repeat the sentences.

1 I had lamb in yoghurt for lunch on Wednesday.
2 Would you prefer spaghetti or vegetable soup?
3 Chocolate makes me feel calm.
4 It takes an hour to get to the island.
5 For camping holidays, take comfortable shoes and a penknife.
6 Could I have a receipt, please?

see Pronunciation bank page 147

Vocabulary | easily-confused words

9 **a** Work in pairs. What is the difference between ...

> argument/discussion   chef/chief
> cook/cooker   educated/polite   now/actually
> plate/dish   recipe/receipt   sensible/sensitive

b Work in groups and compare your ideas.

10 **a** Choose the correct words in *italics*.

Our *cook*/cooker broke when the pizza was cooking.

1 The *chef*/*chief* of the fire department inspected the restaurant kitchen.
2 Can you give me the *recipe*/*receipt* for that chocolate cake you made?
3 The first *plate*/*dish* was delicious pasta with a spicy sauce.
4 I thought he didn't like Indian food, but *now*/ *actually* he loves it.
5 My brother was angry that the bill was wrong and had a big *argument*/*discussion* with the waiter.
6 When a customer complains, the waiters must always be *educated*/*polite*.
7 The waiter is very *sensible*/*sensitive* and gets upset easily if you criticise him.

b Now write sentences for the other word in each pair from exercise 10a.

My mother is the best cook in our family.

Speaking

11 **a** Choose a topic (1–5) and prepare to talk about it. Make notes.

1 A great recipe which I know how to make
2 Someone I know who is an amazing cook
3 A restaurant where you can get fantastic food
4 An argument which I had with a waiter
5 A dish which I loved when I was a child

b Now work in groups of three and take turns to talk about your topics.

1 Work in small groups and tell your classmates about one of your favourite restaurants. Talk about ...

1 the name and location of the restaurant.

2 the type of food (e.g. pizza and pasta, modern French, traditional Indian, fast food).

3 the quality of food (e.g. delicious, varied, well-presented, simple).

4 the prices (e.g. good value, expensive, reasonable, affordable).

5 the quality and type of service (e.g. friendly, efficient, slow, waiter/self-service).

6 the atmosphere and décor (e.g. modern, traditional, lively, touristy, full of young people).

7 any special features/how the restaurant attracts customers (e.g. music, discount before 7:00 p.m., menu in different languages).

2 **a** 1.26 Listen to Anita talking about her plans to open a new restaurant. Answer the questions.

1 Where is Anita's restaurant going to be?

2 What is she going to call her restaurant?

3 Is she going to serve only English food?

4 Is the food going to be very expensive?

5 How many dishes are going to be on the menu?

6 Is there going to be waiter service or self-service?

7 What two extra features does she mention?

b Listen again. Check your answers and complete the menu.

MENU

STARTERS

Fresh mussels in garlic sauce

Italian salad

_____

MAIN COURSES

Cheese and lemon pasta

Grilled fish of the day with green beans

_____

DESSERTS

Chocolate mousse

Homemade ice cream

_____

3 **a** Work in groups of three. Imagine you are going to open a new restaurant. Look at exercise 1 again and make decisions about each topic for your restaurant.

b Tell other groups your ideas. Vote for the group with the best chance of success.

be going to: future plans

We use *be going to* to talk about future plans and intentions (when the speaker makes the decision before speaking).

A: **Are** you **going to see** Sally this week?

B: I don't know. **I'm going to phone** her this evening.

⊕	I He/She/It We/You/They	am is are	going to	see Maria on Saturday.
⊖	I He/She/It We/You/They	am is are	not going to	
❓	Am Is Are	I he/she/it we/you/they	going to	see her?
	Yes, I am./No, I'm not.			

! We often use future time expressions with *be going to* e.g. *this afternoon, tonight, tomorrow, next week,* etc.

Present Continuous: future arrangements

We use the Present Continuous to talk about future arrangements (a time and place are decided).

When **are** you **starting** your new job?

She **isn't coming** to my birthday party.

Are you **meeting** Alan after work? Yes, I **am.**/No, I'm **not.**

⊕	I He/She/It We/You/They	am is are	meeting	Alan at 7:00 p.m.
⊖	I He/She/It We/You/They	am is are	not meeting	
❓	Am Is Are	I he/she/it we/you/they	meeting	him?
	Yes, I am./No, I'm not.			

! *be going to* and the Present Continuous can be used to express similar ideas. Choose depending on what you mean.

I'm going to see Phil again. (a decision has been made but no arrangement)

I'm seeing Phil tonight at the tennis club. (an arrangement has been made with Phil)

With the verbs *go* and *come*, we usually use the Present Continuous.

I **am going to** Australia as soon as I have saved enough money.

Defining relative clauses

Defining relative clauses give essential information to identify the person, thing or place we are talking about.

They answer the questions: *Which person? Which thing? Which place?*

Defining relative clauses come directly after the noun in the main clause.

We use *who* to talk about people, *which* to talk about things and *where* to talk about places.

She's the teacher **who** I like.

This is the book **which** you want.

That's the shop **where** I bought these shoes.

We can use *that* instead of *who* or *which*.

The young man **that**/**who** I work with never stops talking.

Tom bought the jacket **that**/**which** we saw yesterday.

! Don't use commas before or after defining relative clauses.

! In defining relative clauses, we use the relative pronoun (*who, which, where, that*) instead of the subject pronoun (*he, she, it, they*), when the subject is the same in both clauses.

The man lives next door. **He came** to see me yesterday.

The man **who** lives next door **came** to see me yesterday.

~~The man who lives next door he came to see me yesterday.~~

When the subject is different in the second clause, we need to keep the subject pronoun.

She's the person. **I saw** her yesterday.

She's the person **who I saw** yesterday.

~~She's the person who saw yesterday.~~

Key vocabulary

Cooking and eating

allergic   chefs   diets   main course   menu   recipe   traditional dish   vegetarian

Describing food

baked   boiled   fresh   fried   grilled   raw   roast   savoury   spicy   sweet

Easily-confused words

argument/discussion   chef/chief   cook/cooker   educated/polite   now/actually   plate/dish   recipe/receipt   sensible/sensitive

 Listen to these words.

ACTIVE BOOK

 see Writing bank page 137

3 Review and practice

1 Answer the questions with *be going to* and the words in brackets.

Have you finished the report? (tomorrow)
No, I'm going to finish it tomorrow.

1 Have you had something to eat? (later)
2 Have you taken the dog for a walk? (after dinner)
3 Have you bought Mary a birthday present? (at the weekend)
4 Have you painted the spare bedroom? (on Tuesday)
5 Have you cleaned the bathroom? (in the morning)

2 Make questions with *be going to*.

Your friend tells you that she is going shopping.
What _____*are you going*_____ to buy?

1 Your friend has said he definitely wants to give up smoking.
When _____ ?
2 Peter tells you that it's Jane's birthday next week.
_____ a present?
3 Your friend has bought a painting.
Where _____ put it?
4 You see a friend filling a bucket with hot water.
_____ car?

3 Make one sentence from two. Use *who*, *which* or *where*. (You may sometimes need to leave out a word.)

This is the car. I would like to buy it.
This *is the car which I would like to buy.*

1 A waiter brought us our food. He was very friendly.
The _____ .
2 This is the restaurant. John asked me to marry him here.
This _____ .
3 A train goes to the airport. It runs every twenty minutes.
The _____ .
4 Some men robbed the post office. They escaped in a black BMW.
The _____ .
5 This is the corner of the road. The accident happened here.
This _____ .

4 Find the four Present Continuous mistakes and correct them.

A: Hi Tim! What do you do this evening?
B: Not a lot. Actually, I have a quiet evening at home alone.
A: Why don't you come round to my house? I inviting a few friends over for dinner.
B: I'm not sure. I'm quite tired.
A: How about tomorrow night?
B: I'm go to the cinema with my brother. Why don't you come, too?
A: Great! I'd love to.

5 Look at the diary extract. Write complete sentences about what the person is doing on each day.
She's having a day off on Monday.

Monday

DAY OFF!

11 a.m. Dentist
2 p.m. lunch with Jenny
6:30 p.m. Italian class

Tuesday

10 a.m. give presentation to Sales Manager
3 p.m. meeting with Marketing Director
6 p.m. phone US office
8 p.m. cinema with Nathan

6 Complete the sentences with the words from the box. There are two extra words.

> boiled   ~~chef~~   cooker   raw   receipt
> recipe   roast   sweet

I'd like to train to be a _____*chef*_____ when I leave school.

1 Keep the _____ if you want to bring anything back to the shop.
2 I'm not very keen on _____ food like cakes and biscuits.
3 We've just bought a new electric _____ .
4 I'm cooking for Ruth tonight. Do you know a _____ for chicken and spinach?
5 It's good to eat _____ vegetables which you don't cook at all.

Survival

Lead-in

1 Look at the photos and think of three words for each one. In pairs, describe each photo using all of your words.

desert: hot, dry, lonely

2 a 🔘 1.27 Listen to five people. Number the situations in the order you hear them. There is one extra situation.

a surviving in a difficult climate ☐   d doing an extreme sport ☐

b having a job interview ☐   e training for a job ☐

c going travelling abroad ☐   f raising money for charity ☐

b Listen again. Match the phrases with the situations from exercise 2a.

> a challenge ☐   achieve your goal ☐   control your fear ☐
> physical/mental strength ☐   rely on ☐

c Now match the phrases with the definitions (1–5).

1 _____ : make yourself feel less frightened

2 _____ : get the result you wanted or hoped for

3 _____ : something new, exciting or difficult to do

4 _____ : trust or depend on someone or something

5 _____ : the physical or mental ability to deal with difficult situations

3 Work in pairs and discuss the questions.

1 What are you afraid of, e.g. flying, crowded places, heights? Do you do anything to help control your fear? If so, what?

2 What are your goals at the moment? How will you achieve them?

3 Do you enjoy a challenge at work/in your leisure time?

4 Who or what do you rely on most in times of need?

Sir Edmund Hillary and Tenzing Norgay climbed to the top of Mount Everest in 1953. Peter Habeler and Reinhold Messner aren't as famous as Hillary and Tenzing, but their achievements are perhaps more extraordinary. On 8 May 1978, Habeler and Messner became the first people to reach the top of Everest without bottled oxygen. The air at the top of Everest contains very little oxygen and it is much more difficult to breathe up there. When they were about 800 metres from the top, getting dressed took over two hours and they didn't speak in order to save breath. Every time they climbed a bit higher, their progress became a bit slower. They stopped and lay down every few steps because of the lack of oxygen. They were confident of their ability, however, and finally they achieved their 'impossible' goal. They reached the top of Mount Everest without oxygen – feeling physically worse, but also happier, than they ever imagined.

Most people can hold their breath for a bit longer than a minute – long enough to dive down about four metres to the bottom of a swimming pool. But, in April 2009, Sara Campbell went much deeper than that. She held her breath for over three and a half minutes and became the world free-diving champion by diving ninety-six metres below the surface of the sea. Freediving is much more dangerous than you think and Sara is very brave – fifty people a year die doing this sport. What's more extraordinary is that the 'Mighty Mouse' as she is known (she's only one metre fifty-two centimetres tall) only started diving in 2006, when she was thirty-three years old. During her dives, Sara's lungs become the size of oranges, the pain is almost unbearable and she meditates to control her fear. Sara knows that she is very strong mentally, and that her mental strength is as important as her physical strength. She is a talented diver and she is fitter than ever before. She's also determined to go further in this sport: 'I still haven't found the boundaries of possibility,' she says.

Going up

Going down

Reading

1 What goals do you think the people in the photos achieved? Read the texts and check your ideas.

2 Read the text again. Write true (T) or false (F).

1 Habeler and Messner were the first people to reach the top of Everest. ☐
2 It took them two hours to go 800 metres. ☐
3 They stayed silent because breathing and talking was very difficult. ☐
4 Climbing was easier as they got nearer the top of the mountain. ☐
5 Freediving in the sea is a very safe sport. ☐
6 Sara's nickname is 'Mighty Mouse' because she's very small. ☐
7 Sara's body changes as she dives down into the water. ☐
8 Sara has a lot of mental strength. ☐

3 Work in pairs and discuss the questions.

1 How would you feel about diving a long way under the sea and climbing a mountain like Mount Everest?

2 Which person/people from the text do you admire more? Why?

3 Why do you think people do this kind of thing?

Vocabulary | describing people

4 **a** Look at page 130 and read the descriptions (1–9). Which adjective matches each description?

> ~~brave~~ confident determined fit funny
> generous intelligent motivated reliable talented

b Rewrite the descriptions from page 130. Replace the underlined phrases with the verb *to be* and an adjective from exercise 4a.

Sara isn't afraid of anything. Sara is brave.

5 Now describe (a) Sara Campbell and (b) Habeler and Messner, from exercise 1. Use the adjectives from exercise 4a and your own ideas.

Grammar | comparative adjectives

6 **a** Complete the table in the Active grammar box. Check your answers with the text from exercise 1.

b Look at parts A and B of the Active grammar box. What is the difference between …

1 *as … as* and *not as … as*? 2 *a bit* and *much*?

Active grammar

	Adjective	Comparative adjective
One-syllable adjectives	*deep* *fit*	_____ _____
Two-syllable adjectives	*modern*	*more modern than*
Two-syllable adjectives ending with -y	*happy*	_____
Three-syllable adjectives	*dangerous*	_____
Irregular adjectives	*bad* *good* *far*	_____ *better than* _____

A We also make comparisons using *(not) as … as* and the adjective form (not comparative form).

1 *I am as fit as Sara Campbell.*

2 *I am not as fit as Sara Campbell.*

B Modifiers: we can use *a bit* and *much* to modify comparative adjectives.

1 *Most people can hold their breath for a bit longer than a minute.*

2 *Sara Campbell went much deeper than that.*

see Reference page 47

7 **a** Make comparisons with the information from the box.

Carla is much more motivated than Louisa./Louisa isn't as motivated as Carla.

	motivated	fit	determined	brave
Louisa	✓	✓✓✓	✓✓✓	✓
Carla	✓✓✓	✓✓	✓✓	✓✓✓

b 🔘 1.28 Listen and check your answers.

Pronunciation | emphasising important words

8 🔘 1.29 We can give words extra stress when we want to emphasise them. Listen and notice the extra stress.

1 Most people can hold their breath for <u>a bit</u> longer than a minute.

2 Sara Campbell can hold her breath for <u>much</u> more than a minute.

see Pronunciation bank page 148

Speaking

9 Do a personality quiz with your classmates. Divide into two groups: A and B.

Student As: look at the questions below. Match each question with an adjective from exercise 4a and compare your answers with other students in group A.

Student Bs: look at page 130.

1 ▶ Are you usually quite happy to do your homework or do you need someone to push you?

2 ▶ At a party, are you more likely to tell jokes or listen to someone else telling jokes?

3 ▶ When you've made an arrangement to meet a friend, are you: always on time, sometimes late or always late?

4 ▶ How do you feel about giving a speech in front of a lot of people? Do you feel fine, nervous or completely terrified?

10 Now work in A/B pairs and take turns to ask and answer questions. Make notes.

11 Use your notes to make sentences comparing yourself with your partner.

Alessandra is much more motivated than me. She studies a lot without her parents pushing her all the time.

Learn to cope in the wilderness!

THE HILLSIDE SURVIVAL SCHOOL
– *David Johnson*

Vocabulary | survival skills

1 Match the words and phrases from the box with the underlined phrases in the sentences.

> build a shelter   challenge
> cope with   push yourself
> survival skills   ~~the wilderness~~

How long do you think you could survive in <u>an undeveloped, natural place</u>?

How long do you think you could survive in *the wilderness*?

1 What <u>abilities to help you survive</u> do you have?

2 Could you <u>make yourself some protection from the weather and wild animals</u> in a forest?

3 What is the biggest <u>difficult thing to do</u> in your life at the moment?

4 Do you always <u>try very hard</u> in difficult situations?

5 Do you <u>deal with</u> new situations well (e.g. living in a different city)?

2 In pairs, ask and answer the questions from exercise 1. Use the phrases from the box.

How long do you think you could survive in the wilderness?

Listening

3 🔘 1.30 Look at the photos. Listen to a talk by David Johnson of the Hillside Survival School and answer the questions.

1 Who is David Johnson?

2 Who is he talking to and why?

3 Where is he now?

4 Listen again and complete the notes.

5 In groups, discuss the questions.

1 Would you like to go on one of the courses at the Hillside Survival School? Why/Why not?

2 How would you feel about doing the activities you can see in the photos?

Introduction

David's previous work:

(1) _____

His aims: help people discover nature/outdoor life;

(2) _____

Two groups of people the courses are popular with: work colleagues and

(3) _____

Basic survival course:

How long for?

(4) _____

When does it take place?

(5) _____

Cost? (6) _____

Extreme survival course:

When does it take place?

(7) _____

Cost? (8) _____

What do you learn on the Extreme survival course about …

• food? (9) _____

• shelter? (10) _____

Grammar | superlative adjectives

6 **a** Complete the table in the Active grammar box. Check your answers with audioscript 1.30 on page 152.

b Now look at parts A and B of the Active grammar box and complete sentences 1 and 2 with *of* or *in*.

Active grammar

	Adjective	Superlative adjective
One-syllable adjectives	*cold* *wet*	_____ _____
Two-syllable adjectives	*modern*	*the most modern*
Two-syllable adjectives ending with -y	*noisy*	*the noisiest*
Three-syllable adjectives	*popular* *comfortable*	_____ _____
Irregular adjectives	*bad* *good* *far*	*the worst* _____ *the furthest*

Ⓐ Before superlatives, we use *the* or a possessive adjective.

the oldest building
my best friend

Ⓑ After superlatives, we usually use *in* before the names of places and groups of people. In most other cases we use *of*.

1 *He was the most effective person _____ the team.*

2 *It was the most exciting weekend _____ my life.*

see Reference page 47

7 Find the mistake in each sentence and correct it.

1 That is hardest I've ever pushed myself at work.

2 This is the most big challenge of the day.

3 Could you survive in the hottest place of the world?

4 Building a shelter was the more difficult thing we did.

5 Lara is the most good in the class at coping with new situations.

6 Simon is the most experienced person of our office.

7 My sister is the bravest person at our family.

8 That course was the bad experience of my life.

8 Complete the notes with the words from the box. There are two extra words. Does each person feel positive or negative?

> best   difficult   exciting   happy   in
> more   most   noisiest   of   worst

Send | Chat | Attach | Address | Fonts | Colors | Save As Draft

To: David
From: Nicholas Morris
Subject: Last weekend!

Dear David

Just a quick email to say the whole Sales Team really enjoyed the weekend. It was the most (1) _____ thing we've ever done, but it was also great fun. Thanks a million for the (2) _____ fantastic experience which we will never forget (even though you said our shelter was the (3) _____ you've ever seen)!

Best wishes,

Nicholas Morris (Sales Manager – Elite Magazines)

Hi David — a big thank you for helping to make it the most (4) _____ birthday (5) _____ my whole life! We all had a fantastic time and enjoyed it a lot more than we expected. In fact, we loved it all, but cooking over the open fire was the (6) _____ activity. Sorry for being the (7) _____ bunch of girls (8) _____ the group!

Sarah (and Ruth and Lauren)

Speaking

9 Write complete questions. Use the superlative form of the adjectives.

What/difficult situation/you ever cope with?

What is the most difficult situation you've ever coped with?

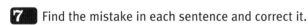

1 What/dangerous thing/ever happen to you?

2 Who/determined person/your family or class?

3 What/challenging job/you ever done?

4 What/difficult exam/you ever take?

10 Work in groups and discuss the questions from exercise 9.

One language – three cultures

One thing that the British, the Americans and the Australians have in common is their language: they all speak English. But, if you're a tourist in one of these places, you'll find there are many differences ... and not only in the language! Have a look at our essential survival guide.

1 _____
You want to know how to be polite wherever you are. It's common for people to queue (UK/Aus) and stand in line (US) at bus stops and in shops – so don't push to the front. Don't be surprised to hear English people saying 'sorry' a lot – even if it's you who steps on their foot. It's best just to say 'sorry', too. And in the US, when every shop assistant asks 'How are you?' it's polite to answer 'I'm good, thanks'. In Australia, it is a bit more informal, as most people greet each other with the traditional Australian 'G'day'.

2 _____
As a visitor in a new country, you try new food and go to different restaurants. You'll soon learn the differences in various kinds of food and drink, such as French fries (US) and chips (UK/Aus), and soda (US), fizzy drink (UK) and soft drink (Aus). Remember, too, about tipping: in the US, it is common to leave a tip of 18–20% of your check (US) wherever you go. In the UK and in Australia, most people leave a tip of about 12–15% of their bill (UK/Aus).

3 _____
In the UK, and in Australia, you drive on the left side of the road, but in the US, you drive on the right. Remember this is also important if you are a pedestrian. When you cross the road, check the direction of the traffic before stepping off the sidewalk (US), the pavement (UK) or the footpath (Aus).

Reading

1 **a** Look at the photos and the title of the text. Answer the questions.

1 What three places can you see in the photos?

2 What do you think the title of the text means?

b Read the text quickly and match the headings (a–c) with the paragraphs (1–3).

a Being polite   c Eating out

b Travel and transport

2 Read the text again and answer the questions.

1 How do you say 'to queue' in the US?

2 In the UK, what sometimes happens when you step on someone's foot?

3 What is a common way of saying 'hello' in Australia?

4 In which country would you hear 'I'd like a soda and French fries, please'?

5 In which country do people usually leave the biggest tip?

6 How do you say 'Can I have the bill, please?' in the US?

7 Which side of the road do the Australians drive on?

8 Where does a pedestrian walk in the US?

3 Work in groups and discuss the questions.

1 Which information in the text do you think is the most useful for a visitor?

2 What other information do you think would be useful to know?

3 Do you know any other English words which are different in the UK, the US and Australia?

4 Look at the Lifelong learning box. Read the tip and write the British English word for each of the American English words.

British and American English

! It is a good idea to be aware of words which are different in British and American English. When you learn a word, try to find out if there are different words.

American English words: *apartment, cell phone, chips, cookie, elevator, gas, pants, purse, restroom, vacation*

British English words: ...

Lifelong learning

Listening

5 🔵 1.31 Listen to three tourists. Match the dialogues (1–3) with the situations (a–c).

a in a clothes shop ☐   c on a train ☐
b at a ticket office ☐

6 Listen again and answer the question for each dialogue.

1 When does the train leave?
2 What does the passenger want to read?
3 Does the customer buy the jacket?

Grammar | indirect questions

7 Listen again and tick (✓) the questions you hear.

1 a How long does the train take? ☐
  b Can you tell me how long the train takes? ☐
2 a Is it OK with you if I sit here? ☐
  b Can I sit here? ☐
3 a Could you tell me how much it is? ☐
  b How much is it? ☐

8 **a** Match the question pairs from exercise 7 (1–3) with the question types in the Active grammar box (A–C).

b Look at exercise 7 again. Which question in each pair is direct and which is indirect?

Active grammar

We use indirect questions when we want to be polite. We begin with an indirect phrase, e.g. *Can you tell me … ?/Could you tell me … ?/ Do you know … ?/Do you mind … ?/Is it OK with you … ?*

A *Wh-* questions: verb *to be* ☐
Direct: question word + *to be* + subject
Indirect: indirect phrase + question word + subject + *to be*

B *Wh-* questions: main verbs ☐
Direct: question word + *do/does/did/can/ could* + subject + verb
Indirect: indirect phrase + question word + subject + verb

C *Yes/No* questions ☐
Direct: *do/does/did/can/could* + subject + main verb
Indirect: indirect phrase + *if* + subject + main verb

see Reference page 47

9 Make the questions indirect. Use the words in brackets.

How long does the journey take? (Do/know?)
Do you know how long the journey takes?

1 What's the time, please? (Can/tell?)
2 Can I borrow your pen for a minute? (Do/mind?)
3 Do you have any 1st class stamps? (Could/tell?)
4 Is there a post office near here? (Can/tell?)
5 Where can I get an application form, please? (Do/know?)

Pronunciation | intonation in indirect questions

10 **a** 🔵 1.32 Our tone of voice changes in indirect questions to make them sound polite. Listen and repeat the question. Try to copy the intonation.

Can you tell me what time it is, please?

b 🔵 1.33 In pairs, ask the other indirect questions from exercise 9 using appropriate intonation. Listen, check and repeat.

see Pronunciation bank page 148

Speaking

11 🔵 1.34 Look at the How to… box. Listen and write the responses.

How to… be polite in English

Use indirect questions and polite responses

Can you tell me if you have this jacket in medium?	1 _____
Could you tell me how much it is, please?	2 _____
Is it OK if I pay by credit card?	3 _____
Do you mind if I read it … ?	4 _____

12 In pairs, practise one dialogue from audioscript 1.31 on page 153. You can change the parts in bold.

1 **a** Label the things in the photo with the words from the box. Which word is not in the photo?

> blankets   box of matches   candles
> chocolate   first-aid kit   mirror
> pen and paper   penknife   plastic bowl
> radio   rope   scissors   sun cream   tent
> torch   umbrella   water

b In pairs, take turns to cover the page and remember the items in the photo.

2 🔊 1.35 Listen to a dialogue about a survival course and answer the questions.

1 Who are they going with?
2 Which items do they decide to take?

3 Listen again and read audioscript 1.35 on page 153. Underline the language they use to ...

1 express their opinions.
2 make suggestions.
3 make comparisons.

4 **a** Work in pairs and prepare to go on a survival course weekend. Make a list of five objects from exercise 1a to take with you.

b Now work with another pair. Compare your lists and agree on a final list of five objects. Try to persuade the other pair that your objects are the best and give reasons for your ideas.

I think sun cream is more important than an umbrella because it's going to be hot and sunny.

Comparative and superlative adjectives

One-syllable adjectives

Adjective	Comparative	Superlative	Spelling
small	smaller (than)	the smallest	ends in consonant: + -er; the -est
nice brave	nicer (than) braver (than)	the nicest the bravest	ends in -e: + -r; the -st
fit big	fitter (than) bigger (than)	the fittest the biggest	vowel + consonant: double consonant

Their garden is **larger than** ours. Brian is **the thinnest** boy in the class.

Two- or more syllable adjectives

Adjective	Comparative	Superlative	Spelling
happy easy	happier (than) easier (than)	the happiest the easiest	two syllables ends in -y: y changes to i
boring interesting	more boring (than) more interesting (than)	the most boring the most interesting	two or more syllables: no change

The beach is **more crowded than** yesterday.
It's **the easiest** way to do it. She is **the most famous** person I know.

Irregular adjectives

Adjective	Comparative	Superlative
bad	worse (than)	the worst
good	better (than)	the best
far	farther/further (than)	the farthest/furthest

(not) as ... as

We can also make comparisons with (not) as ... as.
Marta is **as tall as** Tom, but she isn**'t as tall as** Rachel.

Comparatives with modifiers

We can use a bit and much to modify comparative adjectives.
a bit = a small difference: I'm **a bit taller** than my brother.
much = a big difference: That test was **much easier** than the last one.

Before superlatives

We use the or a possessive adjective: **the** least expensive; **my** oldest son

After superlatives

We usually use in before the names of places and groups of people:
Who is the youngest manager **in** the company?
We use of in most other cases:
She is the cleverest **of** my three sisters.

Indirect questions

We use indirect questions when we want to be polite. We begin with an indirect phrase, e.g. *Can you tell me ... ?/Could you tell me ... ?/Do you know ... ?/Do you mind ... ?/Is it OK with you ... ?*

Wh- questions: verb *to be*

Direct: question word + *to be* + subject
Where is the party?

Indirect: indirect phrase + question word + subject + *to be*
Could you tell me where the party is?

Wh- questions: main verbs

Direct: question word + *do/does/did/can/ could* + subject + verb
What time does this shop open?

Indirect: indirect phrase + question word + subject + verb
Can you tell me what time this shop opens?

Yes/No questions

Direct: *do/does/did/can/could* + subject + main verb
Can Jack speak Spanish?

! Use *if* or *whether* for indirect *Yes/No* questions.

Indirect: indirect phrase + *if/whether* + subject + main verb
Do you know if/whether Jack can speak Spanish?

Key vocabulary

Survival
a challenge   achieve your goal
control your fear
physical/mental strength   rely on
build a shelter   cope with
push yourself   survival skills
the wilderness

Describing people
brave   confident   determined
fit   funny   generous   intelligent
motivated   reliable   talented

Survival equipment
blankets   box of matches   candles
chocolate   first-aid kit   mirror
pen and paper   penknife   plastic bowl
radio   rope   scissors   sun cream
tent   torch   umbrella   water

 Listen to these words.
ACTIVE BOOK

 see Writing bank page 138

1 Complete the sentences with the comparative form of the adjectives from the box.

> bad   exciting   far   happy   ~~old~~   quiet

Her CV says she is only twenty-three years old.
I thought she was ___*older*___ .

1 This café is very noisy. Can we go somewhere _____ ?

2 That film sounds really boring. *Murder City* sounds _____ .

3 My job is quite good. It could be a lot _____ .

4 You seem _____ today – you looked quite sad yesterday.

5 The house was _____ from the station than I thought.

2 Complete the sentences with a comparative adjective and *not as ... as*.

Sarah is 1.65 metres. I am 1.70 metres. (tall)
I'm *taller than* Sarah. Sarah *isn't as tall as me.*

1 The gold watch is €180. The silver watch is €100. (expensive)
The gold watch ... . The silver watch ... .

2 The Brighton train leaves at 3:30 p.m. The London train leaves at 3:00 p.m. (late)
The Brighton train ... . The London train ... .

3 Health is very important to me. Money is not very important to me. (important)
Health ... . Money ... .

4 White bread tastes good. Brown bread tastes very good. (good)
Brown bread ... . White bread ... .

3 Complete the sentences with the superlative form of the adjectives from the box.

> expensive   fast   friendly   hot   ~~long~~   tall

That was *the longest* film I've ever seen. It lasted for four hours!

1 This jacket cost €350. It was _____ one in the shop!

2 August is usually _____ month in the UK. The temperature goes up to around 24°C.

3 Sam is _____ boy in the class. He is nearly two metres tall.

4 This is _____ car I've ever had. It goes from 0–100 kilometres per hour in seven seconds.

5 Michael is _____ man I've ever met. He loves to meet new people.

4 Write complete sentences. Use comparatives or superlatives.

She is/funny/person/my family
She is the funniest person in my family.

1 Today was/hot/day/the year

2 You are/much/brave/me

3 Harry is/intelligent/boy/his school

4 These jeans are/a bit/expensive/those ones

5 This is/old/house/the town

6 She seems/a bit/happy/yesterday

7 It was/bad/shock/my life

8 Greece is/much/hot/England/at the moment

5 Add a word to each sentence to make it correct.

Can you tell me where the bathroom $^{is}_\wedge$?

1 You know why he isn't home yet?

2 Do you know I can pay by credit card?

3 Can you tell me I can find a garage?

4 Can you tell whose car this is, please?

5 Do you know time the next train for Manchester leaves?

6 Write complete questions using the prompts.

What time/shops close? (Do you know ...)
Do you know what time the shops close?

1 where/find/cheap hotel? (Do you know ...)

2 internet café/near here? (Can you tell me ...)

3 we share/taxi to the airport? (Do you mind ...)

4 I/borrow your phone? (Is it OK ...)

5 need visa/go to Ireland? (Could you tell me ...)

7 Complete the sentences with the words from the box. There are three extra words.

> achieve   cope   fear   fit   generous
> ~~motivated~~   push   reliable   rely

He is very *motivated* to practise the piano because he wants to be a professional musician.

1 When he lived abroad, he found it difficult to _____ with learning a new language.

2 My best friend is really _____ . She paid for the whole meal for everyone last night.

3 It's important to control your _____ when you have to give a speech or a presentation.

4 You need to be very _____ if you want to run the marathon next year.

5 When I'm upset, I can always _____ on my friends to make me feel better.

Stages

5

Lead-in

1 Look at the photos. What are the people doing? How old are they?

He's learning to walk.

He's a toddler.

2 **a** What do you think the age range is for each time of life?

A baby is from birth to about one year old.

> adolescent (young) adult baby child middle-aged person
> old/elderly person retired person teenager toddler

b In pairs, compare your answers. Do you agree?

3 In your country, what is the typical age to do the things in the box?

> earn a good salary get a job get a place of your own get engaged
> get married graduate from university have children
> have your first kiss learn to drive a car look after your grandchildren
> retire start wearing make-up

4 Describe your life or the life of an older person.

My grandmother was born in Seville in 1942. When she was a child, she moved to Madrid. She lived there until her twenties and got married at twenty-six.

Grammar *should, have to, can*: obligation and permission

Can do exchange opinions with a friend

Reading

1 Work in pairs and discuss the questions.

1 What has/have been the best year(s) of your life so far? Why?

2 Describe the situations in the photos. What similar experiences have you had?

2 Read text 1 and answer the questions.

1 Who is the website for?

2 What does the website ask readers to do?

3 a Work in groups of three. Read your text and tick (✓) the subjects mentioned.

Student A: read text 2 about Gregor on this page.

Student B: read about Miguel on page 130.

Student C: read about Fei on page 134.

	Gregor	Miguel	Fei
the army			
education			
free time			
career			
money			
family			

b Now take turns to talk about your texts and complete the rest of the table from exercise 3a.

4 In your groups, discuss the questions.

1 Which person do you think you are most similar to: Gregor, Miguel or Fei? In what ways?

2 Did you enjoy your life when you were eighteen? Why/ Why not?

① **HAVE YOUR SAY:** *Life at eighteen*

What's life like for you, now that you are eighteen?

- Is life easy? Perhaps it's the best time of your life. You can study whatever you want and you can socialise with your friends. You live with your parents and you spend their money. You can enjoy your life now, as well as dreaming about your ambitious plans for the future.

- Or is life difficult? Perhaps it's time to stand on your own two feet. You have to become an adult and take responsibility for your life. You should get a job and earn some money. You have to move out of your parents' house and get your own place. You can dream about the future, but you have to deal with the present first.

Have your say and send us your comments. Tell us what life is like for you.

② **Name:** *Gregor Kinski*   **Nationality:** *Russian*

I am from Moscow and my name is Gregor. I am a sculpture student at Moscow University and live with my parents and two brothers. I had my eighteenth birthday last month and I'm enjoying my life at the moment.

In Russia, it is often difficult for men aged eighteen because they usually have to go into the army and do military service. In my opinion, military service shouldn't be compulsory. I mean, I think it should be optional, but it isn't. Luckily for me, I don't have to do military service because I've got health problems. I'm actually quite happy about that! It means it's possible to continue studying sculpture at university. Who wants to be a soldier when you can be a student?

I enjoy my studies and I also have a good social life. In my free time, I like listening to rock and hip-hop. I also like going to restaurants and bars and concerts and playing football – like teenagers everywhere, I suppose. My parents are very kind and tolerant – I can't go out every night, but I can do a lot of things I enjoy. It's difficult to get a place of my own because it's very expensive and anyway, I like living with my family. I'm preparing for my future and my parents are very supportive of that.

Grammar | *should, have to, can*: obligation and permission

5 Look at the text about Gregor from exercise 3a and underline examples of *should, shouldn't, have to, don't have to, can* and *can't*. Then complete the Active grammar box.

Active grammar

Strong obligation

A We use _____ to say when something is necessary and there is no choice.

B We use _____ to say when something is not necessary and there is a choice.

Mild obligation

C We use _____ to say something is the right thing to do in your opinion.

D We use _____ to say something is not the right thing to do in your opinion.

Permission

E We use _____ to say when something is permitted.

F We use _____ to say when something is not permitted.

---

see Reference page 57

6 Choose the correct words in *italics*.

1 There is no choice in my country. I *have to/ should* go into the army for a year.

2 There's no dress code where I work. You *can/ should* wear whatever you want.

3 I think teenagers *have to/should* help with the housework when they're living with their parents.

4 We *don't have to/shouldn't* take a taxi. I've got my car here and I'll drive you.

5 You *don't have to/shouldn't* smoke during meals – it's annoying.

7 Complete the sentences with *should(n't)*, *can('t)* or *(don't) have to*.

1 I think everyone _____ travel for a year before university. It's a brilliant experience.

2 In the UK, children _____ stay at school until they're sixteen. It's the law.

3 Young people in my country _____ do military service. It stopped last year.

4 In my opinion, people _____ come to work in jeans. It looks really bad.

5 In the US, you _____ vote in presidential elections until you're eighteen.

Pronunciation | connected speech (2)

8 **a** 🔘 1.36 When two consonants are next to each other, one of the consonants is often not pronounced. Listen to the sentences and circle the consonant that is not pronounced.

1 You shouldn't sit around doing nothing.

2 You can't go out every night.

b Listen again, check and repeat.

see Pronunciation bank page 148

Listening and speaking

9 **a** 🔘 1.37 Listen and match the dialogues (1–3) with a topic (a–e).

a Eighteen is too young to get married. ☐

b You should look after your parents when they retire. ☐

c Teenagers only worry about girlfriends/ boyfriends and money. ☐

d Children should help with housework. ☐

e Young people should do military service. ☐

b Listen again and answer the questions.

1 What does the woman say happens from the age of eighteen to twenty-five?

2 What does the woman suggest as an alternative to military service?

3 What does the man say is the main pressure on teenagers?

10 **a** Complete the How to... box with the headings (a–c).

a Agree/disagree

b Ask for an opinion

c Give your opinion with reasons

How to... exchange opinions

1 _____	*I think … because …* *In my opinion, …* *The main reason is …*
2 _____	*What do you think?* *Don't you think so?*
3 _____	*I agree (with you)./I think you're right.* *I don't agree./I'm not so sure (about that).*

---

b Work in small groups and discuss one topic from exercise 9a.

Grammar | Present Perfect Simple: *for* and *since*

1 Read the website extract. What is its purpose?

2 Look at the <u>underlined</u> sentence in the text and answer the questions.

1 When did Tina start her job at the advertising firm?

2 Does she still work there?

3 Complete the Active grammar box with *for* or *since*.

Active grammar

We use the Present Perfect Simple for actions that started in the past and continue in the present.

I've worked for the same company for the last two years.

I've lived in Manchester since 2006.

I haven't seen anyone from school for years.

How long have you lived here?

A We use _____ when we give the length of the time.

B We use _____ when we give the beginning of the time.

Common time expressions with *for* and *since*:

for ages, for a long time, for a while

since I left school, since we met, since I last saw her, since then

We use the Past Simple for completed actions in the past when we specify a time.

I joined FriendsBook in April last year.

I bought a flat about a year ago.

---

see Reference page 57 and Irregular verb table page 149

4 Read the dialogue between Tina and an old friend, Martin. Complete the gaps with *for* or *since*.

Tina: I'm so glad you emailed. It's been so long (1) _____ I saw you!

Martin: I know. Well, I've been in Poland (2) _____ almost two years. I'm teaching English there.

Tina: So, are you enjoying it?

Martin: It's been great, especially (3) _____ I met this woman called Dorota. We've known each other (4) _____ about six months now. She works in the same school as me.

Tina: Oh! That's great ... so, when are you both coming to the UK?

Tina Armstrong

Member Profile   Write on Tina's messageboard

What I'm doing now

Since I left school, I've travelled a bit and had a few different jobs including working on a cruise ship in the Caribbean. <u>I've worked for the same company for the last two years.</u> I'm an Accounts Manager in a big advertising firm. It's an interesting job and I work with some great colleagues.

I've lived in Manchester since 2006. I bought a flat about a year ago near the city centre. It's a lovely flat and I share it with Jerry, my cat!

I joined FriendsBook in April last year so I've been a member of this site for nearly a year. It's great and I've made some good new friends. But I haven't seen anyone from school for years. I've lost touch with most of my old school friends and I'd love to get in touch with you – so send me a message!

Tina has **178 friends** | View Tina's friends | Add Tina as a friend

5 Find the mistakes in five of the <u>underlined</u> verbs and correct them.

1 I <u>work</u> in the same office since 2004 and I still love it!

2 He<u>'s bought</u> a new car about six months ago.

3 My sister belongs to a tennis club – she <u>is</u> a member for three years.

4 We<u>'ve lived</u> in Spain before, but now we live in France.

5 When I <u>left</u> school, I started work as a trainee hairdresser.

6 I <u>met</u> some really nice people since I started work here.

6 Choose three things/people from the box. Work in pairs and tell your partner how long you have known the people or had the things. Add one more fact to each description.

I've been a member of my local gym for three months. I try to go twice a week.

> member of a club/social networking website   your doctor
> your flat/house   your mobile phone   your shoes
> your teacher   your town   your watch

Vocabulary | friendship

7 Match the phrasal verbs from A with the definitions from B.

A	B
1 get in touch (with someone)	a) have a good relationship
2 keep in touch (with someone)	b) have no more contact
3 lose touch (with someone)	c) stop being friends after an argument
4 catch up (with someone)	d) continue contact
5 get on (with someone)	e) have a romantic, loving relationship
6 fall out (with someone)	f) start contact again after not speaking for some time
7 go out (with someone)	g) end a loving relationship
8 split up (with someone)	h) find out what has happened during the time you haven't spoken to someone

8 Complete Tina's story with the correct form of the phrasal verbs from exercise 7.

Martin is an old friend of mine. I first met him at school when we were eleven. We (1) _____ really well. In fact, he was my first boyfriend – I (2) _____ with him for six months when we were fifteen. But when I went to university, we (3) _____ and I didn't hear from him for ages. About a year ago, I registered with FriendsBook. Martin saw my profile and (4) _____ again. We spoke to each other on the phone – it was good to (5) _____ with him and all his news. He was in Poland at that time and had a girlfriend called Dorota. Sadly, their relationship didn't last. They (6) _____ because Martin moved back to the UK, but Dorota wanted to stay in Poland. They didn't (7) _____ with each other – they're still friends and they (8) _____ by email.

Listening

9 **a** 🔊 1.38 Listen to Tina and Martin talking about the photo. Who are Alison, Jake and Melanie?

b Listen to the dialogue again and answer the questions.

1 How long has Tina known Alison?
2 How often does she see Alison now?
3 How did she first meet Jake?
4 What does she like about Jake?
5 How long has she known Melanie?
6 What does she think is special about Melanie?

Speaking

1 _____
2 _____

Three of my best friends

3 _____

10 Complete the diagram for you. Write the names of three of your best friends and a word or phrase about each one.

11 **a** Work in pairs. Look at your partner's diagram and write two questions about each person.

b Now ask and answer your questions. Try to ask more questions during the discussion.

How long am I going to live?

A Nobody really knows the answer to that question, but scientists are very interested in trying to understand the various factors involved. Firstly, it depends a lot on what you eat. The country with the longest average lifespan is Japan. On average, women live to 82.5 years and men live to 76.2 years. Scientists think that diet in Japan is a major reason that Japanese people live a long time; <u>they usually eat lots of fish and seafood and not much junk food.</u> As well as diet, lifestyle habits also seem to make a difference to lifespan. On average, married people live longer than single people and pet owners live longer than non-pet owners. <u>Being mentally active and doing physical exercise are also very important.</u>

B Studies of very old people, however, don't always support the scientific theories. <u>Many old people don't eat healthily</u> and don't do much exercise. Jeanne Calment, the world's oldest person ever, certainly goes against logical scientific ideas. She was born in France in 1875 and died aged 122. Did she use to have good lifestyle habits? Well, according to scientists, she had some very good habits: she did plenty of physical exercise and used to ride a bicycle until she was 100. <u>She was good at thinking positively and she didn't use to worry about things.</u> Scientists are surprised, however, by her other habits: she used to be a heavy smoker – and only gave up when she was 120. Also, she didn't use to eat very healthily: she used to eat more than two pounds of chocolate a week.

C So lifestyle is not the only factor in how long we live. Scientists now think that some people are born with genes that protect them from ageing and diseases better than other people. For example, Jeanne Calment probably had a gene that stopped her from getting cancer that other people may get aged forty or fifty. Some experts believe that we can change our genes by eating a low-calorie diet. Experiments with mice show that when they eat one third fewer calories every day, they live forty percent longer. In human terms, that's the same as living to 170 years old. There's no proof that it works in humans, however, and perhaps it's best to enjoy the days you've got rather than be hungry all your life!

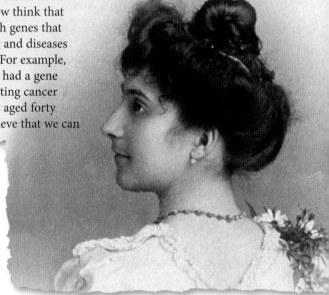

Reading

1 **a** Work in pairs and discuss the statements. To what extent do you think each one is true?

1 How long you live depends on your lifestyle (diet, exercise, etc.).
2 How long you live depends on your genes.
3 Some people have unhealthy habits, but live a long time.

b Read the text quickly and match the statements from exercise 1a with the paragraphs (A–C).

2 Read the text again. Write true (T) or false (F).

1 The Japanese diet has a very good effect on their lifespan. ☐
2 Living with an animal generally decreases your lifespan. ☐
3 Most very old people have always had healthy lifestyles. ☐
4 Some experts think that some people have natural protection from some diseases. ☐
5 Jeanne Calment got cancer when she was about fifty years old. ☐
6 Some people think that eating fewer calories every day will increase your lifespan. ☐

3 Would you like to live to 120 years old? Why/Why not?

Vocabulary | habits

4 Look at the <u>underlined</u> sections of the text from exercise 1b and make verb phrases with the words from A and B.

A

be   do   eat (x2)   think   worry

B

about things   healthily   junk food
mentally active   physical exercise
positively

5 Work in groups and discuss the questions.

1 Which habits from exercise 4 do you have?
2 Which would you like to change? Why?

Grammar | *used to*: past habits

6   **a**   Complete the Active grammar box with *use* or *used*. Check your answers with the text from exercise 1b.

  b   Look at the text from exercise 1b again and find three more examples of *used to/didn't use to*.

Active grammar

used to + infinitive is for habits and situations which happened repeatedly or over a long period of time in the past, but don't happen now or are not true anymore.

➕   *Jeanne Calment _____ to ride a bicycle until she was 100.*

➖   *She didn't _____ to worry about things.*

❓   *Did she _____ to have good lifestyle habits?*

For completed actions in the past, we use the Past Simple (NOT ~~used to~~).

She was born in France in 1875.

For habits in the present, we use *usually* (NOT ~~used to~~).

Japanese people usually eat lots of fish and seafood.

---

see Reference page 57

7   Write complete sentences with *used to*, *didn't use to* or *did (you) use to*.

1   (I/eat/a lot of junk food) _____ , but now I don't.

2   (I/not/worry about things) _____ , but I do now.

3   (you/do regular physical exercise) _____ when you were a child?

4   (My father/do a lot of physical exercise) _____ , but he stopped in 2005 after an accident.

5   (people/be more mentally active) _____ 100 years ago?

6   (My sister/not/like healthy food) _____ , but now she loves it.

8   Choose the correct words in *italics*.

1   I *used to walk/usually walk* to work every day, but I changed my job and now I go by bus.

2   My grandmother *used to go/went* to her first dance class when she was sixty-eight.

3   I *used to cook/usually cook* dinner at home because I really love cooking.

4   I *didn't use to finish/didn't finish* my dinner last night because I didn't feel well.

5   My brother *used to play/usually plays* computer games when he was younger, but now he plays tennis.

6   My parents *didn't use to do/don't usually do* any physical exercise, but now they like swimming.

9   **a**   Look at the Lifelong learning box. Read the tip and answer the questions.

Which of the learning habits ...

1   did you use to do, but don't do now?

2   do you usually do?

3   would you like to do?

Good learning habits

- I write all new words/phrases in my vocabulary notebook.
- I try to speak English as much as I can.
- I watch English-speaking TV programmes and films (with and without subtitles).
- I do grammar revision exercises regularly.

Lifelong learning

---

  b   In pairs, make a list of three more good learning habits.

Speaking

10   🔊 1.39   Listen to a man talking about his childhood and answer the questions.

1   Which three topics from the box does the man mention?

2   Which two statements are true and which one is false?

---

brothers and sisters   food   pets
grandparents   holidays   sports
playing with friends   school

---

11   Work in pairs. Tell your partner three things about your childhood. One statement should be false. Take turns to guess which statement is false.

Penelope Cruz

Maria Sharapova

Michelle Obama

1 What do you know about the women in the photos?

2 a 🔊 1.40 Listen to a radio programme called *This is Your Life*. Which woman is it about? How do you know?

b Listen again and number the phrases in the order you hear them.

a Currently, ... ☐
b After graduating, she ... ☐
c Looking at family matters, ... ☐
d Going back to her early life, ... ☐
e This is where she met ... ☐
f Today on *This is Your Life*, we are talking about ... ☐

3 Prepare to talk about someone in your family or a famous person. Complete the fact file about him/her.

Fact file

Name:	
Year and place of birth:	
Grew up in:	
Now lives in:	
Marital status/children:	
Work/career:	
Hobbies:	
Personality:	
Other information:	

4 a Now make notes about what you want to say. Use your fact file and the phrases from exercise 2b.

b Tell your classmates about the person you've chosen.

Today on This is Your Life, we are talking about a man who ...

should, have to, can: obligation and permission

Form: modal verb + infinitive

➕	I/You/ We/They He/She/It	have to has to	should can	wait.
➖	I/You/ We/They He/She/It	don't have to doesn't have to	shouldn't can't	vote.
❓	Do	I/you/we/ they	have to	go?
	Does	he/she/it		
	Should/ Can	I/you/we/they/he/ she/it		

❗ Do not use the auxiliary *do/does* when making the question form with *should* or *can*.

Should *I wear a hat to the wedding?*

NOT: ~~Do I should wear a hat to the wedding?~~

We use *should/shouldn't* to say something is/isn't the right thing to do in your opinion.

*You **should** wear smart clothes for your job interview.*

*You **shouldn't** go to bed late before an important exam.*

We use *can/can't* to say when something is/isn't permitted.

*You **can** learn to drive when you're seventeen in the UK.*

*You **can't** come in here with your shoes on.*

We use *have to* to say when something is necessary and there is no choice.

*I **have to** get up early tomorrow because my train leaves at 7 a.m.*

We use *don't have to* to say when something is not necessary and there is a choice.

*In Britain, you **don't have to** vote.*

Present Perfect Simple: *for* and *since*

We use the Present Perfect Simple for actions that started in the past and continue in the present.

*I've lived in this country **for** six years.*

*I **haven't seen** Maria **since** last summer.*

*How long **have** you **been** at this school?*

We use *for* when we give the length of the time:

for three years, for a week, for half an hour, for ages, for a long time, for a while

We use *since* when we give the beginning of the time:

since 1996, since this morning, since 10:30, since I left school, since we met, since I last saw her, since then

used to: past habits

used to + infinitive

➕	I/you/ he/she/ we/they	used to		play the piano.
➖	I/you/ he/she/ we/they	didn't use to		do any exercise.
❓	Did	I/you/ he/she/ we/they	use to	live in the countryside?

used to + infinitive is for habits and situations which happened repeatedly or over a long period of time in the past, but don't happen now or are not true anymore.

*Tina **used to** play the violin, but now she doesn't.*

*I **didn't use to** like London, but now I love it.*

For completed actions in the past, we use the Past Simple (NOT ~~used to~~).

He finished his studies in 2010.

For habits in the present, we use *usually* (NOT ~~used to~~).

I usually visit my family at the weekend.

Key vocabulary

Times of life

adolescent   (young) adult   baby   child middle-aged person   old/elderly person retired person   teenager   toddler

Life activities

earn a good salary   get a job   get a place of your own get engaged   get married   graduate from university have children   have your first kiss   learn to drive a car look after your grandchildren   retire start wearing make-up

Friendship

catch up   fall out   get in touch   get on   go out keep in touch   lose touch   split up

Good and bad habits

be mentally active   do physical exercise eat healthily   eat junk food   think positively worry about things

 Listen to these words.

ACTIVE BOOK

 see Writing bank page 139

5 Review and practice

1 Rewrite the sentences using *should(n't), can('t)* or *(don't) have to*.

It's a good idea to join a gym if you want to get fit.

You should join a gym if you want to get fit.

1   In the UK, it is necessary to wear seatbelts in the back of a car.
    In the UK, you _____ .

2   My brother is permitted to watch TV for a maximum of two hours a day.
    My brother _____ .

3   It's a good idea to go to Germany to improve your German.
    You _____ .

4   It's necessary to show your student card to get a reduction.
    You _____ .

5   It isn't necessary to drive me to the airport. I'll get a taxi.
    You _____ .

6   It isn't a good idea to drink coffee just before you go to bed.
    You _____ .

7   It is not permitted to play loud music between 11 p.m. and 7 a.m.
    You _____ .

2 Find the mistakes in five of the sentences and correct them.

You don't have take the dog for a walk. ✗

You don't have to take the dog for a walk.

1   You can't to enter without a ticket.
2   Does he has to work this weekend?
3   You should change your office chair. It isn't good for your back.
4   They doesn't have to wear school uniform.
5   Do you should take a coat with you?
6   Can you wear jeans at your office?
7   Are you sure you have take all your certificates to the interview?

3 Complete the sentences with *for* or *since*.

I've known Susie __since__ we were at primary school.

1   She's lived in London _____ years!
2   We haven't had this car _____ very long.
3   They've worked here _____ 2005.
4   I've had this watch _____ last summer.
5   He hasn't seen his brother _____ nearly a year.

4 Make one sentence from two. Use the Present Perfect Simple.

Sam works for our company. He joined six months ago.

Sam has worked for our company for six months.

1   I play the guitar. I learned when I was a child.
2   My parents live in Bristol. They moved there in April.
3   He had an accident ten years ago. He didn't work after that.
4   I have a dog. I got him two years ago.
5   I know Jack quite well. I met him in October.
6   She doesn't play tennis now. She last played tennis when she was fifteen.
7   I study English. I started studying three years ago.
8   He saw Angie five years ago. He didn't see her after that.

5 Find the mistakes in six of the sentences and correct them.

I didn't use like my piano teacher. ✗

I didn't use to like my piano teacher.

1   They used to go to the same school.
2   Did you use play football at school?
3   She didn't used to get good marks at school.
4   Where you use to live before you came here?
5   He didn't use to enjoy golf very much.
6   I used like my job more than I do now.
7   Did you used to eat a lot of junk food?
8   My parents didn't use have a television.

6 Choose the correct words in *italics*.

My parents are (middle-aged)/-ages now.

1   He used to *make/do* a lot of physical exercise.
2   Mick and Joanne *got/had* engaged last week.
3   I got *on/in* touch with an old friend via the website.
4   I haven't seen Bill for ages. We *lost/missed* touch when he went abroad.
5   She's upset because she split *out/up* with her boyfriend last week.
6   I'd like to get a *piece/place* of my own when I'm old enough.
7   I think it's good to be mentally *action/active* at all stages of your life.

Lead-in

1 **a** Look at the photos. Which continent do you associate with each photo?

> Africa   Antarctica   Asia   Europe   North America
> South America   Oceania

b Work in pairs and answer the questions.

Can you name three countries ...

1   where the main language is Spanish?
2   where you can swim in the Mediterranean Sea?
3   in Europe which are north of Poland?
4   where you have to drive on the left side of the road?
5   which are on the equator?
6   where summer is in December/January?

c Which countries have you visited/would you like to visit?

2 Check the meaning of the <u>underlined</u> words and phrases. Then work in pairs and answer the questions.

1   What is <u>the capital</u> of Australia?
2   Which major city <u>is situated</u> in Europe and Asia?
3   Where are <u>the remains</u> of the Parthenon?
4   What are the main <u>tourist destinations</u> in your country?
5   Which <u>region</u> in your country is an area of <u>natural beauty</u>?
6   What is the most beautiful <u>landscape</u> you've ever seen?
7   What is the <u>population</u> of your country and your town/city?
8   What <u>green spaces</u> are there in your area?

6.1 A Greek island

Grammar	*will*, *may*, *might*: prediction
Can do	make general predictions about the future

Vocabulary | geographical features

1 Look at the photo of a Greek island. Which words from the box can you see?

> bay   beach   cliff   coast
> forest   island   lake   mountain
> peninsula   river   sea

2 Complete the text with the singular or plural form of the words from exercise 1.

Physical location and features

Greece is in southern Europe. It consists of a large (1) _____ called the Peloponnese, surrounded on three sides by (2) _____ and approximately 3,000 (3) _____ . About 140 of these islands are inhabited, and of these, Crete is the largest. Including all the islands, there are about 15,000 kilometres of (4) _____ with thousands of long sandy (5) _____ , high rocky (6) _____ and small (7) _____ , often with many fishing boats.

Eighty percent of Greece is covered in mountains. Olympus, situated in the west, is the highest (8) _____ in Greece, rising to 2,919 metres above sea level. A range of mountains called The Pindus lies across the centre of the country and the longest (9) _____ in Greece, the Aliakmon, starts in this area. The Rhodope Mountains form the border between Greece and Bulgaria in the north. This area is covered with a huge, thick (10) _____ of pine trees and contains one of Greece's largest (11) _____ , called Volvi.

3 In pairs, answer the questions.
1 Is your country an island or not?
2 Is there a famous river or lake near where you live?
3 Do you prefer holidays near a beach or a mountain?
4 Are there any cliffs or bays in your region?
5 Is there a peninsula near where you live?
6 Does your country have a long coast?

Listening

4 🔊 1.41 Listen to a radio programme about tourism in Greece and answer the question.

What positive effect and negative effect of tourism are mentioned?

5 Listen again and complete each sentence with one or two words.
1 Greece is a very _____ holiday destination.
2 Most people know the names of islands like Crete from _____ guides.
3 Skopelos is a _____ island situated to the east of Athens.
4 *Mamma Mia!* was a _____ before it was a film.
5 Before the film, Skopelos was mostly known for plums, pears and _____ .
6 Before the producers chose Skopelos, they researched _____ other islands.
7 In the film, a _____ takes place on the mountain on the peninsula near Glisteri Beach.

6 Work in groups and discuss the question.

Would you like more tourism in your country? Why/Why not?

Grammar | *will, may, might*: prediction

7 Complete the Active grammar box with the verb phrases from the box. Check your answers with audioscript 1.41 on page 154.

> may not keep   might be   will increase
> will the film bring   won't stay

Active grammar

We use *will* + verb and *won't (will not)* + verb to make predictions about the future.

We use *may (not)/might (not)* + verb to talk about future possibilities.

⊕ *The* Mamma Mia! *effect _____ tourism on other islands.*
The film _____ very good for business.

⊖ *They _____ the peaceful atmosphere of the island completely.*
Skopelos _____ the same.

❓ *_____ success for the island of Skopelos?*

see Reference page 67

8 Complete the sentences with *will, won't* or *may/might (not)* and the verbs in brackets.

1 Daniel loves surfing. I'm sure he _____ (come) to the beach with us this weekend.
2 I'm not sure yet, but they _____ (build) a new ski resort in the mountains.
3 We haven't got much money, so I'm certain we _____ (not go) on holiday this year.
4 I'm sure you _____ (have) a fantastic time in the Seychelles. Those islands are amazing.
5 Some people think the Amazon Rainforest _____ (disappear) in fifty years, but they're not certain.
6 I'm not sure about going to the beach today. It's late and we _____ (not find) anywhere to park.
7 I'm certain it _____ (be) cold up in the mountains. It's always freezing, especially at night.

9 Write the words in the correct order to make answers.

1 A: Will tourism change the island of Skopelos?
  B: I/change/Yes/lot/it/think/will/a/it
  _____ .

2 A: Where will you live when you're older?
  B: live/I/by/think/I/coast/will/the
  _____ .

3 A: Where are they going on holiday next year?
  B: go/they/Greece/will/think/to/I
  _____ .

4 A: Do you think you will pass the exam?
  B: will/I/Yes/think/I
  _____ .

5 A: Do you think he will get the job?
  B: is/the/might/he/It/job/not/possible/get
  _____ .

Pronunciation | contractions: *will*

10 ● 1.42 Look at the answers to questions 1–4 from exercise 9. Can you contract the subject + *will* in each case? Listen, check and repeat.

see Pronunciation bank page 148

Speaking

11 Work in pairs and follow the instructions.

1 Draw a simple map of your country/ region. Label the important geographical features.
2 Choose three of the places you labelled. What would you tell a tourist about them? Make notes.
3 What do you think is the future of tourism in your country/region (or a country/region you know well)? Make notes.
4 Now present your map to the class. Tell them about tourism and the future of tourism in your country/ region.

The beaches in my region are very popular. I think the number of tourists will increase because ...

Garden of Freedom
~ my favourite place

Nelson Mandela was in prison in South Africa for twenty-seven years. During that time, and after he was freed, he became a massive influence in Africa, and all over the world. His influence was not only political. When he was in prison, he started a <u>garden</u> which was his favourite place because, as he said, it was, 'a small taste of freedom' for him. Mandela's love for his garden has inspired a lot of <u>people</u>.

Mandela noticed the roof of the prison was flat and empty. It wasn't beautiful, but it was peaceful and more importantly, it got <u>sunshine</u> all day. He realised that he didn't need much <u>equipment</u> or much <u>money</u> to start a small garden. He just needed a few <u>things</u> and a bit of <u>help</u> to get started. After <u>years</u> of asking, the prison guards finally gave him sixteen large oil drums and they cut them in half for him. He filled them with some <u>soil</u> and created thirty-two giant flowerpots.

The garden was a relaxing place to go. It gave Mandela something to do and it produced a little <u>food</u>. But the most important thing was that it gave him some <u>control</u> and <u>freedom</u> in his life. He spent a lot of <u>time</u> there – as often as he could. He loved the satisfaction of planting a <u>seed</u> and watching it grow into a <u>tree</u> or a <u>plant</u> full of <u>vegetables</u>. It was a lot of <u>work</u> but it made him feel better about himself. At first, there weren't any other prisoners who were interested, but after a while some people joined Mandela in his garden.

The charity Seeds for Africa was inspired by the fact that Mandela's prison garden made him and other prisoners feel good. The first prison vegetable garden the charity started was at Kabwe Prison in Zambia. There are 500 <u>prisoners</u> at Kabwe Prison and the prison garden gives them fresh vegetables to eat. And, just as it was for Mandela, the garden is their favourite place. It gives the prisoners somewhere pleasant to go – somewhere which gives them a little <u>happiness</u> and a taste of freedom.

Reading

1 What do you know about Nelson Mandela? Write down as many facts as you can. In pairs, compare your answers.

He was in prison for a long time.

2 **a** Look at the pictures. Why do you think the text is called *Garden of Freedom – my favourite place*?

b Read the text and check your ideas.

3 Read the text again and answer the questions.

1 When was Mandela influential around the world?
2 Why was Mandela's garden his favourite place?
3 In which part of the prison was Mandela's garden?
4 How long did it take him to get the equipment for his garden?
5 Why did the garden make Mandela feel better about himself?
6 Why did Seeds for Africa think about starting a prison garden?
7 What benefits do the prisoners get from their garden?

4 Mandela wrote a book called *Long Walk to Freedom* about his life in prison. Do you think you would like to read it? Why/Why not?

Grammar | countable and uncountable nouns

5 Read the Active grammar box. Then look at the underlined words in the text from exercise 2 and decide if they are countable or uncountable.

> ## Active grammar
>
> | Countable nouns | Uncountable nouns |
> |---|---|
> | • are singular or plural nouns | • are only singular nouns |
> | • can use the indefinite article (*a/an*) | • can't use the indefinite article (*a/an*) |
> | • use *a few*, *some* and *a lot of* in positive sentences | • use *a little*, *a bit of*, *some* and *a lot of* in positive sentences |
> | • use *any* or *many* in negatives and questions | • use *any* or *much* in negatives and questions |

see Reference page 67

6 Choose the correct words in *italics*.

1 I haven't got *any/some* time to sit in the park today.
2 There are *a little/a few* animals living in my garden.
3 I need *a bit of/a few* advice about these fruit trees.
4 We haven't got *much/many* people to help us today.
5 Keeping my garden looking good involves *many/a lot of* hard work.
6 I'd like some more plants, but I don't have *many/much* money at the moment.

7 **a** Correct the mistake in each sentence.

1 I like my city because it's got much trees.
2 There isn't many parks in my city.
3 I've got any beautiful flowers in my garden. They are mostly red and white.
4 There are a little small mountains near where I live.
5 There aren't any of big lakes in my country.
6 I sometimes sit in my garden to get a bit peace.

b Make the sentences from exercise 7a true for you. In pairs, compare your answers.

Vocabulary | describing a place

8 **a** In pairs, check you know the meaning of the words in *italics*. Then choose the correct words.

1 The prison garden gives the prisoners somewhere *pleasant/unspoilt* to go.
2 My favourite place is a beach in Barcelona. It's really *beautiful/wild* – with clear sea and clean sand.
3 The lake near where I live is very *romantic/relaxing*. I go there to calm down after a busy week at work.
4 My favourite beach is empty during the week, but really *crowded/noisy* at the weekends.
5 The most *peaceful/impressive* place I've ever been is the Iguazú Falls in South America. They are huge and amazing.
6 I had a holiday on an *idyllic/exciting* island in the Indian Ocean. Everything about the place was perfect.

b Which two adjectives have a negative meaning?

c Make a sentence for each adjective from exercise 8a. Use places you know.

9 **a** 🌐 1.43 Listen to two people, Gavin and Heather, talking about their favourite places. Match each speaker with a place. Write *G* or *H*.

a Southern Thailand ☐   b Northumberland, UK ☐

b Listen again. Which adjectives from exercise 8a do they use?
1 Gavin _____
2 Heather _____

Pronunciation | diphthongs

10 **a** 🌐 1.44 A diphthong is when we say two vowel sounds together. Listen and repeat the words from the table.

/eɪ/	/aɪ/	/ɔɪ/	/əʊ/	/aʊ/	/ɪə/	/eə/	/ʊə/
bay	like	noise	coast	town	near	hair	sure

b 🌐 1.45 Listen. Match the underlined sounds in the words below with a diphthong from the table. Then work in pairs and practise saying the words.

> w<u>i</u>ld   r<u>o</u>mantic   unsp<u>oi</u>lt   m<u>ou</u>ntain   l<u>a</u>ke
> wh<u>ere</u>   t<u>our</u>   y<u>ear</u>

see Pronunciation bank page 147

Speaking

11 **a** Work in groups and take turns to talk about your favourite places.

b Which two places you heard about would you most like to go to? Why?

Vocabulary | urban environment

1 **a** What is the difference between …

1 sports stadium and leisure centre?
2 library and bookshop?
3 restaurant and café?
4 bar and nightclub?
5 hospital and doctor's surgery?
6 cinema and theatre?
7 museum and art gallery?
8 school and college?
9 bus station and bus stop?
10 train station and tube station?

b Match the areas of a town (1–3) with the buildings you find in them (a–c).

1	residential area	a)	shops and leisure facilities
2	commercial area	b)	factories
3	industrial area	c)	houses and flats

2 Complete the sentences with the words from exercises 1a and 1b.

1 I don't go to the _____ much because I prefer watching films on DVD.
2 There's a good _____ in our town with a swimming pool, a gym and a tennis court.
3 When I was eighteen, I went to the _____ in the town centre to study fashion.
4 We went to a really good _____ last night and danced until 3:00 a.m.
5 There is a large _____ in my town with several very good shopping streets.
6 I bought two good books for my holiday at the _____ in the high street.
7 There were over thirty people waiting for a bus at the _____ this morning.
8 The 8:25 London to Edinburgh train arrives at the _____ in five minutes.
9 I've got an appointment at the _____ to get some medicine for my sore throat.
10 The _____ of my town has wide streets with big houses and a lot of trees.

3 Look at the places from exercises 1a and 1b again. Work in pairs and discuss the questions.

1 Which three places do you often go to in your town? When and why?
2 Which three places do you never go to? Why not?

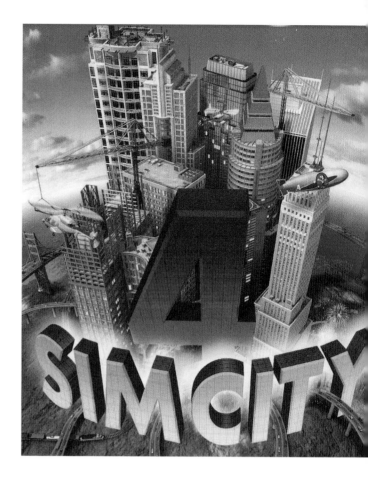

Listening

4 2.2 Listen to two friends talking about the computer game *SimCity*. Answer the questions.

1 What is the basic aim of the game?
2 Why is it so popular?

5 Listen again and complete each sentence with one word.

1 In *SimCity*, you choose what facilities are in your city and how to keep people _____ .
2 You can decide where to put the residential area and the _____ area of the city.
3 You decide how much to spend on basic facilities like roads, hospitals and _____ .
4 The people in *SimCity* don't like paying _____ .
5 When the workers aren't happy about something, they might stop _____ .
6 Newer versions of *SimCity* have areas in your city which become _____ and noisy.
7 Sometimes bad things happen to your city, for example _____ disasters.
8 *SimCity* is popular because it isn't about killing – it's about making decisions in a _____ way.

6 Work in pairs and discuss the questions.

1 Have you ever played *SimCity*?
2 If so, did you like it? Why/Why not?
3 If not, do you think you would like it? Why/Why not?

Grammar | *too, too much/many, (not) enough*

7 **a** Look at the sentences (a–c) and answer the questions.

a Some areas of the city are too noisy for people to live in.

b Some areas of the city aren't quiet enough for people to live in.

c Some areas of the city are quiet enough for people to live in.

1 Which two sentences describe a problem?

2 Which two sentences have the same meaning?

b Look at the Active grammar box and match the rules (A–E) with the examples (1–7).

Active grammar

A We use *too* with adjectives and adverbs. ☐

B We use *too much* with uncountable nouns. ☐

C We use *too many* with countable nouns. ☐

D We use *(not) enough* after adjectives and adverbs. ☐☐

E We use *(not) enough* before nouns. ☐☐

1 *Some areas aren't nice enough to live in.*

2 *Some areas become too crowded for people to live in.*

3 *People don't want to pay too much tax.*

4 *Sometimes they don't spend enough money on schools and hospitals.*

5 *Your city mustn't have too many leisure facilities.*

6 *They want enough facilities in their city.*

7 *They've designed it well enough to appeal to a lot of people.*

We use *very* when we are emphasising an adjective or adverb (but not talking about a problem).

SimCity is a very popular computer game.

See Reference page 67

8 Complete the sentences with the words from the box. You can use some words more than once.

> enough   many   much   too   very

1 The sports stadium isn't near _____ to walk. Let's take the bus.

2 I can't afford to go to the theatre. It's _____ expensive.

3 The neighbours are making too _____ noise for me to sleep.

4 We went to that new nightclub last night. It was _____ good.

5 There were _____ seats on the bus for everyone to sit down.

6 There were too _____ people at the leisure centre so I decided not to go.

9 Complete the sentences with the words in brackets and *enough, too, too much* or *too many*.

1 The area where I live is _____ now. (noisy)

2 My town isn't _____ to have a cinema. (big)

3 There is _____ in the town centre. (traffic)

4 Where I live, it's _____ for me in the winter. (cold)

5 There aren't _____ in our city. (nightclubs)

6 There are often _____ in the café to get a table. (people)

7 My school is _____ for me to walk. (far)

8 There isn't _____ to play football in the park. (space)

Speaking

10 Prepare to talk about your perfect city. First, complete the How to... box with the headings (a–c).

a Give a general reason

b Add a personal reason

c Say your choice

How to... talk about choices and give reasons

1 _____	*I'd like to* build a museum.
	I think we should have a leisure centre.
2 _____	*Because* there aren't enough sports facilities.
	The main reason is that museums are really interesting.
3 _____	*Personally,* I couldn't live without one!
	I love eating out.

---

11 **a** Write five things you would have in your perfect city and make notes about your reasons. Use the How to... box to help you.

b Now work in pairs and discuss your ideas. Agree on five things for your perfect city.

Can do | explain your preferences

A

Cairo

Cairo is full of interesting old monuments, including of course, the famous Great Pyramids at Giza. The people are very friendly and the weather is generally warm and sunny (17°C in March). There are many opportunities for visiting busy markets and getting some good bargains. You can also take interesting boat tours up the river Nile and see more of this ancient country. It's not expensive to stay in Cairo and there are a lot of cheap restaurants with delicious food.

B

Barcelona

Barcelona has something for everyone. There are a lot of interesting museums and art galleries and you can see some amazing modern architecture by Antoni Gaudí, like the Casa Batlló. There are also many beautiful parks, as well as beaches – in the city and all the way up the coast. The nightlife is good – with hundreds of bars and cafés. You can find some cheap places to stay and the climate is very pleasant all year round (12°C in March).

C

Edinburgh

Edinburgh is a very beautiful, old city, full of history. The view of the city from Edinburgh Castle is impressive and there are many good museums and art galleries. There are mountains near the city where you can go walking and the sea isn't far away. It can be cold in Edinburgh (4°C in March), but there is plenty to do, including excellent nightlife and endless shopping possibilities. There is a good choice of places to stay, ranging from cheaper to more expensive.

D

Rio de Janeiro

Rio de Janeiro is famous for beautiful beaches and fantastic nightlife, with great nightclubs and a lot of live music. It's almost always sunny (26°C in March) and the people are very friendly. There are some interesting sites, including the famous Sugar Loaf mountain and of course, Ipanema Beach. Just outside the city, the coast is beautiful and there are forests and mountains. There are a lot of cheap places to stay and plenty of good bars and restaurants.

1 a Match the photos with the cities. What do you know about each city?

> Barcelona ☐   Cairo ☐
> Edinburgh ☐   Rio de Janeiro ☐

b Which topic (a–d) is the most important when you decide where to go for a holiday? What else is important?

a   how far away it is
b   the cost (of getting there, accommodation, food, etc.)
c   the weather
d   activities you can do

2   Work in groups of four and choose one text each to read (A–D). Read your text. Would you like to go on holiday to this city? Why/Why not? Tell the group what you found out.

3 a ⚪ 2.3 Listen to two people deciding where to go on holiday. Which city do they choose?

b Listen again. Write true (T) or false (F).

1   Harry thinks Edinburgh isn't warm enough. ☐
2   Linda loves very hot weather. ☐
3   They both think Rio is too far away. ☐
4   Harry thinks Edinburgh is too expensive. ☐

c Look at audioscript 2.3 on page 155 and complete the sentences. Each sentence is a way of expressing a preference.

1   Cold weather isn't my idea of _____ !
2   I'd _____ somewhere very warm.
3   I like the _____ of going to the beach.
4   I'm not _____ on sitting on a plane for twelve hours.
5   I'd _____ to go somewhere on the coast.

4   Now work in your groups of four again. Imagine you have a week's holiday in March.

1   Decide, on your own, which city (A, B, C or D) you would like to visit and why.
2   As a group, decide on one city to visit. Try to convince other students that your choice is the best.
3   Compare your final decision with other groups. Which city was most popular? Why?

will, may, might: prediction

We use *will* + verb and *won't* (*will not*) + verb to make predictions about the future.

We use *may (not)*/*might (not)* + verb to talk about future possibilities.

➕	I/You/He/She/It/We/They	may/might/will	go.
➖	I/You/He/She/It/We/They	may not/might not/won't	go.
❓	May/Might/Will	I/you/he/she/it/we/they	go?

Yes, it might./No, it might not.
Yes, I will./No, I won't.

! When we make predictions that we are sure about, we use *will*/*won't* + infinitive. We can say we are less sure by saying: *I (don't) think* or *I hope*.

! When we talk about possibilities that we are not sure about, we use *may*/*might (not)* + infinitive.
*It **might** rain today so I'm going to take an umbrella.*
*He **may not** come to the party because he isn't well.*

Countable and uncountable nouns

Countable nouns are words like *person, tree, island*. They can be singular or plural. You can use the indefinite article (*a*/*an*).

Uncountable nouns are words like *information, advice, news*. They are only singular. You can't use the indefinite article (*a*/*an*).

Other examples of uncountable nouns:
accommodation, behaviour, bread, furniture, health, knowledge, luggage, research, salt, spaghetti, traffic, travel, trouble, water, weather, work

Before countable nouns, we use: *a*/*an, a few, some, a lot of* in positive sentences, and *any* and *many* in negative sentences and questions.
*They've got **a lot of** friends in Australia.*
*There weren't **many** people at the party.*
*Have you got **any** tickets?*

Before uncountable nouns, we use: *a little*/*a bit of, some* and *a lot of* in positive sentences, and *any* and *much* in negative sentences and questions.
*We bought **a lot of** bread this morning.*
*I can't give you **any** advice.*
*How **much** salt did you put in this?*

too, too much/many, (not) enough

We use *too* or *not enough* when something is a problem. *too* means there is more than is necessary or wanted. *not enough* means there is less than is necessary or wanted.
*His suitcase was **too** heavy to carry.*
*He was**n't** strong **enough** to carry his suitcase.*

We use *enough* when something is as much/many as necessary, and there is not a problem.
*He saved **enough** money to pay for the ticket.*

We use *very* when we are emphasising an adjective or adverb (but not talking about a problem).
*I'm **very** pleased you came today.*

too	We use *too* with adjectives and adverbs. *I went to bed **too late** last night.* *You did your homework **too quickly**.*
too much	We use *too much* with uncountable nouns. *There's **too much sugar** in my tea.*
too many	We use *too many* with countable nouns. *There are **too many books** on that shelf.*
(not) enough	We use *(not) enough* after adjectives and adverbs, but before nouns. *That bag isn't **big enough**.* *He didn't play **well enough**.* *Sorry, I didn't have **enough time**.* *There were **enough chairs** for everyone.*

Key vocabulary

Geographical features

bay   beach   cliff   coast   forest   island   lake   mountain   peninsula   river   sea

Describing places

beautiful   crowded   exciting   idyllic   impressive   noisy   peaceful   pleasant   relaxing   romantic   unspoilt   wild

Urban environment

art gallery   bar   bookshop   bus station   bus stop   café   cinema   college   commercial area   doctor's surgery   hospital   industrial area   leisure centre   library   museum   nightclub   residential area   restaurant   school   sports stadium   theatre   train station   tube station

Listen to these words.

ACTIVE BOOK

 see Writing bank page 140

6 Review and practice

1 Choose the correct words in *italics*.

Good luck with your exam! I'm sure you (will)/might pass.

1 I've got a long meeting this afternoon, so I *won't/ might* be late home.

2 Why don't you try those jeans on? They *might/ might not* look good on you.

3 What do you think your parents *will/won't* say when they see the mess?

4 I'm sure I *won't/may not* pass my driving test. I'm too nervous.

5 He *might/will* love that present. It's really fantastic.

6 I *might/might not* see you before the weekend because I'm working all week.

7 I invited her to the party, but I don't think she *will/won't* come.

8 It's easy to get there. I'm certain you *might not/ won't* get lost.

2 Delete the extra and unnecessary word in each sentence.

I haven't got much ~~many~~ money at the moment.

1 Are you going to have a few summer holiday this year?

2 I don't need any more of advice.

3 We need some many new furniture for the living room.

4 She's really enjoying a work since she changed jobs.

5 Have you heard Tina's bit news? She's having a baby.

6 Could you give me a little of help with this, please?

7 Have you got any few money you could lend me, please?

8 Would you like me to get you much some tickets for the concert on Sunday?

3 Choose the correct words in *italics*.

I only speak a little/(a few) words of Spanish.

1 We don't have *much/many* rain in summer.

2 She's got *some/a lot* of experience.

3 He gave me a very good *bit/lot* of advice.

4 I need *some/little* paper to write on.

5 Could I have a *little/few* more cake?

6 Do *many/much* tourists come to your town?

7 I don't have *many/much* time this weekend.

8 There isn't *any/some* milk in the fridge.

4 Put the words in the correct order.

got/go/on/money/to/haven't/enough/holiday/I

I haven't got enough money to go on holiday.

1 food/to/The/eat/too/was/hot

2 tea/isn't/enough/There/my/sugar/in

3 far/to/walk/too/home/here/It's/from

4 get/She/old/married/isn't/enough/to

5 pool/the/There/many/in/too/people/were

6 too/chocolate/eat/Don't/much

7 enough/in/waiters/There/this/aren't/restaurant

8 always/her/quickly/dinner/eats/She/too

5 Make one sentence from two.

We couldn't swim in the river. It was too cold.

The river was too cold for us to swim in.

1 I can't carry this suitcase. It's too heavy.

This suitcase _____ .

2 We couldn't sleep in the hotel. It was too noisy.

The hotel _____ .

3 I can't eat this food. It's too spicy.

The food _____ .

4 Nobody could do the homework. It was too difficult.

The homework _____ .

5 I can't reach the top shelf. It's too high.

The top shelf _____ .

6 We couldn't get the table in the car. It was too big.

The table _____ .

6 Put the letters in the correct order.

We walked out to the end of the *peninsula* (slenunapi) and sat looking at the sea.

1 This beach is one of the most _____ (licdily) places I've been in my life.

2 Why don't you go to the _____ (irlbyra) and borrow some books to read on holiday?

3 We set off at 6 a.m. and reached the top of the _____ (anomtuni) at 1 p.m.

4 The _____ (mamelrocic) area of my city is full of really good shops and cafés.

5 My local park is a very _____ (spelnata) place to have a picnic at the weekend.

6 When we were in Greece, we took a boat trip to a beautiful _____ (lidsna).

7 We waited for ages at the _____ (gsyuerr) before we finally saw a doctor.

8 I like going to really _____ (plunosit) places where there aren't many tourists.

Lead-in

1 **a** Put the words into groups: (a) head, (b) torso, (c) arm, (d) leg.

> ankle   back   ear   elbow   eye   face   finger
> forehead   hair   knee   lips   mouth   nose   palm
> shoulder   stomach   thumb   toe   waist   wrist

b Which words can you see in the photos?

2 **a** Match the phrases from the box with the definitions (1–6).

> personality   physical appearance   to get stressed   to go on a diet
> to look like someone   to put on weight

1 _____ : the way someone looks
2 _____ : the kind of person you are, especially in relation to other people
3 _____ : to have a similar appearance to someone else
4 _____ : to become heavier
5 _____ : to eat limited food to lose weight
6 _____ : to get so worried and tired that you cannot relax

b Complete the sentences with the correct form of the phrases from exercise 2a.

1 Most men don't spend enough time on their _____ (hair, clothes, etc.).
2 Most women _____ their mothers.
3 People can _____ by small, everyday things.
4 It's normal to _____ as you get older.
5 Everyone goes _____ at some time in their lives.
6 You can learn about someone's _____ by studying his/her face.

c Work in pairs. Do you agree with the statements from exercise 2b?

69

Grammar First Conditional

Can do talk about possible events and situations in the future

Cover girl

Why do cover girls in magazines always look perfect? Maggie Greene takes a look at the world of models and magazines – and the computers which help them achieve perfection.

Tall and slim, with perfect skin and glossy dark hair, pop star and TV presenter Alesha Dixon is naturally beautiful. But it seems that even she is not good-looking enough to appear in magazines without some help from a computer. Her own experience led Alesha to investigate airbrushing: how photos of celebrities and models are changed to make them more perfect. I was horrified by what she discovered. The evidence, I'm sure you'll agree, is upsetting.

Alesha decided to make a television programme to understand the issue of airbrushing when she noticed a contradiction: people say they like 'natural' beauty, but magazines mostly show 'unnatural' beauty. During her investigations, Alesha discovered that almost all photos in magazines are 'improved' by computers. She found that if you don't agree to airbrushing, magazines won't print photos of you. Magazines are under pressure: they know that if their models look perfect, they will sell more copies. There is pressure, too, from the celebrities themselves: a model or celebrity will be more successful if she looks good. She will be even more successful if she looks perfect. Many airbrushed photos of Alesha herself have appeared in magazines. She admits she looks better after some digital changes: for example, with slimmer legs and better skin.

In my opinion, however, the real danger is not for celebrities, but for ordinary young people. There is a huge pressure for women – and men – to be tall, slim and good-looking. The evidence that Alesha discovered was that airbrushing is increasing this pressure. While making her programme, she talked to young people about beauty. Many of them are desperate to be like the pictures they see in magazines. Most of them, however, have no idea that the pictures aren't real. Looking perfect is a multi-million dollar business for the magazine industry. And it seems that if magazines want to continue to make money, they will have to continue to ignore the dangers of putting pressure on young people to look perfect.

Reading

1 Look at the two photos of Alesha Dixon. In pairs, discuss the questions.

1 Can you see any differences between the two photos?

2 Why do you think the photos look different?

3 Do you read any celebrity magazines or watch programmes about celebrities? Why/Why not?

2 Read the text quickly and answer the questions.

1 What was Alesha Dixon's TV programme about?

2 What does the writer feel about celebrity magazines and young people?

3 Read the text again and answer the questions.

1 How does the writer describe Alesha Dixon's appearance?

2 Why did Alesha first start investigating the issue of airbrushing?

3 How many magazine photos are not airbrushed?

4 Which two areas does the pressure to airbrush come from?

5 What does Alesha think about airbrushed pictures of herself?

6 What does the writer say about young people's attitudes to magazine pictures?

4 Work in pairs. To what extent do you agree with the opinions (a–c)?

a People look better when they are natural and unchanged.

b Airbrushing photos for magazines is always wrong.

c Celebrities should force magazines to use only natural photos.

Vocabulary | appearance

5 **a** Put the words and phrases in the correct column of the table.

> (un)attractive   beautiful   blonde
> dark-haired   dark-skinned
> fair-haired   fair-skinned   fat
> good-looking   handsome
> medium height   muscular
> overweight   red-haired   short
> skinny   ~~slim~~   ~~tall~~   ugly

weight/build	height	attractive or not	colouring
slim	*tall*		

b What is the difference between ...

1 slim and skinny?

2 fat and overweight?

3 handsome and beautiful?

6 **a** Look at the Lifelong learning box. Read the tip and choose one strategy to help you remember the words from exercise 5a.

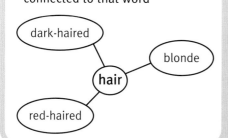

Lifelong learning

Remembering words

❗ You can remember new vocabulary by grouping words in different ways, for example:

- by topic/meaning, e.g. *attractive, beautiful, ...*
- by first letter, e.g. *slim, skinny, ...*
- by part of speech/similar endings, e.g. *dark-haired, fair-haired, ...*
- by creating a story/description, e.g. *My sister is tall and slim, with blonde hair ...*
- by drawing a network of word connections: start with one word and add words which are connected to that word

b Now work in groups and compare the strategies you chose. Which strategies do you think are useful for you?

Grammar | First Conditional

7 Look at the Active grammar box and choose the correct <u>underlined</u> words.

Active grammar

If models look perfect, magazines will sell more copies.
A celebrity will be more successful if she looks good.
If you don't agree to airbrushing, magazines won't print photos of you.

A We use the First Conditional to talk about <u>a possible</u>/<u>an impossible</u> situation in the future.

B The form of the First Conditional is:
If + <u>infinitive</u>/<u>Present Simple</u>, *+* <u>will</u>/<u>won't</u> *+ verb.*

C We use a comma after the first clause:
<u>always</u>/<u>only after the 'if' clause</u>.

see Reference page 77

8 Complete the sentences with the First Conditional form of the verbs in brackets.

1 If you _____ (eat) a lot of junk food, you _____ (put) on weight.

2 You _____ (not have) good skin if you _____ (wear) a lot of make-up.

3 If she _____ (continue) to spend it all on clothes, she _____ (not have) any money left.

4 If you _____ (not start) eating healthily now, you _____ (reduce) your lifespan.

5 You _____ (be) late for the hairdresser if you _____ (not leave) now.

Pronunciation | intonation in conditional sentences

9 **a** 🔊 2.4 Listen and notice the intonation in conditional sentences.

If you eat a lot of junk food, you'll put on weight.

b 🔊 2.5 Listen and repeat. Try to copy the intonation.

see Pronunciation bank page 148

Speaking

10 Choose a prompt (1–3) and make a complete First Conditional sentence about yourself. Add five more sentences. In pairs, take turns to say your sentences.

If I pass my exams, I'll go to university.

If I go to university ...

1 If I pass my exams, ...

2 If I have time this weekend, ...

3 If I make a lot of money, ...

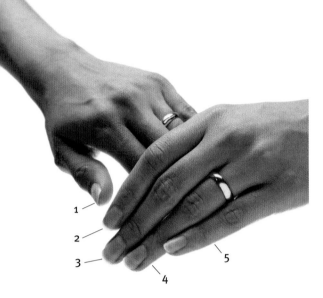

Vocabulary | personality

1 Work in pairs and discuss the questions.

1 Look at the photo. Can you label each finger: *little finger, middle finger, ring finger, index finger, thumb*?

2 Look at your hands and fingers. What do you think they say about (a) your personality and (b) your lifestyle?

2 Match the adjectives with the underlined phrases in the sentences.

> ambitious   chatty   easy-going
> hard-working   lazy   open   organised
> reserved   sensitive   unreliable

1 People with long slim fingers are <u>easily upset</u>.

2 People with short fingers are <u>happy to talk about feelings</u>.

3 People with straight fingers <u>make lots of lists and plans</u>.

4 People with a long index finger <u>work hard</u>.

5 People with a long ring finger <u>don't do what they say they will do</u>.

6 People with a thumb that bends back <u>are easy to talk to and talk a lot</u>.

7 People with a thumb that doesn't bend back <u>don't talk about feelings or problems</u>.

8 People with a long thumb <u>really want to be successful</u>.

9 People with slim hands are <u>not easily annoyed or worried by things</u>.

10 People with soft hands <u>don't like work or physical activity</u>.

Pronunciation | schwa /ə/ on unstressed syllables

3 a 2.6 Listen to the adjectives from exercise 2 and <u>underline</u> the stressed syllables.

am<u>bi</u>tious

b Now look at the unstressed syllables. Which unstressed syllables are pronounced with a schwa /ə/? Listen again, check and repeat.

see Pronunciation bank page 148

4 a 2.7 Listen and write the six questions you hear.

b In pairs, ask and answer the questions.

Listening

5 a 2.8 Listen to two friends, Helen and Daniel, talking about the connection between your hands and your personality. Which topics do they mention?

> the length of fingers ☐   the length of thumb ☐
> the shape of fingers ☐   the softness of skin ☐

b Listen again and look at exercise 2. Which sentences does Daniel think are true for him?

c Work in pairs. What do you think of this way of analysing people's personalities?

Grammar | gerunds and infinitives

6 a Look at the Active grammar box and choose the correct <u>underlined</u> words.

b Find the verbs in audioscript 2.8 on page 155. Add them to the correct list in the Active grammar box.

> afford   consider   finish   offer   promise   seem

> ### Active grammar
>
> *I want to look at the shape of your fingers.*
>
> *I've decided not to do my essay now.*
>
> *I enjoy doing this kind of thing.*
>
> *I avoid telling people about my feelings.*
>
> A Some verbs are followed by the *gerund (-ing form)*/*infinitive with to*, e.g. *enjoy, avoid,* _____
>
> B Some verbs are followed by the *gerund (-ing form)*/*infinitive with to*, e.g. *want, decide,* _____

see Reference page 77

7 Choose the correct words in *italics*.

1 He offered *to read/reading* my palm.
2 I've decided *not to be/not being* so lazy in the future.
3 I enjoy *to go/going* to the gym every day.
4 I'm considering *to learn/learning* German.
5 Have you finished *to write/writing* your essay?
6 I can't afford *to go/going* to that restaurant.
7 She seems *to get/getting* stressed very easily.
8 He avoids *to stay/staying* at work late whenever possible.
9 She promised *not to be/not being* late.
10 I want *to go/going* on a diet to look good for my wedding.

8 a Choose a partner. Complete the sentences about him/her. Don't ask, just guess.

1 He/She really wants _____ after the lesson.
2 He/She really enjoys _____ at the weekends.
3 He/She usually avoids _____ because he/she doesn't like it.
4 He/She's decided _____ for his/her next holiday.
5 He/She's considering _____ next year.

b Now work with your partner. Say your sentences and find out if they are true.

Reading and speaking

9 a Read the text about the connection between your hands and your skills. Write true (T) or false (F).

Some scientists think that ...

1 the length of our thumb gives us most information about our skills. ☐
2 there is no link between the length of our fingers and our skills. ☐

b Read the text again. Is your ring finger longer or shorter than your index finger if you ...

1 are good at football?
2 like learning languages?
3 will probably earn a good salary?
4 are good at communicating with people?

10 a Work in pairs and look at each other's hands. Tell your partner about his/her personality. Talk about fingers, thumbs and hands.

b How accurate do you think the information is about your personality and skills?

Your skills are in your hands

›› Look at your hands and you will learn a lot about your skills, say scientists at Cambridge University in England. They have scientific evidence about the link between talents and the length of fingers – particularly the ring finger and the index finger.

›› If your ring finger is longer than your index finger, you will probably be good at sport, especially running and football. You will probably also be interested in numbers-based subjects like maths and physics. One study found that people with longer ring fingers made up to six times more money than those with longer index fingers. If your index finger is longer than your ring finger, you will probably be more interested in words-based subjects like language and literature. You will also be better at verbal skills and expressing your ideas.

›› There was another study, however, which challenged the Cambridge scientists. It studied twins and showed that for most people, the length of our fingers is inherited from our parents and has nothing to do with our skills and talents at all.

Grammar *stop, try, remember*: gerunds and infinitives

Can do discuss illnesses and give advice

Vocabulary | illness

1 **a** Work in pairs. Check you understand the words for illnesses and symptoms. Which two are illnesses?

> backache   a cold   a cough   earache
> flu   a headache   a high temperature
> a rash   a sore throat   sore eyes
> stomachache   toothache   feel sick
> my arm/foot/leg/neck … hurts

b We say 'I feel sick' and 'my leg hurts'. What verb do we use for all the other phrases?

c Which symptoms from exercise 1a can you see in the pictures?

2 **a** Find the two mistakes in each answer and correct them.

1 **A:** You look terrible. What's the matter?
  B: I've got sick and I've got stomach.

2 **A:** Are you better today?
  B: No … I've got a flu. I've got a high temperature and a headache hurts.

3 **A:** How you are? You don't look well.
  B: I've got cough and sore eyes. I don't think it's serious – I feel a cold. That's all.

4 **A:** Is your back feeling better?
  B: No. I've got terrible backache and my leg feels hurts. I've got some toothache today as well.

5 **A:** How are you feeling?
  B: Terrible! I've got sore throat and earache hurts. I've got a rash as well.

b ⏺ 2.9 Listen, check and practise in pairs.

Listening and reading

3 **a** Read the email and correct the sentences.

1 Georgia is writing an email to her colleagues at work.

2 She is telling them that she is going to be late today.

3 She asks Jenny to come and see her later.

b Read the email again and answer the questions.

1 What are Georgia's symptoms?

2 What is she going to do now?

Message
To: Madison Burns; Ivan Vasilyev; Jenny Dean
From: Georgia Wilde
Subject: <no subject>

Dear all

A quick email to say that I can't come to college today because I don't feel well. I woke up this morning feeling really awful. I've got a headache and a high temperature. Last night, I had a really bad night and didn't sleep much because I've got a sore throat and a cough. In fact, I can't stop coughing! Anyway, I'm not going to go on and on about all my symptoms now! I'm going to go back to bed … I'm going to try to sleep for a couple of hours.

Apologies again that I can't come in today. I hope the class goes well – and Jenny, will you remember to get the homework for me? Hope to see you tomorrow … or very soon. I'll email again and let you know.

All the best

Georgia

4 🔵 2.10 Jenny, Ivan and Madison call Georgia at home. Listen and match each caller with the advice he/she gives and the country the advice comes from.

Advice	Country
Hot water with honey and vinegar	Russia
Hot water with honey and lemon	America
Hot milk with honey and butter	England

5 Listen again and write true (T) or false (F).

1 Jenny is going to buy some honey at the supermarket. ☐

2 Ivan is going to come to Georgia's house after college. ☐

3 Madison tells Georgia not to answer the phone when it rings. ☐

6 In groups, discuss the questions.

1 Have you tried any of the remedies you heard about?

2 What other advice do you have for Georgia?

Grammar | *stop, try, remember*: gerunds and infinitives

7 🔘 2.11 Read the Active grammar box. Then complete the sentences with the gerund (-*ing* form) or infinitive form of the verbs in brackets. Listen and check.

1 I can't stop _____ ! (cough)
2 I'll stop _____ some honey at the supermarket. (get)
3 I'm going to try _____ for a couple of hours. (sleep)
4 Why don't you try _____ your phone off? (turn)
5 Will you remember _____ the homework for me? (get)
6 I remember _____ a sore throat when I was a child. (have)

Active grammar

Some verbs (e.g. *stop, try* and *remember*) can be followed by the gerund or the infinitive with a change of meaning.

A *to stop* + gerund: to stop what you're doing
B *to stop* + infinitive: to stop what you're doing in order to do something else
C *to try* + gerund: to try something as an experiment to see what will happen
D *to try* + infinitive: to try something which might be difficult
E *to remember* + gerund: to remember things in the past and look back on them
F *to remember* + infinitive: to remember something you need to do

see Reference page 77

8 Choose the correct words in *italics*.

1 You must remember *to phone/phoning* the dentist about your toothache.
2 Why don't you try *to put/putting* a cold wet cloth on your forehead?
3 If you've got backache, you should stop *to run/running* every morning.
4 I remember *to feel/feeling* really sick when I last ate shellfish.
5 I can't talk on the phone right now because I have to stop *to cough/coughing* every few minutes!
6 You've got sore eyes, so you should try not *to touch/touching* them at all.
7 You need to remember *to take/taking* your medicine three times a day.
8 You must try *to keep/keeping* warm and drink plenty of liquids.
9 I stopped *to feel/feeling* sick yesterday, but I've still got a high temperature.

Speaking

9 🔘 2.12 Listen to four extracts from the dialogues from exercise 4 and complete the How to... box.

How to... give and respond to advice

Give advice	Respond to advice
Why (1) _____ *you try hot water with honey and lemon?*	*Thanks. That's a good* (2) _____ .
You (3) _____ *go back to bed.*	*Yes, I think I'll do* (4) _____ .
Have you (5) _____ *honey and butter in hot milk?*	*No, I haven't tried that.*
You should have honey and vinegar in hot water.	*Oh, I don't* (6) _____ *that!*

10 Work in pairs and follow the instructions.

Student A: ask a question from exercise 2a. Listen to Student B's illnesses/symptoms and then give advice.
Student B: listen to Student A's question. Tell him/her about your illnesses/symptoms and respond to his/her advice.

7 Communication

Stress? What stress?

For each situation, write your Stress Factor (1–5).
1 **No problem!**
2 **Not happy, but keeping cool!**
3 **Getting a little tense!**
4 **Heart is beating faster!**
5 **Major stress alert!**

1 You wait in a bus queue for twenty minutes. When the bus comes, you can't get on because there are too many people on it. *Stress Factor:* ___

2 You walk to work. It starts raining heavily and you haven't got an umbrella. You get completely soaked. *Stress Factor:* ___

3 You take some clothes back to a shop. The assistant won't give your money back because you've lost the receipt. *Stress Factor:* ___

4 You phone a customer services line to try to fix your computer. You don't manage to speak to a person, just a machine. *Stress Factor:* ___

5 You're in your car at traffic lights. Another driver shouts at you for not driving away quickly enough. *Stress Factor:* ___

6 You go to the cinema to see a really good film. Some people next to you don't stop talking and eating loudly. *Stress Factor:* ___

7 You play a game of tennis with a friend. You don't play well and he/she beats you easily. *Stress Factor:* ___

8 You're just about to go to work/school. You realise you can't find an important document/piece of homework. *Stress Factor:* ___

9 You're in bed and you can't sleep because the dog next door is barking. *Stress Factor:* ___

10 You want to pay for your shopping but the shop assistant is chatting on the phone and not looking at you. *Stress Factor:* ___

1 Work in pairs and discuss the questions.
1 Are you someone who gets stressed easily?
2 What things make you stressed?
3 How do you feel when you are stressed?
4 How bad do you think stress is for your health?

2 a ● 2.13 Listen to two people doing part of the quiz about stress. Which questions do they talk about?

b Listen again. For each question they talk about, do they agree about the level of stress or not?

3 Now work in pairs and do the quiz to find out how stressed you really are. Ask your partner to explain his/her answers.

4 a Add up your 'Total Stress Factor'. Then find out what it means on page 130.

b How accurate do you think the 'Total Stress Factor' results are for you? Do you think your level of stress is healthy or not? Why?

5 a Work in small groups and discuss the questions.
1 What advice could you give to someone who gets a score of 36–50 in the quiz?
2 Which of the following things do you think are good for healthy stress levels?

> close your eyes and breathe deeply   do yoga
> have a bath   have a massage   listen to music
> play computer games   play a physically hard sport
> sing   talk to a friend   watch TV

3 What do you do to relax and reduce your stress levels?

b Report back to the class. What are the most popular ways of relaxing?

First Conditional

We use the First Conditional to talk about a possible situation in the future.

If + Present Simple, *will/won't* + verb

! We don't use *will* in the '*if*' clause.

*If we **leave** at 9:30, we'll be late.*

NOT: ~~If we'll leave at 9:30, we'll be late.~~

The '*if*' clause can come first or second.

When the '*if*' clause is first, we need a comma at the end of the clause.

*If I **don't go** to bed now, I'll be too tired tomorrow.*

*He'll fail his exam if he **doesn't work** harder.*

! We can also use other modal verbs in the 'result' clause (not just *will*), e.g. *may, might, could*.

*If I **finish** this soon, I **might go** and see Tony.*

*Bobby **may bring** his son if he **comes** on Sunday.*

*If you **want** to go out tomorrow, you **should do** your homework now.*

We can also use other time words (with a present tense) to talk about the future, e.g. *when, as soon as.*

When I see him, I'll tell him.

As soon as he arrives, we'll have dinner.

Gerunds and infinitives

Some verbs are followed by the gerund (*-ing* form) and some are followed by the infinitive with *to*.

Verbs followed by the gerund include:

enjoy, avoid, finish, consider, miss, imagine, suggest, understand, give up, risk, practise

*I **enjoy playing** tennis.*

*I can't **imagine going** to the moon.*

*Would you **consider** not **working** at all?*

Verbs followed by the infinitive with *to* include:

want, decide, seem, offer, promise, afford, hope, expect, agree, arrange, choose, manage, ask

*I **want to see** that new film.*

*I'm **hoping to go** to university next year.*

*He **decided** not **to have** piano lessons anymore.*

stop, try, remember: gerunds and infinitives

Some verbs can be followed by the gerund or the infinitive with a change of meaning.

Three of the most common are: *stop, try* and *remember*

stop

to stop + gerund: to stop what you're doing

*Please **stop shouting** at me!*

*He didn't **stop playing** computer games until 3 a.m. last night.*

to stop + infinitive: to stop what you're doing in order to do something else

*I **stopped to talk** to Carole on the way to the meeting.*

*When I'm at work, I usually **stop to have** a coffee at about 11 a.m.*

try

to try + gerund: to try something as an experiment to see what will happen

*If the car won't start, **try pushing** it down the hill.*

*We haven't got any butter, so I'm going to **try using** oil instead.*

to try + infinitive: to try something which might be difficult

*Please **try to finish** all your homework by Friday.*

*I **tried to talk** to Ben, but he didn't listen.*

remember

to remember + gerund: to remember things in the past and look back on them

*My mother **remembers coming** to this beach when she was a child.*

*I **remember putting** my keys in my bag this morning.*

to remember + infinitive: to remember something you need to do

*I must **remember to phone** Anabel today.*

*Did you **remember to buy** that magazine?*

Key vocabulary

Parts of the body

ankle back ear elbow eye face finger forehead hair knee lips mouth nose palm shoulder stomach thumb toe waist wrist

Describing appearance

(un)attractive beautiful blonde dark-haired dark-skinned fair-haired fair-skinned fat good-looking handsome medium height muscular overweight red-haired short skinny slim tall ugly

Describing personality

ambitious chatty easy-going hard-working lazy open organised reserved sensitive unreliable

Illness

backache a cold a cough earache flu a headache a high temperature a rash a sore throat sore eyes stomachache toothache feel sick my arm/foot/leg/neck … hurts

 Listen to these words.
ACTIVE BOOK

---

 see Writing bank page 141

7 Review and practice

1 Find the missing word in each sentence.

If I eat any more, I be sick.

If I eat any more, I'll be sick.

1 We'll be late we don't leave now.

2 If it rains, we not play tennis this afternoon.

3 You buy me a newspaper if you go shopping later?

4 If I don't see Holly today, I phone her.

5 You put your hand on the cooker, you'll burn yourself.

6 I won't meet you at the cinema I don't finish my work.

7 If you lend me five pounds, I pay you back tomorrow.

8 If you get home before me, you make the dinner?

2 Write complete First Conditional sentences using the prompts.

she/eat all that cake/be sick

If she eats all that cake, she'll be sick.

1 they/offer me the job/take it

_____ .

2 I/have a party/pass my exam

_____ .

3 you/not use sun cream/get burnt

_____ .

4 I/be late for work/not get up now

_____ .

5 we/not invite her/she be upset

_____ .

6 I/see Jon/not tell him about the party

_____ .

7 you/not have any money left/buy those jeans

_____ .

8 we/not leave now/be late

_____ .

3 Choose the correct words in *italics*.

I really want *passing/(to pass)* my driving test.

1 I enjoy *going/to go* to the cinema.

2 I promise *not telling/not to tell* anyone.

3 He offered *washing/to wash* the dishes.

4 I considered *doing/to do* a computer course.

5 She's decided *going/to go* running every day.

6 He seems *liking/to like* living with his parents.

7 Have you finished *using/to use* the computer?

8 He avoided *talking/to talk* to girls as much as possible.

4 Complete the sentences with the gerund or infinitive (with *to*) form of the verbs in brackets.

We've decided ___to eat___ (eat) at home this evening.

1 I'm considering _____ (go) to Thailand for my next holiday.

2 I can't afford _____ (go) on holiday this year.

3 Gabriela offered _____ (help) me with my homework.

4 We'll leave at 10 a.m. to avoid _____ (arrive) in the dark.

5 I want _____ (do) a lot of work this weekend.

6 Let me know when you've finished _____ (talk) on the phone.

5 Find the mistakes in four of the sentences and correct them.

I don't remember ~~to see~~ *seeing* him here before.

1 I can't stop to think about that horror film I saw last night.

2 If you want to talk to her, try phoning her.

3 Please remember bringing an umbrella tomorrow.

4 She talked all evening and didn't stop listening to me at all.

5 Do you remember walking along here when we were children?

6 Could you stop to shout at me, please?

6 Complete the sentences with the words from the box. There are two extra words.

ambitious   ~~chatty~~   high temperature
feel sick   muscular   reliable   reserved
sensitive   skinny   sore throat

My brother is always talking. He's so *chatty* .

1 I think she's too thin. She's very _____ now.

2 I've got a terrible _____ and I've nearly lost my voice.

3 You can always trust Mick. He's very _____ .

4 James goes to the gym almost every day. He's getting very _____ .

5 She's quite _____ at first and doesn't say much.

6 I was in bed with a really _____ yesterday. It was nearly 40°C.

7 My sister is very _____ . She wants to be the Director in two years.

Speed

Lead-in

1 Look at the photos. What is the connection between them?

2 **a** Complete the sentences with the phrases from the box.

> speed camera   speed limit   speeding   top speed

1. A McLaren Formula One car has a _____ of 400 kilometres per hour (kmph).
2. The _____ on motorways in Spain is 100 kmph.
3. About ten percent of British drivers are fined for _____ every year.
4. One _____ in England caught 76,000 drivers in five years.

b Two of the sentences from exercise 2a are false. In pairs, decide which ones. Then check your answers on page 131.

3 **a** Check you understand the underlined phrases.

1. Are you the type of person who is always in a hurry?
2. Do you usually arrive on time for things? How do you feel if you're late?
3. Do you usually make decisions immediately or do you like taking your time?
4. How often do you eat meals on the go?
5. What time is the rush hour in your town? What is it like?
6. Do you usually speed up or slow down when you see an amber traffic light? Why?

b In pairs, ask and answer the questions from exercise 3a. Which of you has a faster pace of life?

8

Grammar	Present Simple Passive
Can do	discuss the use of technology

Slow Movement

Take your

Food

Fast facts:

Health problems are on the increase – and fast food is one of the major reasons. It is a sad fact that a huge amount of fast food is consumed every day around the world. In the US alone, sixty-five million fast-food meals are eaten every day. Forty years ago, Americans spent about $6 billion on fast food. They now spend more than $110 billion a year and this figure continues to rise. McDonald's had about 1,000 restaurants forty years ago. Today it has about 31,000 around the world and this number goes up by almost 2,000 each year.

Slow tips:

Cook your own food from fresh ingredients. Sit down and eat with other people. Take your time to enjoy your food and enjoy the people you're eating with. At work, don't eat on the go or at your desk – have a proper lunch break.

For more information about the Slow Movement, go to

Listening

1 Choose the words in *italics* that are true for you. In groups, compare your answers. Give reasons for your answers.

1 My life is *fast and busy/slow and calm*.

2 I mostly talk to people *face to face/via my computer*.

3 I usually eat my dinner *around a table with my family/in front of the TV*.

2 a 🔊 2.14 Listen to a radio interview with Petra van Stroud from the Slow Movement. Write true (T) or false (F).

1 Petra has a negative opinion of all technology. ☐

2 She thinks that people should slow down sometimes. ☐

b Listen again and complete each sentence with one or two words.

1 Petra thinks that new technology makes people _____ about the important things in life.

2 The Slow Food organisation started in 1986 as a protest against _____ .

3 They were concerned with both the quality of the food and the _____ side of eating.

4 The Slow Movement is concerned with areas like food and _____ .

5 The interviewer says that many people _____ their busy, fast lives.

6 Petra says that people should sometimes leave their _____ at home.

3 Work in pairs and discuss the questions.

1 Do you agree that most people think 'fast is good'? Why/Why not?

2 What do you think about the aims of the Slow Movement?

Reading

4 Look at the Lifelong learning box and read the tip. Then read the Slow Movement text and answer the questions.

1 Approximately how many McDonald's restaurants are there in the world now?

2 How many times a day does an average office worker check his/her email?

Speed reading

❗ Speed reading is a useful skill when you want to find information quickly or you have a long text to read.

• Be clear about why you are reading and stay focused on that.

• Don't stop to look at every word and don't try to understand every word.

Lifelong learning

Communication

Fast facts:

Social problems are on the increase – and virtual communication is one of the major reasons. Instead of talking to each other face to face, people are communicating more and more via technology. In the UK, over 200 million text messages are sent each day and this figure is rising by nearly forty percent a year. An average office worker gets 160 emails a day (including a lot of junk mail) and checks their emails more than fifty times daily. On average, nearly two hours are spent dealing with emails a day. Email isn't switched off at home either: about sixty percent of people check their work emails when they're out of the office or on holiday.

Slow tips:

Organise your email time at work: perhaps have an 'email-free' day and don't check your work emails at home. Arrange to meet your friends instead of sending messages via a computer or mobile phone.

www.slowmovement.com

5 Read the text again and correct the sentences.

1 British people eat about sixty-five million fast-food meals every day.

2 The amount of money spent on fast food in the US is going down.

3 The text recommends having lunch in front of your computer.

4 British people send more than two million text messages every day.

5 In one day, an average office worker spends an hour on email.

6 The text says you should have some days when you don't use your phone.

6 Work in pairs. Look at the 'Slow tips' in the text and discuss the questions.

1 Do you do the things they suggest? Do you think they are good ideas? Why/Why not?

2 Can you think of one more tip for each section? Tell the class your tips.

Grammar | Present Simple Passive

7 **a** Complete the Active grammar box with the correct form of the verbs in brackets.

b Find four more examples of the Present Simple Passive in the text from exercise 4.

Active grammar

Most sentences in English are active.

active subject + verb + object

1 *Americans _____ (spend) more than $110 billion on fast food every year.*

We use the passive form when …

- who/what causes the action is unknown or not important.
- we want to emphasise the passive subject (at the beginning of the sentence).

2 *Sixty-five million fast-food meals _____ (eat) in the US every day.*

passive subject + *am/is/are (not)* + past participle

see Reference page 87

8 Complete the sentences with the Present Simple Passive form of the verbs in brackets.

1 Traffic speed _____ (reduce) by seven percent in areas where there are speed cameras.

2 Cars in London rush-hour traffic _____ (drive) at an average of seven miles per hour.

3 Eighty-one percent of the cars in the world _____ (own) by people in the US, Canada, Europe and Japan.

4 The London Underground _____ (use) by over a billion passengers every year.

5 About 50,000 plane journeys _____ (make) every day.

9 Make the <u>underlined</u> verbs passive, if necessary.

1 Over three million people <u>employ</u> in the fast-food industry in the US.

2 The average American <u>eats</u> about 4,000 calories a day.

3 Most Domino's pizzas <u>deliver</u> in less than thirty minutes.

4 Most British people <u>know</u> how to cook spaghetti bolognese without a recipe book.

5 Customers <u>charge</u> thirty-five yen per minute to eat in the Totenko restaurant in Tokyo.

Speaking

10 **a** ⊕ 2.15 Listen and write the eight questions you hear.

b Now work in small groups and try to answer the questions. Check your ideas on page 131.

Vocabulary | phrasal verbs: relationships

1 Match the phrasal verbs from A with the definitions from B.

A	B
1 ask someone out	a) have a romantic, loving relationship
2 go out with someone	b) stop having a romantic, loving relationship
3 take someone out	
4 grow apart from someone	c) slowly stop having a good relationship
	d) invite someone to go on a date with you
5 put up with someone/something	e) stop feeling sad about someone/something
6 split up with someone	f) accept a bad situation without complaining
7 get over someone/something	g) go with someone to a restaurant, cinema, club etc. and pay for him/her

2 Complete the sentences with the correct form of the phrasal verbs from exercise 1.

1 Jade's been single since she _____ her boyfriend last year.

2 Pete _____ me _____ yesterday and I said 'yes' because I really like him.

3 Oliver never does the washing-up and Maria just _____ it.

4 When my sister got divorced, she found it difficult to _____ her ex-husband.

5 On our first date, Jack _____ me _____ to a really expensive French restaurant.

6 Linda and Guy are a couple. They started _____ each other last month.

7 We used to be good friends, but we've _____ over the last year.

Pronunciation | phrasal verbs: stress

3 **a** 🔊 2.16 Listen to the first sentence from exercise 2. <u>Underline</u> the part of the phrasal verb which has the main stress.

Jade's been single since she split up with her boyfriend last year.

b 🔊 2.17 <u>Underline</u> the main stress in the other phrasal verbs from exercise 2. Listen, check and repeat.

see Pronunciation bank page 148

4 Work in small groups and discuss the questions.

1 Do women ever ask men out in your country?

2 What do you think is the minimum time you should go out with someone before you get married?

3 If your partner never did any housework, would you put up with it? Why/Why not?

4 Why do people usually split up with their partner?

Listening

5 **a** In pairs, think about (a) speed-dating and (b) arranged marriages. Discuss the questions.

1 What do you know about each topic?

2 What would you like to know? Write two questions.

b 🔊 2.18 Listen to a conversation between two friends, Fiona and Deepa. Do you hear the answers to your questions from exercise 5a?

6 Listen again and write true (T) or false (F).

1 Fiona split up with her last boyfriend on Easter Day. ☐

2 In most arranged marriages now, the woman must marry the man her parents choose. ☐

3 A lot of Indian weddings happen in the winter. ☐

4 When Deepa was in India, she met lots of men at parties. ☐

5 Deepa got married in Britain after spending two months in India. ☐

6 Fiona says each date in a speed-dating event lasts three minutes. ☐

7 When she went speed-dating, Fiona talked to twenty men. ☐

7 Work in pairs and discuss the questions.

1 What do you think about the kind of arranged marriage Deepa had? Do you think it might be a good way to get a husband/wife? Why/Why not?

2 What do you think about speed-dating? Do you think it might be a good way to get a boyfriend/girlfriend? Why/Why not?

Grammar | prepositions of time

8 **a** Complete the sentences with *on, in* or *at*.

1 I arrived in India _____ December.

2 I got married _____ the end of January.

3 I got married _____ 28 January actually.

b Look at audioscript 2.18 on page 157 and check your answers. Then find six more examples of prepositions of time (*on, in* and *at*).

9 Complete the Active grammar box with *on, in* or *at*.

Active grammar

A _____: for long periods of time	B _____: for specific days and parts of specific days	C _____: for times and special holiday periods
Month: *December* Year: *2009* Season: *the winter* Part of day: *the morning, the evening*	Day: *Monday* Part of specific day: *Tuesday morning* Date: *17 June* Special day: *Valentine's Day*	Time: *9:30, midnight, lunchtime* Holiday time: *Christmas, Thanksgiving* Also: *night, the weekend, the beginning/end*

see Reference page 87

10 Complete the sentences with *on, in* or *at*.

1 In Britain, a lot of people traditionally get married _____ June.

2 Valentine's Day is celebrated _____ 14 February.

3 _____ the end of the evening, we knew we wanted to get married.

4 The most popular place to go _____ your first date is a café.

5 More than 300,000 couples got married in Britain _____ 2007.

6 In Britain, women can traditionally propose marriage to a man _____ 29 February.

7 We arranged to meet _____ 8 o'clock _____ the evening in an Italian restaurant.

8 My parents will celebrate their golden wedding anniversary _____ the summer.

11 Work in groups and ask and answer questions. Use the dates and times from the box.

A: *What do you usually do on your birthday?*

B: *I usually have a meal with my family and go out with my friends in the evening.*

> 2008   31 December   7:30 this morning   Fridays
> Saturday evening   the summer   the weekend   your birthday

Speaking

12 **a** 🔊 2.19 Listen and answer the questions.

1 Which topic from the box is the man talking about?

2 How does he feel about the topic: mostly positive/mostly negative/neutral?

> a special celebration
> an arranged marriage
> speed dating
> traditional dating in your country
> Valentine's Day
> wedding anniversary celebrations
> wedding traditions

b Listen again and answer the questions.

1 In which country did Valentine's Day start?

2 Why did the emperor kill Valentine?

3 What are two traditional presents on Valentine's Day?

4 Where do people go in the evening of Valentine's Day?

5 What does the speaker think of Valentine's Day?

13 **a** Prepare to talk about a topic from exercise 12a. Make notes about what you want to say.

b Now work in groups and take turns to talk about your topics.

Lightning Bolt!

Usain Bolt is the world's fastest man. He first came to the public's attention at the Beijing Olympics in 2008, where he won three gold medals. The most amazing of these was for the 100-metre race, which he ran in just 9.69 seconds – even though his shoelaces were undone and even though, while he was getting to the finish line, he was slowing down and already celebrating his victory. During that race, he reached a top speed of 43.9 kmph. So, we ask, how does the man whose nickname is 'Lightning Bolt', run so fast and just what does it feel like?

Usain Bolt was born in Jamaica on 21 August 1986. He has a brother and a sister and while they were growing up, they spent most of their time playing cricket and football in the street. Bolt was running around at primary school, when a teacher noticed he had a talent for sprinting. He became one of the best sprinters at his high school even though he didn't train very hard. At the age of fifteen, Bolt was 196 cm tall and he dominated the 2002 World Junior Championships, becoming the youngest person ever to win the 200 metres. He turned professional when he left high school, aged seventeen. During the first couple of years of Bolt's professional life, he got a few injuries, but his health soon improved and he began to win all the major championships. He went from strength to strength, amazing the world with his speed.

So, how does he do it? Bolt says that he is naturally fast – just something he was born with.

He's also got a number of people looking after him: his parents and family have always supported him. And one of the main reasons for his success is Norman Peart, his manager. Peart has looked after Bolt since he was fifteen, working hard to keep him focused.

However you explain it, Bolt's performances in Beijing were truly incredible. What's more incredible is that, since then, he has continued to get even faster. In August 2009, he smashed his own record by running the 100 metres in 9.58 seconds. At the fastest point in this race, he ran at an amazing 44.9 kmph. If you do this speed on a bicycle, it feels very quick. So, what does it feel like on your own two feet? 'It's just great running that fast,' says Bolt. 'It's lovely, just lovely.'

Reading

1 a What do you think this man's top speed is: 24, 34 or 44 kmph?

b Find the answer in the text quickly.

2 Read the text again and answer the questions.

1 When did Usain Bolt first become well-known around the world? What for?

2 How did he become fast?

3 Explain the significance of the phrases from the text.

his shoelaces were undone

It was amazing that Bolt won the gold medal in Beijing because he didn't tie his shoelaces correctly before the race.

1	Lightning Bolt	5	from strength to strength
2	a talent for sprinting	6	something he was born with
3	didn't train very hard	7	keep him focused
4	turned professional	8	smashed his own record

4 In pairs, retell the story of Usain Bolt using the phrases from exercise 3.

Vocabulary | measurements

5 **a** 🔘 2.20 Listen and (circle) the numbers you hear.

> 8,880/88,018 centimetres   3,235,999/3,235,899 metres
> 6¹/₂/6¹/₄ kilograms   9³/₄/9¹/₄ hours
> 75¹/₄/75¹/₂ minutes   0.15/0.015 seconds
> 449.9/44.9 kilometres per hour

b Listen again, check and repeat.

c In which numbers, and where, do you need to say (a) *point* and (b) *and*?

6 **a** Choose the correct words in *italics*.

1   How *fast/long* do you usually walk?
2   How *tall/far* is your home from here?
3   How *long/fast* does it take you to say the alphabet?
4   How *tall/much* is the tallest person in your family?
5   How *far/much* do you think your bag weighs today?

b In groups, ask and answer the questions from exercise 6a.

Grammar | Past Continuous and Past Simple

7 Complete the Active grammar box with *Past Simple* or *Past Continuous*.

> ### Active grammar
>
> A We use the _____ to talk about an action in progress at a particular time in the past.
> *While they were growing up, they spent most of their time playing cricket and football.*
>
> B We use the _____ to talk about complete actions in the past.
> *He won three gold medals at the Beijing Olympics.*
> *In high school, he didn't train very hard.*
>
> C We use the _____ to talk about a longer action interrupted by another action in the _____ .
> *He was running around at primary school, when a teacher noticed he had a talent for sprinting.*
> *What was he doing when you saw him?*
>
> We usually use *when* to refer to events or periods in your life.
> *When he left high school, he turned professional.*
>
> We usually use *when/while* to refer to two longer actions happening at the same time.
> *While/When he was getting to the finish line, he was slowing down.*

see Reference page 87

8 Complete the paragraph with the Past Simple or Past Continuous form of the verbs in brackets.

Lewis Hamilton (1) _____ (become) the youngest ever Formula One World Champion in 2008, at the age of twenty-three. While he (2) _____ (grow up), Hamilton was very keen on go-karting. When Hamilton was six, his father (3) _____ (buy) him his first go-kart. While Hamilton (4) _____ (compete) in karting races, his father (5) _____ (work) hard to support his son's career. At that time, his father (6) _____ (go) to all Hamilton's races. One day, when Hamilton was ten, he (7) _____ (walk) around at a race meeting, when he (8) _____ (meet) Ron Dennis, the head of the McLaren Racing Team. He (9) _____ (tell) him, 'I want to race for you one day!'

Pronunciation | was/were

9 🔘 2.21 We can say *was/were* in different ways. Listen and repeat.

1   A: Was he training when you last saw him?
    /wəz/ weak pronunciation
    B: Yes, he was.
        /wɒz/ strong pronunciation

2   A: Were they watching the race?
    /wə/ weak pronunciation
    B: Yes, they were.
        /wɜː/ strong pronunciation

see Pronunciation bank page 148

Speaking

10 Invent a story in small groups. Each sentence must start with the last letter of the previous sentence.

A: *It all happened last summer.*
B: *Roberto and his friends were spending the day at the seaside.*
C: *Everyone was feeling happy.*

In your groups, choose a sentence (1–4) to start your story. Then tell your story together. Which group can make the longest story?

1   It all happened last summer.
2   It was a dark night and she couldn't sleep.
3   When I walked into the room, I saw him.
4   It was a beautiful day and we were walking to school as usual.

8 Communication

Can do talk for an extended period on a familiar topic

1 🔘 2.22 Listen to two presentations and answer the questions.

1 What is the topic of each presentation?
2 Which do you think is better? Give two reasons.

2 **a** 🔘 2.23 Listen to the introduction of one presentation again. Look at the script below and notice where the speaker pauses.

The topic of my presentation is / 'The benefits of technology in my life'. / The main points I will talk about are: / firstly, how technology benefits my work life / and secondly, how technology benefits my personal life.

b Now listen to the rest of the presentation. Look at audioscript 2.22 on page 157 and mark the pauses.

3 Complete the How to... box with the headings (a–d).

a Introducing each point   c Starting the presentation
b Stating the main points   d Finishing the presentation

How to... organise a presentation

1 _____ _____	The topic of my presentation is ... What I'm going to talk about today is ...
2 _____ _____	The main points I will talk about are: firstly ... , secondly ...
3 _____ _____	Let's begin with ... Now let's move on to ... Now we're going to look at ...
4 _____ _____	I'd like to finish by saying ...

4 Now prepare your own presentation. Choose a topic from exercise 1 and make notes. Use the How to... box to help you organise your ideas.

5 **a** Work in small groups and take turns to give your presentations. Make sure you speak slowly enough and pause where necessary.

b Now work in different groups and give your presentations again. Before you start, think about how you can improve your presentation.

86

Present Simple Passive

Most sentences in English are active. In active constructions, the subject is the person or thing that does the action.

active subject + verb + object

She cleans my room every day.

We use the passive form when who/what causes the action is unknown or not important.

passive subject + *am/is/are* + past participle

Most computers are made in Asia.

The gates are locked at 6:00 p.m.

We also use the passive form when we want to emphasise the passive subject (at the beginning of the sentence).

! We use *by* to say who did the action.

Most text messages are sent by teenagers.

The object of active sentences becomes the subject of passive sentences. Compare:

Active: *She cleans my room every day.*

Passive: *My room is cleaned every day.*

Prepositions of time

in – We use *in* for:

long periods of time (months, seasons, years, etc.)

My exams are in June.

They went abroad three times in 2009.

I'm going skiing in the winter.

parts of (general) days

See you in the morning!

on – We use *on* for:

specific days and dates

I'm starting my new job on Monday.

My mum's birthday is on 17 March.

My boyfriend took me out for dinner on Valentine's Day.

parts of specific days

Her driving test is on Friday morning.

at – We use *at* for:

times

I usually leave work at 5:30 p.m.

I'm meeting Jon at lunchtime.

special holiday periods

My whole family gets together at Christmas.

other fixed phrases with *at*:

at the beginning/at the end/at the weekend/at night/at that time

Past Continuous and Past Simple

➕ ➖	I/He/She/It You/We/They	was wasn't were weren't	waiting ...
❓	Was Were	I/he/she/it you/we/they	eating ...?
Yes, No, Yes, No,		I/he/she/it you/we/they	was. wasn't. were. weren't.

We use the Past Continuous to talk about an action in progress at a particular time in the past.

Adam was cooking when I got home.

I was waiting for the bus at half past six.

! Past Continuous actions are not complete at that time in the past. We use the Past Simple to talk about complete actions in the past.

I sent David an email yesterday.

Martin cooked dinner last night.

We use the Past Continuous to talk about a longer action interrupted by another action in the Past Simple.

I was watching TV when he arrived.

We usually use *when* to refer to events or periods in your life.

When he got married, he moved to Spain with his wife.

We usually use *when/while* to refer to two longer actions happening at the same time.

While/When she was talking to me on the phone, she was also cooking dinner.

Key vocabulary

Speed

arrive on time   be in a hurry   be on the go   immediately   rush hour   slow down   speed camera   speed limit   speed up   speeding   take your time   top speed

Phrasal verbs about relationships

ask someone out   get over someone/something   go out with someone   grow apart from someone   put up with someone/something   split up with someone   take someone out

Measurements

centimetres   hours   kilograms   kilometres per hour   metres   minutes   seconds   four thousand two hundred and twenty-six   five and a half   two point one four

 Listen to these words.

ACTIVE BOOK

---

 see Writing bank page 142

1 Complete the sentences with the Present Simple Passive form of the verbs.

> clean   cover   cut down   invite   lock
> ~~make~~   open   sell   serve

Cheese _is made_ from milk.

1   The rooms in this hotel _____ at 10:00 a.m. every morning.
2   You _____ to Paul and Sheila's wedding.
3   All of these products _____ in France.
4   Thousands of trees _____ every year.
5   Most of the Earth's surface _____ by water.
6   The park gates _____ at 6:00 p.m.
7   Breakfast _____ from 7:00 to 9:00 a.m.
8   Sometimes, important public buildings _____ by the Queen.

2 Complete the sentences with the Present Simple Passive or the active form of the verbs in brackets.

My house _is painted_ (paint) every year.

1   You _____ (not pronounce) the 'k' in knife.
2   Photos _____ (take) of speeding cars by speed cameras.
3   John _____ (not invite) to parties very often.
4   Fifty people _____ (employ) in the new factory.
5   People _____ (not use) this bus route much.
6   At least three trains a day _____ (cancel) at this station.
7   Glass _____ (make) from sand.
8   Many sports _____ (play) on this field on Saturday.

3 Choose the correct words in _italics_.

The race is _in/on/at_ 15 May.

1   The film starts _in/on/at_ half past six.
2   I'm going to see my cousins _in/on/at_ the weekend.
3   We're going skiing _in/on/at_ Christmas this year.
4   I'm going to get a job as a waiter _in/on/at_ the summer.
5   She's going shopping _in/on/at_ Saturday afternoon to buy some shoes.
6   Every year _in/on/at_ April, they spend a week in New York.
7   We're having a party _in/on/at_ Saturday to celebrate the end of exams.
8   They're getting married _in/on/at_ the end of this year.
9   He moved from Madrid to Barcelona _in/on/at_ 2008.
10 My grandmother makes a delicious roast dinner _in/on/at_ Thanksgiving Day.

4 Complete the paragraphs with the Past Continuous or Past Simple form of the verbs in brackets.

At about 6:30 yesterday evening, I _was cycling_ (cycle) home from work. It (1) _____ (rain) and a lot of people (2) _____ (drive) too fast. Suddenly, a car (3) _____ (stop) in front of me. I (4) _____ (not hit) the car, but I (5) _____ (fall) off my bicycle. Luckily, I (6) _____ (not be) hurt.

A couple of years ago, I (7) _____ (walk) home along a dark street. Somebody (8) _____ (follow) me and I was quite frightened. I (9) _____ (start) to run, but when I (10) _____ (look) back, I (11) _____ (see) my friend Daniel. I was so happy!

5 Complete the questions with the Past Continuous or the Past Simple.

A: What _were you doing_ when I phoned you?
B: I was having a shower.

1   A: When you last saw Jane, where _____?
    B: She was working for a big advertising company.
2   A: _____ very fast when the accident happened?
    B: No he wasn't. He was driving slowly.
3   A: _____ you while you were living in Sydney?
    B: Yes. He visited me twice.
4   A: What _____ while I was doing the washing-up?
    B: I was cleaning the bathroom.
5   A: Where _____ for you when you arrived at the station?
    B: She was waiting by the ticket office.
6   A: _____ to Italy while you were travelling around Europe?
    B: No, I didn't have time to go there.
7   A: _____ to music while you were writing your essay?
    B: Yes I was. It helped me to concentrate.

6 Correct the _underlined_ words.

I really like him. I hope he asks me <u>up</u> soon. _out_

1   When her cat died, it took ages for Lucy to <u>put</u> over it.
2   I'm exhausted. I've been <u>at</u> the go all day!
3   Tom's so lazy! Why do you put <u>on</u> with it?
4   I never drive into Lisbon during the rush <u>time</u>. It's too busy.
5   There's no rush. You can <u>have</u> your time to discuss this.
6   Why don't you relax? You're always <u>at</u> a hurry.
7   Jane and I were best friends at school, but we've grown <u>away</u> now.
8   This car has a <u>high</u> speed of 120 kmph.

Lead-in

1 **a** Match the jobs with the photos.

> construction worker   fashion designer   nurse   stockbroker

b Which things from the box do you associate with each job?

> flexible/long hours   high/low salary   a lot of training
> uniform   shift work   working outside

2 Work in pairs and answer the questions.

Can you name three more jobs ...

1   which involve wearing a uniform?   4   which involve working long hours?
2   which pay a high salary?   5   which involve a lot of training?
3   which involve shift work?   6   which involve working outside?

3 Do you have a job? How do you say it in English? Work in groups of three and find out what job each student does. If you don't know what the job is, ask the student to explain.

4 **a** Put the phrases in a logical order. In pairs, compare your answers.

First, you have to prepare a CV, then ...

> apply for a job   be offered a job   get promoted   have an interview
> ~~prepare a CV~~   resign   run your own company   take a job

b Which of the things from exercise 4a have you done? Tell another student about your experiences.

Ben gets dream job

By Greg Miller

The sun is shining and Ben Southall is looking out over the clear sea from his huge £2.5 million house on an idyllic island. It may not look like it, but Ben is hard at work. His job, he says, is, 'to make people jealous'! Just a few months ago, Ben couldn't even imagine being in this beautiful place.

Things changed for Ben when the Australian state of Queensland advertised a job for someone to look after Hamilton Island in the Great Barrier Reef. They knew it sounded like the best job in the world, but they were surprised when over 35,000 people applied for the job. Then they had to make a difficult decision – which person to choose from so many candidates? After a lot of testing and interviewing, they announced 34-year-old Ben Southall from England as the winner. Ben now works for the Queensland Tourist Board and his job is to look after the island and to promote tourism there. Because of the unique nature of the job, the Tourist Board wanted a unique person, with a range of skills and qualities. It was a long interview process, involving a variety of tasks to find out about each candidate.

Fitness was very important; swimming ability was particularly essential. Ben can swim very well and he also likes running, climbing, scuba diving and mountain biking. It is clear that, physically, he can do almost anything. The ability to communicate was as important as fitness. For the last part of the interview process, the final sixteen candidates did various tests and tasks, including talking to TV and radio reporters. The competition was tough and the candidates needed to show what they could do. The interviewers were interested in how the candidates performed in the tasks, how they handled the press attention and their ability to write about their adventures in a daily blog. The candidates did their best to impress the interviewers and they knew they couldn't make any mistakes at this final stage.

Before he went, Ben was confident about his abilities to handle the challenge. He couldn't do everything they asked him in the interview, as he can't speak any other languages, but he felt that his other skills and his personality were impressive. He made a huge effort during the interview process and he was able to convince the interviewers that he was the best person for the job. Even so, he says he was amazed when he got the job; he couldn't believe it! He hopes to do a good job and promote the island successfully: he has to get to know every part of the island and tell the world about it in numerous media interviews. When you read Ben's blogs from his interview tasks, it is easy to see why they chose him. He is funny and easy-going and he will certainly get the attention of any potential tourist to this beautiful place.

Reading

1 Look at the photo and the title of the text. What do you think the job is?

2 Read the text and answer the questions.
1. What is the job?
2. How did Ben feel before the interview?

3 Read the text again and write true (T) or false (F).
1. The state of Queensland thought more people would apply for the job. ☐
2. Part of Ben's job is to encourage more tourists to come to the island. ☐
3. The Tourist Board found the right person for the job quite quickly. ☐
4. Swimming was the most important physical ability they were looking for. ☐
5. The candidates had to talk to journalists. ☐
6. One of the tasks was to write a blog every week. ☐
7. When he was offered the job, Ben was very surprised. ☐
8. Ben is a relaxed type of person. ☐

4 Work in pairs and discuss the questions.
1. Would you like to have Ben's job? Why/Why not?
2. Do you think the job is a good way of promoting tourism on the island? Why/Why not?

Grammar | *can, could, be able to*: ability

5 Complete the Active grammar box. Check your answers with the text from exercise 2.

Active grammar

Ability in the present
To talk about ability in the present, we use *can/can't*.

1 *Ben _____ swim very well.*
2 *He _____ speak any other languages.*

Ability in the past
To talk about general ability in the past in positive sentences, we use *could* or *was/were able to*.

3 *The candidates needed to show what they _____/were able to do.*

To talk about general ability in the past in negative sentences, we use *couldn't* or *wasn't/weren't able to*.

4 *He _____/wasn't able to imagine being in this beautiful place.*

To talk about ability in the past on one specific occasion in positive sentences, we use *was/were able to* only (NOT ~~could~~).

5 *He _____ convince the interviewers that he was the best person for the job.*

To talk about ability in the past on one specific occasion in negative sentences, we use *couldn't* or *wasn't/weren't able to*.

6 *He _____/wasn't able to do everything they asked him in the interview.*

---

see Reference page 97

6 Look at the words in *italics*. Decide if one or both of the options is/are correct.

1 I think I'm perfect for the job. I *can/can't* imagine myself doing it.
2 I *couldn't/wasn't able to* hear what the candidate was saying.
3 I *could/was able to* speak three languages fluently by the time I was nine.
4 The interview went well. I *could/was able to* impress them with my answers.
5 When I was younger, I *could/was able to* swim very long distances.
6 I *can/can't* speak Spanish or French, so I don't think I'll get the job.
7 I *could/was able to* complete all the tasks quickly and easily.
8 He wasn't the best candidate. He *can't/wasn't able to* do everything we needed him to do.

7 Complete the sentences with *can('t)*, *could(n't)* or *was(n't) able to*. Sometimes there are two possible answers.

1 There was a fire in the office, but luckily everyone _____ get out.
2 I stayed late at work last night, but unfortunately I _____ finish the report.
3 When I lived in Paris, I _____ walk to work in about half an hour.
4 Alex wasn't at work, but I _____ contact her on her mobile phone.
5 I look online everyday, but I _____ find a job that I want to apply for.
6 Most of the interview went well, but I _____ remember one of the interviewer's names.
7 I had a meeting with my boss. I didn't get the promotion, but I _____ get a higher salary.
8 In my last job, I _____ take responsibility in the way that I can now.

Speaking

8 Look at the Lifelong learning box. Read the tip and write three answers for the question.

Last month, I wasn't able to order a meal in a restaurant, but now I can ...

Checking progress

! It is a good idea to review your learning sometimes.

- Every week/month/year, look back at what you have learned.
- Ask yourself: *What can I do now that I couldn't do a week/month/year ago?*

Lifelong learning

---

9 a Prepare to talk about your abilities. Choose two areas of your life (e.g. work, studies, hobbies, sport) and make notes. Think about your abilities in these areas in the past and the present.

Five years ago, I couldn't give presentations at work very well because I was very nervous. Now, I can speak in public with more confidence.

b Now work in groups and tell each other about your abilities.

Vocabulary | work

1 a Work in pairs. What is the difference between ...

1 an interviewer and an interviewee?
2 an employer and an employee?
3 an application form and a CV?
4 experience and qualifications?
5 a salary and a wage?
6 a bonus and commission?
7 a receptionist and a secretary?
8 a sales rep and a sales assistant?
9 a managing director and a marketing director?

b Choose the correct words in *italics*.

1 Most of our *employers/employees* have been with the company since we started three years ago.
2 I'm afraid we need someone with much more *experience/qualifications* in related jobs.
3 It's very important that a *receptionist/secretary* should be welcoming to visitors.
4 If we reach our sales targets, we will get a twenty percent *bonus/commission*.
5 A good *interviewer/interviewee* knows how to ask good questions to find out about people.
6 I must fill out the *application form/CV* for that job at CoffeeCo today.
7 In my new job, the yearly *salary/wage* is twice as much as in my previous job.

Pronunciation | changing word stress

2 a 🔊 2.24 The main stress on words in the same word family is sometimes different. Listen and underline the main stress on each word/phrase.

1 to interview/an interviewer/an interviewee
2 to employ/an employer/an employee
3 to apply/an applicant/an application form
4 to qualify/a qualification
5 a secretary/a secretarial job

b Listen again, check and repeat.

see Pronunciation bank page 148

3 Work in groups and discuss the questions.

1 What personal qualities do you think make a good interviewer?
2 When was the last time you were an interviewee? How did you feel?
3 What information should you include in a CV?
4 Would you rather have a high salary and no bonus, or an average salary and possible bonuses?

A ☐

B ☐

C ☐

Listening

4 a In pairs, discuss what is happening in each picture.

b 🔊 2.25 Listen to three people's stories about their worst job interviews. Match the stories (1–3) with the pictures (A–C).

5 Listen again and match the sentences (a–i) with the stories (1–3).

a <u>Slowly</u>, I took it from him. ☐
b He shouted at me <u>angrily</u>. ☐
c I poured it very <u>carefully</u>. ☐
d I <u>quickly</u> moved to one side. ☐
e The whole interview went really <u>badly</u>. ☐
f I prepared myself for the interview really <u>well</u>. ☐
g I was really <u>embarrassed</u>. ☐
h I was <u>desperate</u> to get to the interview. ☐
i I was really <u>worried</u> about being late. ☐

6 Work in groups and discuss the questions.

1 Do you prefer group interviews or individual interviews? Why?
2 What do you think of interview techniques like throwing a tennis ball at someone? Has anything like that ever happened to you?

Grammar | adverbs of manner

7 **a** Look at part A of the Active grammar box and the sentences from exercise 5. Which of the <u>underlined</u> words are adverbs of manner and which are adjectives?

b Look at part B of the Active grammar box and write the adverbs.

c Look at part C of the Active grammar box. Which sentence is incorrect?

1 I poured the water carefully.
2 I poured carefully the water.
3 Carefully, I poured the water.
4 I carefully poured the water.

Active grammar

A 1 Adverbs of manner tell us about verbs. They describe how somebody does something or how something happens.
2 Adjectives (not adverbs) tell us about nouns.

B 1 Most adverbs of manner are formed by adding *-ly* to the adjective, e.g. *quick* → _____
2 When the adjective ends in *-y*, we change the *y* to *i* and add *-ly*, e.g. *angry* → _____
3 There are some irregular adverbs, e.g. *good* → _____

C 1 Adverbs of manner generally come at the end of a clause.
2 To emphasise the meaning, we can also put adverbs of manner (a) directly before the main verb or (b) at the beginning of the sentence.
3 We cannot put an adverb of manner between the main verb and the object.

see Reference page 97

8 Choose the correct words in *italics*.

1 I completed the application form very *careful/carefully*.
2 I've got *good/well* qualifications and I speak Italian very *good/well*.
3 *Sad/Sadly*, he stood up and left the interview room.
4 I'm going to complain because the interviewer was very *rude/rudely* to me.
5 The receptionist put the phone down *angry/angrily*.
6 He was *happy/happily* to receive a bonus at the end of the year.
7 He walked into the interview room *quick/quickly* and *confident/confidently*.
8 The first candidate was very *nervous/nervously* and he spoke very *quiet/quietly*.

9 Find the mistakes in four of the sentences and correct them.

1 He wrote carefully his CV.
2 She spoke to the interviewees angry.
3 Slowly, he opened his book.
4 She pronounced the word careful.
5 She sat down on her chair nervously.
6 He asked confidently the question.

Speaking

10 Work in pairs. Make a list of five pieces of advice to give someone who is going to a job interview. Include an adverb of manner in each one.

Speak clearly during the interview.

11 **a** In pairs, prepare to roleplay a job interview. Choose a job advert from page 131. Then follow the instructions.

Student A: you are the interviewer. Decide which of the questions (1–8) are relevant for the job. Write two or three more questions of your own.

Student B: you are the interviewee. Decide which of the questions (1–8) you think the interviewer might ask you and prepare answers.

1 What qualifications have you got for this job?
2 Have you got any relevant experience?
3 What personal qualities have you got that make you a good candidate?
4 What skills do you think are important for this job?
5 What are your hobbies?
6 Which languages do you speak? To what level?
7 Why do you want this job?
8 Have you got any questions you want to ask?

b Now roleplay the interview.

Vocabulary | crime

1 **a** Work in pairs and make sure you understand the underlined words/phrases from exercise 1b.

b Look at the words and answer the questions.

> judge   jury   police officer   ~~thief~~   victim   witness

Who <u>steals</u> things? *thief*

1 Who <u>arrests</u> criminals?

2 Who suffers because someone has <u>committed a crime</u> against them?

3 What group of people can decide if a <u>criminal</u> is <u>guilty</u> or <u>innocent</u>?

4 Who can decide what <u>punishment</u> to give a criminal, e.g. <u>a fine</u>, <u>a prison sentence</u>, <u>a suspended sentence</u> or <u>community service</u>?

5 Who sees a crime or accident and can describe what happened?

2 Complete the sentences with the correct form of the words/phrases from exercise 1b.

1 A _____ broke into our office through the window and took three computers.

2 This _____ is dangerous – do not go near him.

3 He regularly _____ money from people in the street to pay for his expensive lifestyle.

4 The _____ for illegal parking is a £50 fine.

5 The _____ was standing at a bus stop when her handbag was stolen.

6 The _____ said he must go to prison for five years.

7 The police officer _____ him and took him to the police station.

8 I know he is _____ of taking her handbag because I saw him do it.

9 The _____ consisted of six men and six women.

10 The _____ gave a detailed description of the man's appearance.

3 Work in pairs and discuss the questions.

1 What punishment would you give …

   a a thief who broke into a shop and stole some CDs?

   b a businessman who avoided paying £1,000 of taxes?

2 Would you like to be a police officer? Why/Why not?

3 Have you ever done jury service? Would you like to?

4 Do you think there are any disadvantages to trial by jury?

5 What do you think of the prison system in your country?

Car cleaner sent to prison

Last week, cleaner Peter Blain was sent to prison for six years after being found guilty of stealing. Blain is no ordinary criminal, however, and at first, police were confused about the case. The fact was that over a period of months, Blain cleaned thirty-six cars. This may not sound like a crime, but they were not his cars, it was not his job and he was not paid to clean them.

All the cars were stolen from expensive car showrooms in the Midlands area of England and many of them had a price of more than £40,000 each. Blain was able to steal the cars using a technique which he perfected over time. He walked into car showrooms and pretended that he wanted to buy a car. He then chose a car and asked to test-drive it. He drove away from the showroom and didn't come back. Every car was later found in different residential roads, absolutely spotless inside and out. Blain washed and cleaned each one before leaving it. He was called, 'the man you would most want to steal your car' by one judge.

When the case went to court, Blain revealed that the reason he stole cars was in order to make himself feel important. He explained that he was a cleaner who didn't have his own car. He wanted to make people think he was a rich businessman with an expensive car. So, he drove each car to a different street and spent time cleaning it. He said he felt happy when people saw him and thought the car was his.

When the police finally worked out what was happening, Blain was arrested at his home in Sheffield. The cars weren't damaged and he didn't sell the cars for his own financial benefit. But Judge Alan Goldsack told Blain that a long prison sentence was inevitable. The judge explained that the owners of the car showrooms were the victims and that Blain's actions affected their businesses. Blain's wife Mary, a 48-year-old nurse, said after the case that their thirteen-year marriage was over and she wanted a divorce. She told reporters that he looked after the cars better than her.

Reading

4 **a** In pairs, look at the words/phrases from the box. What do you think the text is about?

> absolutely spotless   businessman
> car showroom   expensive new car
> prison sentence   thief

b Read the text and check your ideas.

5 Read the text again. Complete each sentence with one or two words.

1 Peter was given a _____ -year prison sentence.

2 The value of many of the cars he stole was over _____ pounds.

3 The staff in the car showrooms thought he wanted to _____ a new car.

4 He usually left the clean cars in the _____ in residential areas.

5 When Peter had the cars, he felt _____ .

6 He was a cleaner, but he wanted to look like a _____ .

7 Blain didn't _____ or sell the cars.

8 When he was arrested, his wife decided to _____ him.

6 Work in pairs and discuss the questions.

1 What do you think about Peter's punishment?

2 Do you think a different punishment would be better? If so, what?

Grammar | Past Simple Passive

7 **a** Complete part A of the Active grammar box with the correct form of the verbs in brackets. Check your answers with the first paragraph of the text from exercise 4.

b Complete part B of the Active grammar box with an appropriate ending.

Active grammar

Ⓐ We use the active form to say what the subject did.

1 *Over a period of months, he _____ (clean) thirty-six cars.* (*he* = subject)

We use the passive to say what happened to the subject.

2 *He _____ (send) to prison for six years.* (*he* = subject)

Ⓑ When we want to use the passive form and also include the agent (who/what caused the action), we use *by*.

3 *A description of the thief was given to police by _____ .*

passive subject + *was/were (not)* + past participle (+ *by ...*)

8 Underline six more examples of the Past Simple Passive in the text from exercise 4.

see Reference page 97

9 Choose the correct words in *italics*.

Germany's worst bank robber (1) *gave/was given* a one-year suspended sentence after a judge (2) *felt/was felt* sorry for him. The court (3) *told/was told* how Marko, aged 28, (4) *waited/was waited* outside the bank for three hours trying to get over his nerves. He then (5) *ran/was run* into the bank with a woolly hat over his face. Unfortunately, he couldn't see anything. He (6) *took/was taken* off the hat in front of the security camera and demanded money from the cashier. He was holding a cigarette lighter in the shape of a gun. She could see it wasn't a real gun and just (7) *told/was told* him to go away. Finally, he ran off, but (8) *arrested/was arrested* by police outside the bank. He (9) *took/was taken* in a van to the nearest police station. 'Give up being a bank robber,' the judge told him. 'You have no talent for the job.'

Speaking

10 **a** Work in pairs and follow the instructions.
Student A: look at the two stories on page 131.
Student B: look at the two stories on page 134.
Complete your stories with the Past Simple or Past Simple Passive form of the verbs in brackets.

b Take turns to retell your stories, using your own words.

11 Work in groups and discuss the questions.

1 Which crime do you think was the worst? Why?

2 Which criminal do you think was the most stupid? Why?

3 What punishment do you think is suitable for each criminal? Why?

9 Communication

Can do take part in a simple negotiation

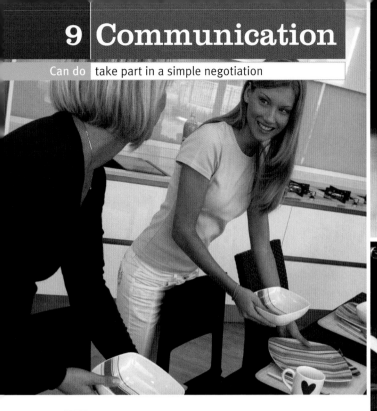

1 Work in pairs and discuss the questions.

1 What is the relationship between the people in each photo: (a) work colleagues, (b) family, (c) friends?

2 What types of negotiation do you think these people might have?

2 Look at the suggestions in the text. Do you agree with them? Can you add any more points?

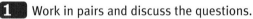

The five rules of negotiation

1 Be clear about what you want. Before you negotiate, decide…
  a) what you must have.
  b) what you would like, but is not essential.

2 Make sure you have things to offer the other person, as well as things you want.

3 Keep calm and reasonable in your voice and behaviour. Do not let emotions take over. Be aware of your body language.

4 Listen carefully and ask questions. It's important to really understand what the other person is saying. Listening to someone shows respect. That person will feel valued and important and is more likely to listen to you.

5 Try to find a 'win-win' situation. Both sides should feel happy and successful when the negotiation is finished.

3 a ⊙ 2.26 Listen to a negotiation between an employee and his boss. Answer the questions.

1 What does each person do to make the negotiation unsuccessful?

2 What advice would you give each of them to make the negotiation more successful?

b ⊙ 2.27 Now listen to a different negotiation and answer the question.

What does each person do to make this negotiation more successful?

4 Look at the How to... box and listen to the second negotiation again. Number the phrases in the order you hear them.

How to... negotiate with other people

Say what you want	*If possible, I'd like to have* the day off.	☐
Offer something	*I'll work late this week if* **necessary.**	☐
Show that you're listening	*I understand what you're* **saying.**	☐
Be positive	*I'm very pleased with* your work.	☐
Say thank you	*Thank you very much for* your understanding.	☐

5 You are going to practise negotiating. Divide into two groups and prepare for your negotiation.

Group A: look at the information on page 131.

Group B: look at the information on page 134.

6 a Work in groups of four: two from Group A, two from Group B. Negotiate with each other and try to achieve a decision on all the points. Use the language from the How to... box.

b Report back to the class on your decisions. Who were the most successful negotiators?

can, could, be able to: ability

Ability in the present

can('t) + infinitive

To talk about ability in the present, we use *can/can't*.

*She **can't speak** any other languages.*

***Can** you **see** the river?*

Ability in the past

could(n't) + infinitive

was(n't)/were(n't) able to + infinitive

To talk about general ability in the past in positive sentences, we use *could* or *was/were able to*.

*I **could swim** when I was five years old.*

*She **was able to speak** three languages fluently when she was a child.*

To talk about general ability in the past in negative sentences, we use *couldn't* or *wasn't/weren't able to*.

*I **couldn't ride** a bicycle until I was twelve years old.*

*He **wasn't able to play** the guitar when he was younger.*

To talk about ability in the past on one specific occasion in positive sentences, we use *was/were able to* only (NOT *could*).

*I **was able to finish** the race in less than an hour yesterday.*

NOT *I could finish the race in less than an hour yesterday.*

To talk about ability in the past on one specific occasion in negative sentences, we use *couldn't* or *wasn't/weren't able to*.

*The lights went out and I **couldn't see** anything.*

*They **weren't able to see** the film because there were no tickets left.*

Adverbs of manner

Adverbs of manner tell us about verbs. They describe how somebody does something or how something happens.

*He **answered** the phone **quickly**.*

*She **sang beautifully** in the concert.*

Adjectives (not adverbs) tell us about nouns.

*They had a **quick conversation**.*

Most adverbs of manner are formed by adding *-ly* to the adjective.

*quick – quick**ly**; nervous – nervous**ly**; careful – careful**ly***

! There are also some adjectives which end in *-ly* (*friendly, lively, lonely, lovely, silly*). In these cases, we usually use a phrase instead of an adverb: *in a friendly way, in a lively way …*

When the adjective ends in *-y*, we change the *y* to *i* and add *-ly*.

*angry – ang**ri**ly; happy – happ**i**ly; noisy – nois**i**ly*

There are some irregular adverbs.

good – well; fast – fast; late – late; hard – hard

Position of adverbs of manner

Adverbs of manner generally come at the end of a clause.

*She spoke about the topic very **intelligently**.*

To emphasise the meaning, we can also put adverbs of manner …

1   directly before the main verb.

   *I **slowly** turned round and then I saw him.*

2   at the beginning of the sentence.

   ***Silently**, she moved towards the door.*

We cannot put an adverb of manner between the main verb and the object.

*You speak English **well**.* NOT *You speak **well** English.*

Past Simple Passive

We use the active form to say what the subject did.

***Sarah made** a beautiful mirror for Sam's birthday.*

subject   active verb

We use the passive form to say what happened to the subject.

***This camera was made** in China.*

subject   passive verb

When we want to use the passive form and also include the agent (who/what caused the action), we use *by*.

*We were greeted warmly **by** the receptionist.*

Key vocabulary

Work

flexible/long hours   high/low salary   a lot of training
uniform   shift work   working outside
apply for a job   be offered a job   get promoted
have an interview   prepare a CV   resign
run your own company   take a job
an application form   a bonus   commission
a CV   an employee   an employer   experience
an interviewee   an interviewer   a managing director
a marketing director   qualifications   a receptionist
a salary   a sales assistant   a sales rep   a secretary
a wage

Crime

arrest   commit a crime   community service
a criminal   a fine   guilty   innocent   a judge   a jury
a police officer   a prison sentence   a punishment
steal   a suspended sentence   a thief   a victim
a witness

 Listen to these words.

ACTIVE BOOK

---

 see Writing bank page 143

9 Review and practice

1

Complete the sentences with *can('t)* or *could(n't)* and the verbs from the box.

> finish   help   ~~lift~~   play   sleep   stand
> take   tell

I _can't lift_ this box. It's too heavy.

1   Alice has an amazing memory. She _____ you the capital city of every country in the world.

2   I didn't take my camera on holiday, so I _____ any photos.

3   I _____ with the housework now. I've got some free time.

4   When Michael was younger, he was very good at gymnastics. He _____ on his hands!

5   I hurt my leg last week, so I _____ tennis today, I'm afraid.

6   **A:** You look awful.
    B: Yes, I _____ at all last night!

7   I _____ this report. I don't have all the statistics.

2

Make questions with *can, could, was/were able to* and the verbs in brackets. Sometimes more than one form is possible.

We're thinking of moving to Spain. (speak)

Can you speak Spanish?

1   Ellie would like to learn the saxophone. (read music)

2   We had a fantastic room in the hotel. (see the sea)

3   Pete wants to buy a car. (how much/afford)

4   My interview went really well. (answer all the questions)

5   My dog is very clever. (what/do)

6   Tania loved speaking languages as a child. (how many/speak)

3

Find the mistakes in five of the sentences and correct them.

She spoke ~~clear~~ to the whole group. *clearly*

1   Tina looked at me sad and walked away.

2   My brother plays the guitar good.

3   The thief entered the house quietly through the back door.

4   He sat down and opened carefully the letter.

5   The children played in the park happy all afternoon.

6   Nervously, he talked about what happened that day.

7   The security guard polite asked him to leave.

4

Rewrite the sentences in the Past Simple Passive starting with the words given.

Somebody took the keys from my desk.
The keys *were taken from my desk* _____ .

1   The police arrested more than fifty people.
    More _____ .

2   They opened the store at exactly 9 a.m.
    The store _____ .

3   They paid me a lot of money to do the job.
    I _____ .

4   Nobody met us at the airport.
    We _____ .

5   They rescued everybody from the ship.
    Everybody _____ .

6   Somebody cleaned all the classrooms yesterday.
    All _____ .

5

Correct the underlined words.

Tom got <u>applied</u> to Marketing Director with a much higher salary. He's really pleased. *promoted*

1   She's a very good <u>interviewer</u>. She's got every job she has applied for.

2   I don't have the right <u>experience</u> for this job. I don't have a degree in mathematics.

3   They pay us a <u>wage</u> of twenty percent of our annual salary if we reach our targets.

4   A <u>secretary</u> is usually the first person you meet when you go in the building.

5   She's been voted 'employ of the month'! She's met all her targets.

6   I'm not going to take the job because I don't want to do shift <u>job</u>.

6

Put the letters in the correct order.

They all thought that a large ___*fine*___ would be the best punishment. (einf)

1   There are normally twelve men and women on a _____ . (yruj)

2   He had to clean the streets as part of his 200 hours of _____ service. (motymunic)

3   There was only one _____ but he saw the thief very clearly. (nstiswe)

4   Three men were _____ by the police for breaking into a jewellery shop. (radetser)

5   He was found _____ and sent to prison for five years. (tulygi)

6   The _____ lost a lot of money because the thieves used his credit card. (micivt)

Lead-in

1 **a** Which words can you see in the photos?

> bicycle   bus   car   coach   ferry   lorry   moped
> motorbike   plane   taxi   train   van

b In pairs, ask and answer questions about what pairs of words from the box have in common.

A: *What do a van and a car have in common?*

B: *They both use petrol and …*

2 **a** Make verb phrases with the verbs from the box and the forms of transport from exercise 1. Each verb can be used with several forms of transport.

> catch   get into/out of   get on/off   go by   miss   ride   take

b What is the difference between …

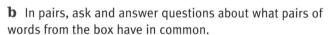

> commuter/traveller   journey/voyage   passenger/pedestrian

3 Correct the underlined words. Then ask and answer the questions in pairs.

1   Have you ever <u>lost</u> a plane or train?
2   Do you ever go to work/school <u>on</u> bicycle?
3   Have you ever got <u>in</u> a train without a ticket?
4   Have you ever got <u>out of</u> a moving train or bus?
5   What transport do <u>travellers</u> in your city use to go to work?
6   What do you do when you're a <u>pedestrian</u> on a long car journey?

Reading

1 Work in pairs and discuss the questions.

1 Have you ever been on holiday with friends? What was it like?

2 Who would your perfect travel companion be? Why?

3 Which things from the box would annoy you most about a travel companion?

> he/she talks a lot   he/she is lazy
> he/she snores
> he/she complains a lot

2 Read the extract from Lucy's travel blog. Which things about travel companions from question 3 in exercise 1 are mentioned?

3 Now read a summary of Lucy's blog. Which three things are different from her blog?

> Lucy and Andy are friends from school. They met each other by chance when they were both in Rio de Janeiro. On Saturday, Lucy was worried because they decided to travel together. When they were travelling to Salvador, Andy annoyed Lucy because he talked a lot. When he fell asleep on Monday afternoon, he started talking in his sleep. When they were sunbathing on the beach on Tuesday, Lucy was very tired. She was upset because Andy was complaining about lots of things. On Wednesday afternoon, Andy was shouting a lot and annoying Lucy. Now, she feels she can't travel with him anymore.

4 **a** Lucy decides she doesn't want to travel with Andy anymore. Work in pairs and write (a) what you think she says and (b) how he reacts. Then practise your conversation.

b 2.28 Listen to Lucy and Andy's conversation and compare it with yours. What is the same/different?

My backpacking holiday in Brazil by *Lucy Briggs*

Sat 3rd

I can't believe it! I'm in an internet café in Rio, 3,500 miles from home, and I've just met Andy, an old school friend from years ago. I didn't know he was here. It's great to see him again and it's good to have a travel companion. We're going sightseeing in Rio this afternoon and we're going to travel to Salvador together. It's a long way, but we've decided not to rent a car. We're going to use local transport and go by bus. I might practise my Portuguese with some of the other passengers.

Posted in Rio | no comments

Mon 5th

We're staying in a really nice hotel here. But there's bad news. It's 10:15 a.m. and Andy has already started to annoy me. He never stops talking! He didn't stop talking on the bus all the way from Rio to Salvador … that's nearly twenty-four hours! Oh well … I'm sure it'll get better. I hope it will … . More later!

Posted in Salvador | no comments

Mon 5th

Me again! 3:30 p.m. I can't stand it! Andy hasn't stopped talking yet. I now know everything about his friends, his family, even his neighbour's cat! He's just fallen asleep, but it isn't really any better because now he's started snoring! Aggh!

Posted in Salvador | 2 comments

Tues 6th

12:30 p.m. – I'm exhausted! I didn't get any sleep because of HIM. And I've just spent the whole morning sunbathing on a really idyllic beach listening to Andy complaining about the weather, the food and even the beach! What am I going to do?

Posted in Salvador | 1 comment

Wed 7th

In a café – 2:30 p.m. Now he's started singing to himself. I have to tell him I can't travel with him anymore. It isn't going to be easy, but he's driving me crazy. I'll have to think of a reason for travelling on my own because I really don't want to offend him by telling the truth. I'm not sure what I'm going to say though!

Posted in Salvador | no comments

Grammar | Present Perfect Simple: *just, yet, already*

5 Look at the sentences (1–4) and complete the Active grammar box with *just, yet* and *already*.

1 I've just met Andy.
2 Andy has already started to annoy me.
3 He hasn't stopped talking yet.
4 Has Lucy told him yet?

Active grammar

We often use *just, yet* and *already* with the Present Perfect Simple.

A _____ means something has happened before now (probably sooner than expected). It is usually used in positive sentences, directly before the main verb or at the end of the sentence.

B _____ in negative sentences means something has not happened, but will probably happen at some point in the future. In questions, we use it to find out if something has happened before now. It usually comes at the end of the negative sentence/question.

C _____ means something has happened a short time ago. It is usually used in positive sentences, directly before the main verb.

see Reference page 107

6 Add *just, already* or *yet* to each sentence. Use the notes in brackets to help you.

I've bought my plane ticket. (I bought my plane ticket five minutes ago.) *I've just bought my plane ticket.*

1 Simon's arrived at the bus station. (I saw him arrive a minute ago.)
2 Diana hasn't phoned from the airport. (I expected her to phone earlier.)
3 I've spent all my holiday money. (I didn't expect to spend it all so early.)
4 Have you written any postcards? (I'm not sure if you wrote them before now.)
5 My parents have come back from holiday. (They came back two hours ago.)
6 She's booked the flight. (I didn't expect her to book so soon.)

7 Work in A/B pairs and look at page 132. Read the list of things to do for you and your partner. Ask and answer questions about the things you have/haven't done.

A: *Have you booked your holiday yet?*
B: *Yes, I have.*

Speaking and listening

8 ● 2.29 Listen to Lucy telling a friend about the holiday she's just had and answer the questions.

1 Is she generally positive or negative about her holiday?
2 Who were Lucy's two travel companions?
3 What does she say about her photos?

Pronunciation | showing interest

9 **a** ● 2.30 To show interest, we change the tone of our voice. Listen and notice the intonation in two dialogues. Which one sounds more interested?

1 A: I met an old school friend of mine called Andy.
   B: That's great!
2 A: I met a really nice woman called Emily.
   B: That's great!

b Listen again and repeat. Try to copy the intonation.

see Pronunciation bank page 148

10 **a** Imagine you've just come back from a holiday and you want to tell your partner about it. Make notes (e.g. Where did you go? Who did you go with? What did you do?).

b Work in pairs and take turns to talk about your holidays. When you're listening, make sure you ask questions and make comments to show you're being a good listener.

10.2 Customs worldwide
Grammar | verbs with two objects
Can do | make generalisations about customs

Vocabulary | greetings and gifts

1 Match the words with the photos (A–E).

> a bow ☐   a gift ☐   a handshake ☐
> a kiss ☐   a wave ☐

2 **a** Complete the sentences with the correct form of the verbs.

> bow   shake hands (with)   kiss
> ~~give a gift~~   wave

In Japan, you should *give a gift* using both hands.

1 In most countries, people _____ when they say goodbye.
2 In most Western countries, people usually _____ when they meet in a business situation.
3 In Asia, people usually _____ when they meet in a business situation.
4 In the UK, men don't _____ on the cheek when they meet in a business situation.

b Work in pairs and discuss the questions.

1 Which of the customs from exercise 2a exist in your country?
2 How do you usually greet your friends/your colleagues/your boss?
3 When do you give gifts to people (apart from birthdays)?

ADVICE FOR
UK BUSINESS TRAVELLERS

GIVING GIFTS

Japan
Unlike the UK, in Japan it is very important to give people gifts and it usually happens at the end of a visit. Pens are a good idea or something not available in Japan. Japanese people are generally quite superstitious, so if you give them flowers, avoid giving four or nine flowers as these are unlucky numbers.

China
Chinese people will probably refuse your gift several times, but it is polite to continue offering it to them. Do not give clocks to Chinese people as the Chinese word for 'clock' is similar to the word for 'death'.

Middle East
Give gifts of highest quality leather, silver or crystal. Remember to avoid alcohol and leather from pigs.

South America
Gift-giving is less formal in South America, but still an important part of the culture. Avoid leather, as many of the world's best leather products come from South America.

Australia, Canada, US and Europe
Gift-giving in these countries is informal and not always expected. However, it is polite to bring your host flowers, chocolates or wine when visiting their house. In some European countries, you should avoid red flowers (associated with romance).

Reading

3 Work in two groups and follow the instructions.

Group A: read the text above. Which customs from exercise 2a are mentioned in your text?

Group B: complete exercises 3 and 4 on page 132.

4 **a** Group A: read the text again. What is the significance of the words/phrases from the box?

> a clock   four flowers   a leather briefcase   pens
> red flowers   silver goods

b Work with a student from Group B. Ask your partner the questions about his/her text.

1 Should you use first names in Germany?
2 In which part of the world do people stand closest to each other?
3 Why don't American people like you to stand too close to them?
4 Should you show how strong you are when you shake hands?
5 Do Asian people ever shake hands?
6 Do business people kiss each other in Russia?

c Now answer your partner's questions about your text.

5 In groups, read the saying and discuss the questions.

'When in Rome, do as the Romans do.'

1 What does the saying mean?
2 Do you agree with it? Why/Why not?

Grammar | verbs with two objects

6 Look at the Active grammar box. How many of the sentences (1–4) are correct?

1 Do not give Chinese people clocks.
2 Do not give them clocks.
3 Do not give to Chinese people clocks.
4 Do not give clocks to Chinese people.

Active grammar

Some verbs can be followed by two objects.

In Japan, it is very important to give people gifts.
indirect direct
object object

The indirect object is usually a person and usually comes first, especially when the indirect object is a pronoun (*me*, *him*, *them*, etc.).

verb + indirect object + direct object

It is polite to bring your host flowers./It is polite to bring her flowers.

We can also put the direct object first, but we need to add *to*.

verb + direct object + *to* + indirect object

It is polite to bring flowers to your host.

Common verbs which take two objects are: *give, bring, offer, lend, owe, send, show, tell, promise*

see Reference page 107

7 **a** Find the mistake in each sentence and correct it.

1 You should always a tip give to your waiter after a meal.
2 It's traditional to send to your mother a bunch of flowers on Mother's Day.
3 It's usual for people a seat on the bus to offer old people.
4 When guests come to my house for dinner, I like them to me bring a gift.
5 It's best to tell to someone the truth if you don't like the food they've cooked.
6 It's bad manners to owe to people who are not in your family money.

b Work in groups. Do you agree with the statements from exercise 7a? Why/Why not?

8 **a** Write five *Have you ever …?* questions. Use the verbs from the end of the Active grammar box.

Have you ever lent someone some money which they never paid back?

b In pairs, ask and answer your questions.

Speaking

9 Look at the How to... box and complete each sentence with one word. Check your answers with the texts from exercise 3 (pages 102 and 132).

How to... make generalisations

1 _____ Asians follow the bow with a handshake.
2 People in South America _____ to stand quite close to each other.
3 In the Middle East, they _____ stand even closer.
4 You _____ only kiss people you know well.
5 Chinese people will _____ refuse your gift several times.

10 Work in pairs. Prepare advice for visitors to your country. Use the topics from the box and your own ideas.

> an important national festival   birthdays
> giving gifts   visiting someone's house

10.3 Travel movies

Grammar | Past Perfect Simple

Can do | recommend a film

Listening

1 Look at the photo and answer the questions.

1 What do you know about the film in the photo?
2 Do you think it is a film you would like to see? Why/Why not?

2 ● 2.31 Listen to part of a radio programme called *Travellers' Tales* in which TV reporter, Ben Gardner, is talking about the film *The Motorcycle Diaries*. Which topics does he mention?

> the main actors/characters ☐   the scenery ☐
> the name of the director ☐   the soundtrack ☐
> the supporting actors/characters ☐
> where and when the film is set ☐

3 Listen again and write true (T) or false (F).

1 *The Motorcycle Diaries* is set in the 1960s. ☐
2 The main characters travel through five countries on their trip. ☐
3 Ben is interested in how the men change throughout the trip. ☐
4 Ben talks about a hospital on the border of Peru and Colombia. ☐
5 Ben says the actors in supporting roles were very good. ☐
6 Ben says the best scenery in South America is in Colombia and Venezuela. ☐

4 Work in pairs and discuss the questions.

1 Has the radio programme changed your opinion about question 2 from exercise 1? Why/Why not?
2 Which other films about travelling would you recommend? Why?
3 Would you like to do a road trip on a motorbike? Why/Why not?

Vocabulary | *-ed* and *-ing* adjectives

5 Look at the underlined adjectives in the sentences. Which adjective describes (a) how the speaker feels, (b) what makes the speaker feel this way?

1 I was inspired by the two main characters.
2 All their adventures were really inspiring.

6 Choose the correct words in *italics*. Check your answers with audioscript 2.31 on page 158.

1 The film follows them on their *amazed/amazing* eight-month-long trip.
2 They have some really *excited/exciting* adventures.
3 I was *fascinated/fascinating* to see how their personalities grow and change.
4 The hospital was a *depressed/depressing* place.
5 I was *surprised/surprising* by the incredible beauty of this continent.
6 I'm sure you won't be *disappointed/disappointing*.

7 In pairs, ask and answer questions.

Student A: look at page 132.
Student B: look at page 134.

In each answer, use at least two adjectives from the box and give details.

> amazed/amazing   annoyed/annoying
> bored/boring   depressed/depressing
> disappointed/disappointing
> excited/exciting   frightened/frightening
> inspired/inspiring   interested/interesting
> relaxed/relaxing   surprised/surprising
> tired/tiring

Grammar | Past Perfect Simple

8 **a** Look at the sentences (1–4) in the Active grammar box. In each sentence, which of the actions in **bold** came first?

b Look at the rules (A and B) in the Active grammar box and choose the correct <u>underlined</u> words.

Active grammar

1 *Before he **arrived** in Cuba, he **had lived** in Argentina with his family.*
2 *They **had become** much more grown up by the time they **reached** the end of the trip.*
3 *Before I **saw** this film, I **hadn't thought** of visiting South America.*
4 ***Had** he **starred** in any other films, before he **made** this one?*

A We use the Past Perfect Simple to talk about an action (or actions) that happened *before*/*after* another action in the past.

B Past Perfect Simple: *had + past participle*/*infinitive*

---

see Reference page 107

9 Choose the correct words in *italics*.

1 We *arrived*/*had arrived* at the cinema late and the film *began*/*had begun*.
2 I *saw*/*had seen* a motorbike by the side of the road. It *broke down*/*had broken down*.
3 He *read*/*had read* the book, so he *knew*/*had known* the plot of the film.
4 I *didn't go*/*hadn't been* to Argentina before. It *was*/*had been* my first time.
5 Before I *went*/*had been* to the airport, I *checked-in*/*had checked-in* online.
6 She *arranged*/*had arranged* something else, so she *didn't come*/*hadn't come* to the cinema.

10 Complete the sentences with the Past Perfect Simple or Past Simple form of the verbs in brackets.

1 As soon as I saw her, I _____ (realise) I _____ (meet) her before.
2 A: _____ (he/finish) the book when you _____ (see) him?
   B: Yes, he _____ .
3 When I _____ (arrive) at the station, the train _____ (leave).
4 When the driver _____ (ask) to see my ticket, I realised I _____ (lose) it.
5 When we _____ (get) there, we realised we _____ (not pack) enough warm clothes.
6 I _____ (want) to read a book on the plane, but I _____ (forget) to buy one at the airport.

Pronunciation | using fillers: *anyway*

11 🔊 2.32 We often say *anyway* as a filler when we tell a story. Listen to two extracts from the radio programme from exercise 2 and tick (✓) the correct answer.

We use anyway to show that …

a we are responding to someone's questions. ☐

b we are returning to the story after giving some extra, background information. ☐

see Pronunciation bank page 148

Speaking

12 **a** Prepare to talk about a film which you enjoyed or which inspired you. Look at the topics from exercise 2 and make notes. Include at least two sentences with the Past Perfect Simple.

b Now work in small groups and talk about your films.

c Which film that you heard about do you most want to see? Why?

1 Look at the photos and answer the questions.

1 What problems are the people having?

2 What other problems might you have when travelling?

2 a ● 2.33 Listen to a man talking about an unusual/difficult journey. What two problems did he have?

b Listen again and complete the How to... box.

How to... tell a story in an engaging way

Start the story in an engaging way	*Something really frightening happened to me the other day.*
	Do you know what happened to me yesterday?
	I heard an amazing story last week.
Emphasise something interesting or amazing	(1) *It's hard to believe, but* _____ .
	(2) *Believe it or not,* _____ .
	(3) *It's incredible, I know, but* _____ .

---

3 a Prepare to talk about an unusual, difficult or interesting journey that you've had. Make notes for each question.

1 Where were you going and why?

2 How did your journey start?

3 What happened next?

4 What happened in the end?

b Add two or three sentences from the How to... box to make your story more engaging for your listener.

4 a Now work in small groups and tell your stories.

b Whose story was the most engaging to listen to? Why?

Present Perfect Simple: *just, yet, already*

We often use *just*, *yet* and *already* with the Present Perfect Simple.

Present Perfect Simple: *has/have* + past participle.

already means something has happened before now (probably sooner than expected). It is usually used in positive sentences, directly before the main verb or at the end of the sentence.

*You've **already** told me that.*

*He's taken his driving test six times **already**.*

yet in negative sentences means something has not happened, but will probably happen at some point in the future. In questions, we use it to find out if something has happened before now. It usually comes at the end of the negative sentence/question.

*I haven't bought the tickets **yet**.*

*Have you seen Dave **yet**?*

just means something has happened a short time ago. It is usually used in positive sentences, directly before the main verb.

*I've **just** seen a really great film.*

*Have you **just** arrived?*

Verbs with two objects

Some verbs can be followed by two objects (a direct object and an indirect object).

The indirect object is usually a person and usually comes first, especially when the indirect object is a pronoun (*me, you, him, her, it, us, them*).

verb + indirect object + direct object

He gave <u>his wife</u> <u>some earrings</u> for her birthday.

He gave <u>her</u> <u>some earrings</u> for her birthday.

We can also put the direct object first, but we need to add *to*.

verb + direct object + *to* + indirect object

He gave <u>some earrings</u> <u>to his wife</u> for her birthday.

He gave <u>some earrings</u> <u>to her</u> for her birthday.

Common verbs which take two objects are:

give, bring, offer, lend, owe, send, tell, promise, buy, teach, show, write.

*Don't forget that you **owe** <u>him</u> <u>ten pounds</u>.*

*Could you **lend** <u>me</u> <u>that book</u>, please?*

*She **showed** <u>the photos</u> <u>to everyone</u> in the office.*

*I **wrote** <u>a long letter</u> <u>to the train company</u>.*

Past Perfect Simple

We use the Past Perfect Simple to talk about an action or actions that happened before another action in the past.

*When I saw him I realised **I'd met** him before.*

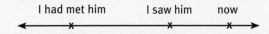

| I had met him | I saw him | now |

Past Perfect Simple: *had* + past participle.

*By the time we got to the restaurant, I **hadn't eaten** all day.*

***Had** you **been** to that cinema before yesterday?*

! The Past Perfect Simple is common after verbs of saying/thinking:

*I told her we **had bought** the tickets.*

*She realised she**'d met** him before somewhere.*

The Past Perfect Simple is common after *when*:

*When he**'d finished** the washing-up, he turned the TV on.*

Key vocabulary

Transport and travel

bicycle   bus   car   coach   ferry   lorry   moped   motorbike   plane   taxi   train   van

commuter   traveller   passenger   pedestrian   journey   voyage

catch a bus/a ferry/a plane/a taxi/a train

get into or get out of a car/a lorry/a taxi/a van

get on or get off a bicycle/a bus/a coach/a ferry/ a moped/a motorbike/a plane/a train

go by bicycle/bus/car/coach/ferry/moped/motorbike/ plane/taxi/train

miss a bus/a coach/a ferry/a plane/a train

ride a bicycle/a moped/a motorbike

take a bus/a coach/a ferry/a plane/a taxi/a train

Greetings and gifts

shake hands (with someone)   a handshake
bow (to someone)   a bow   kiss (someone)   a kiss
wave (to someone)   a wave   give a gift (to someone)
a gift

-ed and -ing adjectives

amazed   amazing   annoyed   annoying   bored   boring   depressed   depressing   disappointed   disappointing   excited   exciting   frightened   frightening   inspired   inspiring   interested   interesting   relaxed   relaxing   surprised   surprising   tired   tiring

 Listen to these words.

ACTIVE BOOK

---

 see Writing bank page 144

10 Review and practice

1 Choose the correct words in *italics*.

A: Where are you going on holiday this year?

B: I've haven't decided *yet*/*already*.

1 A: Do you want to see that film?

 B: No, I've seen it *yet*/*already*.

2 A: Have you booked the tickets *just*/*yet*?

 B: No, I'll do it today.

3 A: Why is your hair wet?

 B: I've *just*/*already* had a shower.

4 A: Have you cleaned the kitchen?

 B: No, I haven't done it *already*/*yet*.

5 A: Would you like some lunch?

 B: No, thanks. I've *yet*/*just* eaten.

6 A: I'd like to buy Louise that new CD.

 B: She's *yet*/*already* got it.

7 A: Have you started jogging *just*/*yet*?

 B: No, I'll start next week.

2 Write complete sentences using the prompts. Make any necessary changes.

Tom's only seventeen and he/visit eleven countries. (already)

Tom's only seventeen and he's already visited eleven countries.

1 I hope Katya is OK. She/not phone me. (yet)

2 Do you like these flowers? Natalia/bring them. (just)

3 I'd love to see your new flat. You/move in? (yet)

4 A: The sitting room looks lovely.

 B: I/paint it. (just)

5 I really want to read that book. You/finish it? (yet)

6 A: Could I speak to Alex, please?

 B: She/go home. (already)

7 I hope it isn't too late to invite Pietro. I/not ask him. (yet)

3 Put the words in the correct order.

anyone/You/money/shouldn't/to/lend

You shouldn't lend money to anyone.

1 all my secrets/told/I/him

2 owes/a lot of money/me/Juan

3 I/Can/some tea/you/offer?

4 a pay rise/He/this month/me/promised

5 always/me/My grandmother/really good advice/gives

6 the nurse who looked after me/I/some flowers/sent/to

7 the bill/us/Could/bring/please/you?

4 Complete each sentence with one verb in the Past Simple and one verb in the Past Perfect Simple.

I ___wanted___ (want) to read something, but I *hadn't packed* (not pack) my book.

1 She _____ (decide) to buy the bag she _____ (see) the day before.

2 When I _____ (arrive) at the airport, I realised I _____ (miss) my plane.

3 As soon as I _____ (close) the door, I remembered I _____ (leave) my keys inside.

4 When I _____ (eat) my breakfast, I _____ (feel) better.

5 When I _____ (see) the exam question, I realised I _____ (not study) enough.

6 When she _____ (try) to pay for something in the shop, she realised she _____ (forgot) her credit card.

5 Find the mistakes in six of the underlined verbs and correct them.

I <u>went</u> to the ticket office to buy my train ticket. When I <u>had tried</u> to pay for the ticket, I <u>had realised</u> I <u>didn't have</u> my wallet. I <u>remembered</u> that when I <u>got off</u> the bus, someone <u>pushed</u> past me. I <u>had realised</u> that this person <u>took</u> my wallet.

6 Complete the sentences with the correct form of the words from the box. There are three extra words.

> bow   catch   ~~commuter~~   drive   miss
> passenger   pedestrian   ride   shake   wave

Most *commuters* in my city travel to work by bus.

1 Should I _____ hands with the boss when I meet her?

2 The new traffic lights make it safer for _____ to cross the road.

3 Sorry I'm late. I _____ the bus and had to wait for another one.

4 I prefer driving a car to being a _____ .

5 The train left the station and we all _____ goodbye to them.

6 I don't like _____ my bicycle in the city as it's too dangerous.

Lead-in

1 Work in pairs and discuss the questions. Use the words from the box to help you.

> an advert   a celebrity   childhood   a hero   the media
> a mentor   a peer   a role model

1   In what ways is each photo connected with the word 'influence'?
2   In what ways do you think people are influenced by the media?
3   What kinds of people do you think have the biggest influence on (a) children, (b) teenagers and (c) adults? Think about family members, friends/peers, celebrities, etc.

2 **a** Tick any of the following that you think describe you. Are you someone who ...

- is a natural leader?   ☐
- is usually a follower?   ☐
- usually sticks to his/her own opinions?   ☐
- is easily influenced by other people?   ☐
- likes to follow the crowd?   ☐
- can usually persuade other people to do things?   ☐
- is often a fashion victim?   ☐

b Work in groups. Compare your opinions and explain your reasons. Which other student gave similar answers to you?

11

Grammar *would*: past habits

Can do talk about people who influenced you

Reading

1 Look at the pictures. What is the relationship between the people and the animals?

2 Read the text. How many examples of children raised by animals are mentioned?

3 Read the text again and answer the questions.

1 Who was the father of Romulus and Remus?
2 Where were they left when they were very small?
3 Who found them at first?
4 Who was the first human they saw?
5 What did the boys do when they became adults?
6 What was the result of the boys' argument?
7 Who was looking after Kamala and Amala when they were found?
8 How was the girls' relationship with other children?
9 What special abilities did they have?
10 What happened to Amala and Kamala?

4 Work in pairs and discuss the questions.

1 Do you think there is any truth in the story of Romulus and Remus? Why/Why not?
2 Do you know of any similar stories: in myths/legends, in real life or in films?
3 Do you think that an animal could look after a human baby/child? Why/Why not?

Vocabulary | phrasal verbs

5 Look at the underlined phrasal verbs in the text from exercise 2. Read the sentence around each verb, then match the phrasal verbs (1–6) with the definitions (a–f).

1 to look after (someone) ☐
2 to come across (something) ☐
3 to bring (someone) up ☐
4 to grow up ☐
5 to look up to (someone) ☐
6 to pick (something) up ☐

a to raise/educate children
b to learn without trying
c to respect and admire
d to take care of
e to change from child to adult
f to find by chance

Raised by animals

There are a number of stories of children who are raised by animals. One of the earliest stories is about the twin brothers Romulus and Remus. They were the sons of the god Mars. When they were very young, they were left by the banks of the River Tiber. Luckily, they were found by a wolf. The wolf <u>looked after</u> them and fed them with her milk.

Later, a shepherd <u>came across</u> the boys. He took them home and <u>brought them up</u> as his own children. The boys <u>grew up</u> to be very strong and clever. They decided to build a town in the place where the shepherd found them. Shortly after building the town, the twins had a big argument. Romulus killed his brother Remus in the fight. Romulus then became the first king of this town, which was named Rome, after him.

More recently, according to many reports in the media, two young girls were discovered in the care of a wolf in 1920, in Godamuri, India. The girls (Kamala, eight, and Amala, aged eighteen months) were taken to a children's home, but they didn't like their new life there at all. They preferred to be with cats and dogs and they seemed to <u>look up to</u> animals, not people. They never got on with the other children and they would sometimes bite and attack them.

The girls slept during the day and were awake at night. They walked on their hands and feet and enjoyed raw meat. They had extremely good eyesight and hearing. The younger child, Amala, died after one year in the children's home. After her sister died, Kamala became a bit friendlier towards other people and <u>picked up</u> a small number of words. She remained very different from other children, however, and died eight years later.

6 **a** Complete the questions with the correct form of the phrasal verbs in brackets.

1 Where _____ ? (you/grow up)

2 Do you think it is better _____ children in a city or a village? (bring up)

3 Have _____ a small child? (you/ ever/look after)

4 As a child, who _____ ? (you/ look up to)

5 Have _____ any English from TV or songs? (you/pick up)

6 Have _____ any money in the street? (you/ever/come across)

b In pairs, ask and answer the questions from exercise 6a.

7 Look at the Lifelong learning box. Read the tip and complete the exercise.

Learning phrasal verbs

! To help you learn phrasal verbs, you should write (1) a definition and (2) some example sentences.

For each of the phrasal verbs from exercise 5, copy the definition and write two example sentences in your vocabulary notebook.

to bring (someone) up = to raise/ educate children

Jane is bringing up her five children on her own./My grandmother brought me up.

Lifelong learning

Listening

8 **a** 🔊 2.34 Listen to Emma and George talking about their childhoods and answer the question.

Who influenced each speaker the most?

b Listen again and correct each sentence by changing one word.

1 Most of the time, Emma's father worked in Japan and Korea.

2 Emma usually lived with just her grandmother.

3 When George first started ice hockey he found it difficult.

4 George's sports coach sometimes went to his training sessions.

Grammar | *would*: past habits

9 **a** Complete the Active grammar box with *would* + the verbs *not say* and *look after*. Check your answers with audioscript 2.34 on page 159.

b Look again at audioscript 2.34 on page 159 and find more examples of *would* + infinitive.

Active grammar

We use *would* + infinitive for actions in the past which happened over a long period of time, but don't happen now.

1 *She _____ me when my mum was working.*

2 *When you asked him something, he _____ much.*

We also use *used to* + infinitive for habits in the past.

I used to wear my skates more than my shoes.

We use *used to* + infinitive (NOT ~~would~~) with state verbs.

I used to be really good at ice hockey. ~~I would be ...~~

He used to have a job which took him to different countries. ~~He would have ...~~

We use the Past Simple for an action which happened only once.

I started playing when I was about five. ~~I would start ...~~/ used to start ...

see Reference page 117

10 **a** Rewrite the sentences with *would* + infinitive, where possible.

1 My cousins and I played together for hours.

2 The footballer Pelé was my role model when I was growing up.

3 My maths teacher helped me when I didn't understand something.

4 When I was twelve, my family moved to the US.

5 My older brother was my hero, but he didn't talk to me much.

6 My parents were very supportive of me when I was a child.

7 I spent hours every day listening to The Beatles in my bedroom.

b Which of the sentences above can you rewrite with *used to* + infinitive?

Speaking

11 **a** Prepare to talk about someone who influenced you when you were growing up. Make brief notes about the person you want to talk about.

b Work in pairs and take turns to talk about the people you chose.

11.2 The power of advertising
Grammar articles
Can do discuss adverts and their influence

Vocabulary | the media

1 Divide the words into two groups, depending on where you usually see them:

a on television   **b** on a computer

> a blog   a channel   a commercial break
> a computer game   a direct email advert
> a documentary   a drama series
> a podcast   a pop-up advert
> a search engine   a soap opera
> a TV advert

2 Choose the correct underlined words.

1 A TV advert/drama series for Chanel No. 5 perfume starring Nicole Kidman cost over £18 million to make.

2 During a podcast/commercial break on television, most viewers switch to another channel/advert.

3 I can't stand getting pop-up adverts/direct email adverts on the screen while I'm looking at a website.

4 People who have their own search engine/blog on the internet update them twice a month on average.

5 Millions of people have played *Super Mario Brothers* – one of the best-selling soap operas/computer games ever.

6 Seventy-three percent of people who are looking for something on the internet use a podcast/search engine.

7 *March of the Penguins* is a channel/documentary lasting eighty-five minutes about how penguins live.

8 Twenty percent of people listening to a blog/podcast use a portable player, e.g. an MP3 player.

3 Work in pairs and discuss the questions.

1 What are your two favourite types of TV programme? Why?

2 What experience have you got with blogs? Do you read any? Do you write one?

3 Do you ever listen to podcasts? What type?

4 How do you feel about (a) pop-up adverts and (b) direct email adverts? Why?

5 Do you think adverts on television are mostly: annoying, informative or entertaining? Why?

Listening

4 🔵 2.35 Listen to a radio programme about advertising and answer the questions.

1 Tick (✓) the ways that TV adverts are described.

a annoying ☐   b informative ☐   c entertaining ☐

2 How many new types of TV advertising are mentioned?

5 Listen again and write true (T) or false (F).

1 Companies need to advertise so they get more customers to buy their product. ☐

2 The expert says that all adverts have a lot of influence on everyone. ☐

3 It is possible that adverts might appear in the middle of a TV programme. ☐

4 A logo may appear anywhere on the television screen, including over someone's face. ☐

5 Almost everyone is positive about the development of pop-up adverts. ☐

6 Research in Japan shows that it is important to give consumers choice. ☐

7 The new Japanese adverts will include more information than before. ☐

8 Developers in Japan think that people will avoid adverts more and more. ☐

6 Work in pairs and discuss the questions.

1 To what extent do you think you are influenced by adverts on TV? Which are most effective? Why?

2 How do you think you would feel about pop-up adverts during a TV programme? Why?

3 Do you think you would choose to watch the new style Japanese adverts? Why/Why not?

Grammar | articles

7 Match the sentences (1–4) with the rules in the Active grammar box (A–D).

1 Adverts may become one of <u>the most popular</u> things on TV.

2 A new computer game uses <u>a new system</u> for advertising.

3 With <u>the new system</u>, no adverts are shown on the screen.

4 <u>Consumers</u> choose to watch adverts only if they want to.

Active grammar

A We use *a/an* the first time we mention something. ☐

B We use *the* to refer to something or someone we have mentioned before and to refer to a particular person or thing. ☐

C We use *the* with superlatives. ☐

D We use no article with a plural or uncountable noun to talk about things in general. ☐

---

see Reference page 117

8 Complete the sentences with *a/an*, *the* or no article (–).

1 I think Cartoon Network is _____ best channel on television.

2 Did you see _____ advert I told you about?

3 These days, _____ companies spend huge amounts of money on advertising.

4 I saw _____ interesting documentary on TV last night.

5 That's _____ most annoying advert I've ever seen.

6 I'll get a drink when there's _____ commercial break.

7 Celebrities have a lot of influence on _____ young people.

8 Adverts use _____ music to create different effects on people.

9 Find the mistake in each sentence and correct it.

1 What's funniest advert you've seen?

2 Would you like a job thinking of ideas for the adverts?

3 What do you do during commercial break on TV?

4 Do you think it's effective to use the celebrities in adverts?

5 Do any of your clothes have the advert on them?

Pronunciation | using fillers: *well, so* and *erm*

10 a 🔊 2.36 We often say *well, so* and *erm* as fillers in conversations. Listen to two extracts from the radio programme from exercise 4 and tick (✓) the correct answer.

We use *well, so* and *erm* to show that …

a we have finished speaking. ☐

b we are asking a question. ☐

c we want to have time to think. ☐

b Look at audioscript 2.35 on page 159 and find more examples of *well, so,* and *erm*.

see Pronunciation bank page 148

Speaking

11 🔊 2.37 Listen to two radio adverts and answer the questions.

1 What product is each advert for?

2 What different groups of people do you think each advert is aimed at? Why?

3 Which advert do you think is the most effective? Why?

12 Complete the How to… box with the headings (a–d).

a Use emotional adjectives

b Use repetition

c Exaggerate and make statements sound like facts

d Ask the listener questions

How to… use persuasive language

1 _____	*My hair looks terrible!*
2 _____	*Are you worried about your hair?*
3 _____	*This is the car you've wanted all your life!*
4 _____	*Designed by an expert car designer … Engineered by an expert car engineer.*

---

13 Work in groups and prepare an advert for television. Discuss the questions.

1 What product is your advert for?

2 What group of people is your advert aimed at?

3 What approach do you want to use, e.g. giving information, using humour, using a celebrity?

4 What language will you use in your advert? Use the ideas from the How to… box to help you.

Reading

1 Work in pairs. Look at the film poster and discuss the questions.

   1 Have you seen the film or read the book *Yes Man*?

   2 If not, what do you think they are about?

   3 If so, did you like it/them? Why/Why not?

2 Read Adam's email quickly. Does he describe the film as funny, serious or both?

3 Read the text again and complete each sentence with one, two or three words.

   1 Adam has just finished doing _____ .

   2 Adam read the book *Yes Man* and thought it was

       _____ .

   3 The man who Danny met on the bus was a _____ to him.

   4 At the beginning of the book, Danny describes his life as _____ .

   5 When the man said, 'Say "yes" more,' Danny _____ 'yes' to everything.

   6 In the film, Carl decides to say 'yes' more when he goes to a _____ .

   7 Adam thinks the story in the film is _____ , but the acting is good.

   8 After seeing the film, Adam says he wants to be _____ and do more things.

4 Work in pairs and discuss the question.

How would your day be different if you said 'yes' to everything?

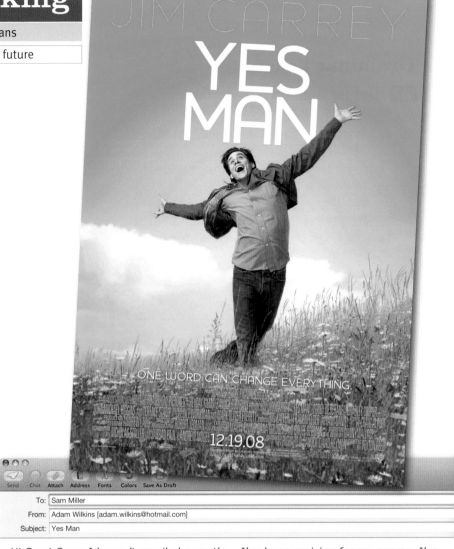

JIM CARREY

YES MAN

ONE WORD CAN CHANGE EVERYTHING.

12.19.08

To: Sam Miller
From: Adam Wilkins [adam.wilkins@hotmail.com]
Subject: Yes Man

Hi Sam! Sorry I haven't emailed recently – I've been revising for my exams. I've finished them now and I've got some time to relax and some money to spend on going out. Last weekend, I went to see a great film called *Yes Man*. If you haven't seen it, you must go! Jim Carrey plays the main character and it's very funny and entertaining – and also quite inspiring. It's based on a book by Danny Wallace which is also called *Yes Man*. I read the book a few months ago and that's hilarious, too – I really laughed out loud!

The book is a true story about what happens to the author, Danny. Basically, he found that he was doing nothing all the time, just worrying about things and complaining about his life. He wasn't seeing his friends much, so he was lonely and bored. Then one day, he was on a bus in London when he sat down next to a man. The man was a total stranger, but they started talking. Danny told him about his boring life and the man responded to him with just three words: 'Say "yes" more.' And for Danny this was a turning point in his life. Those three words influenced everything he did. <u>At that moment, he made a decision: 'I'll say "yes" to everything!'</u> And he wrote a book about what happened to him in the next year or so. Three years later, the book was made into a hit film.

The film is based on the book although there are some differences. Firstly, it's set in the US instead of England. Secondly, the main character is based on Danny, but he is called Carl in the film and he doesn't meet a man on a bus. His turning point comes when he goes to a self-help class and they persuade him to say 'yes' more. He succeeds in changing his life and doing lots of crazy things: he has flying lessons, he learns to speak Korean and he rides a motorbike with no clothes on! The storyline isn't very strong. It's quite weak, I suppose, but all Carl's adventures are very entertaining – especially because Jim Carrey is a very funny actor.

I think the film really appealed to me because there's a serious message, too. <u>When I saw the film, I said to myself: 'I won't be negative anymore!'</u> I believe in making the most of life and <u>I've decided I'm going to be more positive</u>. <u>I've decided I'm not going to stay at home so much</u> – I'm going to do more things, see my friends more and everything. Actually, that's why I'm emailing you! It would be great if we could meet up soon. Let me know when you're free.

All the best, Adam

Grammar | *will* and *be going to*: decisions and plans

5 Look at the underlined sentences in the text from exercise 2. Complete the rules in the Active grammar box (A and B) with the correct ending (1 or 2).

> ### Active grammar
>
> A We use *will* to talk about decisions about the future, when ... ☐
>
> B We use *be going to* to talk about future plans and intentions, when ... ☐
>
> 1 ... we decide at the moment of speaking.
> 2 ... we've decided before we speak.
>
> In questions, we usually use *be going to* to ask about plans and intentions.
> *What are you going to do this weekend?*

see Reference page 117

6 Complete the dialogue with the correct form of *will* or *be going to* and the verbs in brackets.

A: So, Tom. The exams are over! What (1) _____ (you/do) this summer?

B: Well, I (2) _____ (go) on holiday. My friend Pete and I have decided to go to Spain.

A: Oh, which part of Spain?

B: We're not sure yet – maybe I (3) _____ (go) online and see what I can find.

A: That's a good idea. And (4) _____ (you/get) a job?

B: Yes. I need some money for the holiday, so I (5) _____ (work) at my uncle's restaurant – starting next Monday.

A: Oh! I didn't think of that ... . I think I (6) _____ (get) a job, too. I might ask your uncle ... .

B: That's a good idea.

7 Work in small groups. Ask and answer questions about your plans. Ask each student three questions and use three time references from the box.

> after the class   after your exams
> next week   on Friday evening
> this evening   this summer   this weekend

Vocabulary | verb + preposition (1)

8 Complete the sentences with the prepositions. Check your answers with the text from exercise 2.

> about (x2)   for   in (x2)   on   to (x2)

1 I've been revising _____ my exams.
2 I've got some money to spend _____ going out.
3 He found he was worrying _____ things.
4 He was complaining _____ his life.
5 The man responded _____ him with just three words.
6 He succeeds _____ changing his life.
7 The film appealed _____ me because there's a serious message.
8 I believe _____ making the most of life.

9 **a** Choose the correct words in *italics*.

1 What kind of films usually appeal *for/to* you?
2 What have you succeeded *in/about* doing in your life that you are proud of?
3 What tips have you got when revising *about/for* an exam?
4 What have you spent money *in/on* in the last seven days?
5 What are the kinds of things you worry *for/about* most?
6 What would you complain *on/about* in a restaurant?
7 Do you believe *in/on* horoscopes based on zodiac signs?
8 How long does it usually take you to respond *about/to* an email or text message?

b In pairs, ask and answer the questions from exercise 9a. Explain your reasons in each case.

Speaking

10 🔊 2.38 Listen to two people playing the 'Yes-No' game and answer the questions.

1 How do you play the game?
2 Number the questions in the order you hear them.
   a Are you going to go on holiday this summer? ☐
   b Have you seen any good films recently? ☐
   c Have you ever seen a film that changed your life? ☐
   d Do you believe in fate? ☐

11 **a** Prepare to play the 'Yes-No' game.

1 Look at audioscript 2.38 on page 160. Underline all the different answers they use to avoid saying *yes/no*.
2 Look at the questions from exercise 10 and add six more. Make sure they are *Yes/No* questions.

b Work in pairs and play the 'Yes-No' game.

1 Read the text. What does the magazine want you to do?

English International

→ Our magazine, *English International*, is twenty-five years old next month. To celebrate our twenty-fifth birthday, we've decided to give you the chance to decide who will be on the cover of next month's issue. We want this person to be an influential and important person who is still living. He/she should be someone with special qualities who has made a significant contribution to the world. It doesn't matter what his/her job is – he/she could be a sportsperson, an actor, a scientist, a political leader, etc. The important thing is that you can justify why you think the person you have chosen should be on the cover.

2 **a** Work in groups of three or four. Choose a famous, influential person who you think should be on the magazine cover. Use someone from this page (look at the information on page 133) or your own ideas. Make sure each member of the group chooses a different person.

b Make notes using the questions. Add any other information you want to.

1 What important things has he/she done?
2 What special qualities does he/she have?
3 In what ways has he/she affected other people's lives?
4 Why does he/she deserve to be on the cover more than the others?

3 Work in groups and talk about the people you chose. Agree on which person should be on the magazine cover.

would: past habits

We use *would* + infinitive for actions in the past which happened over a long period of time, but don't happen now.

We also use *used to* + infinitive for habits in the past.

*When I was a child, I **would walk** to school every morning with my best friend.*

*When my mother was angry, she **wouldn't say** much.*

*I **used to go** out every Friday evening when I was in my twenties.*

We use *used to* + infinitive (NOT ~~would~~) with state verbs.

*I **used to be** much fatter than I am now.*

~~*I would be much fatter than I am now.*~~

We use the Past Simple for an action which happened only once.

*My cousin **got** married in June last year.*

! For habits in the present, we use *usually* (NOT ~~would~~ or ~~used to~~).

*I **usually** get up early and go for a run before breakfast.*

Articles

The indefinite article – *a/an*

We use *a/an* the first time we mention something.

*Could you buy **a newspaper** when you go out, please?*

*Oh no! It's raining and I haven't got **an umbrella**.*

The definite article – *the*

We use *the* to refer to something or someone we have mentioned before.

*I bought some ham and some **chicken**. We had **the chicken** for lunch.*

We use *the* to talk about a particular person or thing.

***The president** is going to give an important speech tomorrow.*

*There's a problem with **the cat**. He isn't eating anything.*

We use *the* with superlatives (because we are only referring to one and it is usually clear which one we are talking about).

*She's **the best player** in the team.*

No article

We use no article with a plural or uncountable noun to talk about things in general.

***Cats** make very good pets for children.*

***Money** doesn't make you happy.*

! We do not usually use *the* with singular proper names.

*Which department does **James Cameron** work in?*

will and *be going to*: decisions and plans

will/won't + infinitive

We use *will/won't* + infinitive to talk about decisions about the future, when we decide at the moment of speaking.

! We often add phrases like *I (don't) think, maybe* and *I'm not sure*.

A: *What are you going to do tonight?*

B: *I'm not sure. **I think I'll go** out, but **I won't stay** out late.*

be going to + infinitive

We use *be going to* + infinitive to talk about future plans and intentions, when we've decided before we speak.

! In this case, we often add phrases like *I've decided*.

A: *What are you going to do after the exams?*

B: *Well, **I've decided I'm going to get** a job and **I'm not going to go** on holiday.*

In questions, we usually use *be going to* to ask about plans and intentions.

***What are you going to do** this weekend?*

! We use the Present Continuous to talk about plans when arrangements are already made, e.g. when a time and place are decided.

*I'm **starting** my new job on Monday.*

Key vocabulary

Influence

an advert   a celebrity   childhood   a hero
the media   a mentor   a peer   a role model

Phrasal verbs

to bring (someone) up   to come across (something)
to grow up   to look after (someone)
to look up to (someone)   to pick (something) up

The media

a blog   a channel   a commercial break
a computer game   a direct email advert
a documentary   a drama series   a podcast
a pop-up advert   a search engine   a soap opera
a TV advert

Verb + preposition (1)

appeal to   believe in   complain about   respond to
revise for   spend on   succeed in   worry about

 Listen to these words.
ACTIVE BOOK

 see Writing bank page 145

11 Review and practice

1 Decide if one or both of the options in *italics* is/are correct.

She *would go/used to go* swimming twice a week when she was at school.

1 When I was a child, I *would play/used to play* in the street after school.

2 I *would always eat/used to always eat* lunch in the park when I was at university.

3 My family *would move/moved* house four times when I was a child.

4 My mother *would sing/used to sing* to me every night when I was young.

5 This town *wouldn't be/didn't use to be* as busy as it is now.

6 I *would start/started* playing the guitar when I was eleven.

7 When I worked in the town centre, I *wouldn't get/didn't use to get* home until 7:30 p.m.

8 I *would watch/used to watch* TV for hours every evening when I was a teenager.

2 Complete the sentences with *a/an, the* or no article (–).

What's _____*the*_____ longest river in South America?

1 I had _____ sandwich and _____ banana for lunch, but _____ sandwich was awful!

2 Simon is looking for _____ job in publishing.

3 Did you pass _____ exam you took last month?

4 Listening to _____ music helps me relax.

5 Excuse me, where is the main entrance to _____ university?

6 I heard that yesterday was _____ hottest day of the year.

7 You should eat _____ vegetables and _____ fruit as part of a healthy diet.

8 Could I speak to _____ manager, please?

3 Complete the sentences with the correct form of *will* or *be going to* and the verbs in brackets.

A: What are you going to do after work today?

B: I'm not sure. Erm … maybe I *'ll go* (go) round to Dave's house.

1 A: What are you going to do this weekend?

   B: I haven't decided, but … maybe I _____ (go) to the cinema.

2 A: Have you got any holiday plans?

   B: Yes, I _____ (stay) with my aunt in Scotland.

3 A: What are you going to do on Friday night?

   B: Nothing. I've decided I _____ (not do) anything.

4 A: Have you got any plans for your birthday this year?

   B: No not really … but I think I _____ (invite) some friends for dinner.

5 A: What are you going to do when your exams finish?

   B: I've decided that I _____ (have) a big party. Definitely!

6 A: Where are you going to have dinner?

   B: I don't know … erm … I think I _____ (have) dinner at home.

4 Choose the correct words in *italics*.

Don't worry *for/about* finishing the report at the moment.

1 She succeeded *in/to* passing her driving test the third time.

2 When I was in Paris, I came *about/across* a small art gallery.

3 Some people believe *on/in* the power of mind over matter.

4 It's important to have someone you can look up *for/to* when you're a child.

5 When she lived in Italy, she picked the language *on/up* very quickly.

6 I'm sorry, but I'd like to complain *about/for* the service here.

7 My mother brought me *on/up* in a very relaxed way.

8 How much do you spend *for/on* clothes every month?

5 Complete the sentences with the words from the box. There are two extra words/phrases.

> blog   channel   commercial break
> direct email advert   documentary
> drama series   podcast
> pop-up advert   search engine

There were two emails in my inbox this morning, but one of them was a *direct email advert*.

1 Which _____ is the football match on tonight?

2 I'm writing a _____ on the internet about my travels in Australia.

3 I'll phone him during the next _____ so I don't miss the programme.

4 When I was looking at that website, a _____ came up on the screen.

5 There was a really good _____ on TV last night about tigers in India.

6 Which _____ do you use when you're looking for something on the internet?

Lead-in

1 **a** In pairs, discuss which things from the box you can see in the photos.

> a bargain/a discount   a coin/a note   a cashpoint/a cash till
> a credit card/cash   a currency/an exchange rate
> a receipt/a bill   a wallet/a purse

b What is the difference in meaning between each pair of words from exercise 1a?

2 Work in pairs and ask and answer the questions.

1 Do you usually pay for things in cash or by credit card? Why?
2 When did you last buy something which was a bargain? What was it?
3 Can you name five different currencies?
4 Do you know what the exchange rate is between the US dollar and your currency?

3 **a** Choose the correct words in *italics*.

1 What do you enjoy *spending/borrowing* money on?
2 Do you try and *lend/save* any money each month? If so, is it difficult?
3 Do you ever buy things that you can't really *afford/spend*?
4 How do you feel when you *owe/earn* money to someone?
5 How often do you *win/withdraw* money from a cashpoint?
6 Have you ever *earned/won* any money in a lottery or a competition?
7 How much do nurses, teachers or lawyers typically *earn/lend* each year in your country? Do you think this is right?

b In pairs, ask and answer the questions from exercise 3a.

How much do you want to pay?

Not everyone is totally honest all of the time. Anthony Jenkins finds out what determines how honest people really are.

We're all taught that honesty is the best policy. Telling the truth is important and it's essential not to steal or cheat your way through life. I would say, 'I am always totally honest' if you asked me how honest I am. That's certainly how I'd like to be … and probably how most people would like to be. But when you look at honesty box schemes, in some situations, people are not as honest as they'd like to think. So, what determines how honest people are?

Honesty boxes are sometimes used to sell products like newspapers at train stations and vegetables at the farmer's gate. You take what you want and you pay by putting your money in a box. Sometimes, similar systems are used for paying a fare on a bus or train. Schemes like this are good because they avoid long queues. But it's a risk for the seller: if someone didn't pay, the seller wouldn't know who that customer was. Honesty boxes are now part of the online world, too. In 2007, Radiohead decided to sell their new album, *In Rainbows*, by using a digital version of an honesty box. They released the album as a download and a blank price box appeared on the screen saying, 'It's up to you'. Most people paid a fair price.

Why, in this case, were most people honest? There are two major factors that determine how honest people are. Firstly, people are more honest if they think someone is watching them. To test this theory, some researchers did an experiment. A poster was put above an honesty box for tea and coffee in an office and two different posters were tested: one with some flowers and the other with a pair of eyes. The results showed that when the poster was a pair of eyes, people were more honest than when it was some flowers. They clearly felt that someone was watching them.

The second factor is loyalty: people are more honest when they care about the seller in some way. It could be that people buying the Radiohead album were loyal customers and true fans of Radiohead. To test this idea, in another experiment, shoppers were given too much change. Most people check their change and know when they are given too much or too little. The results of the tests showed that in large supermarkets people usually kept the extra change. In small shops, however, people were more honest and gave it back.

So, what about you? Are you as honest as you'd like to be? Or would you only be honest if you cared about the person? Or if somebody was there to see you? Come on, be honest … .

Reading

1 Work in pairs and discuss the questions.

1 What does the title of this lesson mean? Do you agree with it?

2 Do you think it's always necessary to be honest about (a) money and (b) your opinions?

2 Read the text. What two factors does it say determine how honest people are?

3 Read the text again and complete each sentence with one word.

1 Honesty box schemes are used for paying for newspapers, food and _____ .

2 One of the benefits of honesty boxes is not having to _____ to pay for something.

3 Fans of Radiohead could _____ how much they wanted to pay for the album.

4 People were more honest about paying for their coffee when the poster with _____ was there.

5 In one experiment, shops gave people too much _____ to see how honest they were.

6 Customers have a more honest attitude towards _____ shops.

4 Work in pairs. Do you think the idea of honesty boxes would work where you live? Why/Why not?

Vocabulary | money

5 **a** Make questions by matching the beginnings (1–8) with the endings (a–h).

1 Do you always check your ☐
2 Do you always leave a ☐
3 Do you pay any of your bills ☐
4 Do you have to pay a fare ☐
5 Do you pay a lot of interest ☐
6 Do you think people have to pay too much tax ☐
7 Do you know what salary an average person earns for ☐
8 Do you know how much pension people get ☐

a when they retire?
b by direct debit?
c to the government?
d tip in a restaurant?
e working a thirty-five hour week?
f change in a shop?
g on money that you borrow from a bank?
h before you get on a bus or train in your country?

b In pairs, ask and answer the questions from exercise 5a for you and your country. Give reasons.

Grammar | Second Conditional

6 Look at the Active grammar box and choose the correct underlined words.

> ### Active grammar
>
> *I would say, 'I am always totally honest' if you asked me how honest I am.*
>
> *If someone didn't pay, the seller wouldn't know who that customer was.*
>
> *Would you only be honest if you cared about the person?*
>
> A We use the Second Conditional to talk about situations in the *past*/*future* which are possible, but unlikely to happen.
>
> B We also use the Second Conditional to talk about imaginary situations in the *past*/*present*.
>
> C Second Conditional: *If + infinitive*/*Past Simple*, *+ would (not) + verb*
>
> D We use a comma after the first clause: *always*/*only after the 'if' clause*.

see Reference page 127

7 Complete the sentences with the correct Second Conditional form of the verbs in brackets.

1 If a shop assistant _____ (give) me too much change, I _____ (give) it back.
2 If I _____ (have) a bank account, I _____ (pay) all my bills by direct debit.
3 He _____ (not pay) his bus fare if nobody _____ (ask) him for it.
4 If I _____ (earn) a lot of money, I _____ (give) more to charity.
5 I _____ (eat) out more if it _____ (not be) so expensive.
6 _____ (you/leave) a tip in a restaurant if the service _____ (be) poor?

8 Complete the second sentence in each pair so it has the same meaning as the first.

I don't have any money, so I can't buy a new car.
If I *had some money, I would* buy a new car.

1 I won't change my bank because it gives good rates of interest.
If my bank didn't _____ change it.
2 I've decided to leave a big tip for the waiter because he works so hard.
If the waiter didn't _____ him a big tip.
3 We're not going to Australia because it costs so much.
We'd go _____ so much.
4 He hasn't got enough change, so he isn't going to pay in cash.
He'd _____ enough change.
5 I'm going to work longer hours because I want to earn more money.
If I didn't _____ longer hours.

Speaking

9 Work in pairs. What would you do/say in each situation?

1 A shop assistant gives you too much change.
2 You find a wallet in the street. There is no name or address in it, but there is a lot of cash.
3 Some builders are doing some work on your house. They ask you to pay in cash, so they don't have to pay any tax.
4 Your friend doesn't have much money. He/She suggests going on a train without paying the fare.
5 At the beginning of a meal in a restaurant, you realise that you haven't got enough money to leave a tip.

Listening

1 Look at the newspaper headlines. What do you think each story is about?

Prizes for grades

Paid to go to school

Do your homework for $100

Average graduate owes £15,000

Music students pay more

2 **a** Prepare to listen to a radio programme about the stories from exercise 1. Look at the Lifelong learning box. In pairs, read the tips and try to predict what you are going to hear.

Lifelong learning

Predicting before listening

! When you listen, you will understand more if you can predict what you're going to hear. To help you predict ...

- list any words and phrases connected to the topic that you think you'll hear.
- think about the types of people who are going to talk and their possible opinions.
- look at any questions/activities, headlines, titles, pictures or photos which accompany the listening.

b 2.39 Listen to the radio programme. Which of the news stories from exercise 1 are mentioned?

3 Listen again and answer the questions.

1 Where do most university students get their money from?
2 How much money does the average medical student owe when he/she leaves university?
3 How much in total has St Luke's School given to its A-level students?
4 How much did it give to each student who got into university?
5 Why does Caroline Clarke particularly like this scheme?
6 What does the parent think about the scheme?
7 What is Holly going to buy with her reward money?
8 In the US scheme, what prize did the oldest children get?

4 Work in pairs and discuss the question.

Do you think you would be motivated by the schemes you heard about? Why/Why not?

Vocabulary | money in education

5 In pairs, look at audioscript 2.39 on page 160 and find the verb phrases from the box. Make sure you understand each phrase.

be in debt   get a grant   get a loan   get a prize
get a scholarship   pay back a loan   pay fees
take part in a reward scheme

6 **a** Complete the questions with words from the verb phrases from exercise 5.

1 Is it easy to get a _____ or a scholarship to help pay for university _____ ?
2 Is it usual for university students to get a _____ from the bank?
3 How would you feel about being in _____ as a student and owing the bank money?
4 Have you ever taken part in a _____ scheme at school?
5 Have you ever got a _____ (e.g. money) for studying hard?

b In pairs, ask and answer the questions from exercise 6a.

Grammar | reported speech

7 **a** Look at part A of the Active grammar box and complete the sentences (1–7).

1 'The students **are working** much harder than before.' → He said the students _____ much harder than before.

2 'My school **will continue** with the scheme.' → He said his school _____ with the scheme.

3 '**I'm** really pleased.' → Holly said that she _____ really pleased.

4 'The scheme **made** me work much harder.' → She told me the scheme _____ her work much harder.

5 'I **have earned** over £500.' → She said she _____ over £500.

6 '**I'm going to buy** a new laptop computer.' → She told me she _____ a new laptop computer.

7 'Now I **can afford** to buy a new computer.' → She said she _____ to buy a new computer.

b Complete parts B and C of the Active grammar box.

Active grammar

A When we change direct speech into reported speech, we usually change the tense/form of the verb:

- Present Simple → Past Simple
- Present Continuous → Past Continuous
- Past Simple → Past Perfect
- Present Perfect → Past Perfect
- *is going to → was going to*
- *will → would*
- *can → could*

B To report what someone said, we use *say* or *tell*. With both verbs, we can use *that*, but it is not necessary. *Tell* is followed by an object. *Say* is not followed by an object.

1 *She _____ (that) it was a great idea.*

2 *She _____ me (that) it was a great idea.*

C Sometimes we need to change the pronouns.

'I'm pleased my school took part.' →

3 *She said _____ was pleased _____ school had taken part.*

see Reference page 127

8 Change the direct speech to reported speech. Start with the words given.

1 'I'm going to save money for university.' He said ...

2 'My school gave prizes to the top students.' She told ...

3 'I don't want to be in debt for years.' He said ...

4 'I'll pay back the loan as quickly as possible.' She told ...

5 'They've offered me a scholarship to study medicine.' He said ...

6 'Our school is taking part in a reward scheme.' She told...

7 'I can't afford to pay the fees for my university course.' He said ...

Speaking

9 Look at what Holly says in audioscript 2.39 on page 160 and complete the How to... box.

How to... report back on discussions

Reporting on how many people	**All of us** thought it was a good idea to pay students to do well in exams.
	(1) _____ thought the reward scheme was really good.
	(2) _____ weren't sure at first.
	None of us thought that the scheme would work.
Reporting on (dis)agreement	(3) _____ that the scheme had made us work harder.
	We disagreed about giving rewards to children for doing their homework.

10 **a** Work in small groups and discuss the questions. Make a note of the group's opinions.

1 Do you think it's a good idea to pay students to do well in exams? Why/Why not?

2 Do you think it's a good idea to give children prizes when they do their homework? Why/Why not?

3 Do you think students should be paid to stay at school after the age of sixteen? Why/Why not?

4 Do you think education at university should be free? Why/Why not?

b Report back to the class on your group's opinions and give reasons.

| Grammar | *both, either, neither* |
| Can do | describe similarities and differences |

Making baseball history

Reading

1 In groups, discuss the questions.

1 What is the game in the photo?
2 What is the aim of the game? Use these words to help you: *pitcher*, *batter*, *base*, *run*, *home run*.
3 Why do you think a baseball might be worth $1 million?

2 Read the text and answer the questions.

1 What was the argument between Alex Popov and Patrick Hayashi about?
2 Did the argument have a happy ending for them?

3 Read the text again and answer the questions.

1 What record did Barry Bonds break?
2 Why was the ball worth $1 million?
3 Who caught the ball first?
4 Why did he then lose the ball?
5 What did Hayashi get from the officials?
6 What did Popov do after the game?
7 How long did the court case last?
8 What did the judge decide?

4 Work in pairs. Do you think the judge made the right decision? Why/Why not?

Vocabulary | verb + preposition (2)

5 Some verbs are often followed by a preposition. Look at the text from exercise 2 and find the prepositions which often follow the verbs in **bold**.

1 Bonds was **playing** _____ the San Francisco Giants. (line 14)
2 The judge didn't **agree** _____ either man. (line 37)
3 Legally, the ball **belonged** _____ neither of them. (line 39)

6 Complete the sentences with the prepositions.

> for (x3)   from   on   to (x2)   with

1 She apologised _____ not paying me back sooner.
2 I don't like lending money _____ people.
3 I've applied _____ a job in a large Swiss bank.
4 I borrowed some money _____ a friend to pay for the ticket.
5 He's always arguing _____ his flatmate about money.
6 I waited _____ ages to get a refund for the cancelled show.
7 I'm going to listen _____ *The Money Programme* on the radio.
8 I don't know if I'll go to the show. It depends _____ the price.

This is the story of how a baseball came to be worth
5 $1 million … and of how two men both felt that they owned the ball. When Alex Popov and Patrick Hayashi went to a baseball game, neither of them owned the ball. But when the match was over, both Popov and Hayashi were sure the ball was theirs.

10 The story started when baseball champion, Barry Bonds, hit a baseball into the stands. At that moment, he had no idea he was starting one of the strangest legal battles in sporting history. Bonds, who was playing for the San Francisco Giants at the time,
15 completed his seventy-third home run of the season, beating the existing record. As this record-breaking champion hit the ball towards the crowd, it instantly became worth a million dollars – and the fans knew it. The fight over who owned the ball began as soon as it
20 was caught. But who had caught it?

Either Alex Popov or Patrick Hayashi had caught it. But which one was it? They were both confident: both of them said they had caught the ball. The truth is, according to TV video recordings, Popov caught
25 the ball first and it was in his hands for a fraction of a second. It was then knocked out of his hands by other fans. Then Hayashi got it and held it in the air. He was taken away by officials and they gave him a certificate saying it was his. At that point, the ball was worth
30 $1million if Hayashi wanted to sell it. However, Popov wasn't happy. He claimed that the ball was his, because he had got it first, and he took Hayashi to court.

First, history was made with a record-breaking home run. Then, legal history was made with two
35 men fighting in court over a $1 million ball. For four months, Judge Kevin McCarthy considered the case. In the end, he didn't agree with either man. He said that neither man was the clear winner in this case and that, legally, the ball belonged to neither Popov nor
40 Hayashi. The judge ordered them to sell it and share the money. In the end, however, it wasn't a happy ending for either of them. Unfortunately for both men, any profit went to pay their lawyers' fees.

7 In pairs, ask and answer the questions.

1 How do you feel about lending money to (a) your friends and (b) your family? What does it depend on?
2 How do you feel about borrowing money from (a) your friends and (b) your family? What does it depend on?
3 Have you ever argued with anyone about money? What happened?

Grammar | *both, either, neither*

8 Read the rules (A–C) and complete the Active grammar box.

Active grammar

When we are talking about two people or two things, we can use:

A *both (... and ...)* with a plural noun. It means 'one **and** the other'.

B *either (... or ...)* with a singular noun. It means 'one **or** the other'.

C *neither (... nor ...)* with a singular noun. It means '**not** one and **not** the other'.

1 *Two men _____ felt that they owned the ball.*

2 *_____ Popov _____ Hayashi were sure the ball was theirs.*

3 *In the end, the judge didn't agree with _____ man.*

4 *_____ Alex Popov _____ Patrick Hayashi had caught it. But which one was it?*

5 *He said that _____ man was the clear 'winner' in this case.*

6 *Legally, the ball belonged to _____ Popov _____ Hayashi.*

both/either/neither can be followed by *of* + pronoun/*the/these*, etc.

7 *When they went to a baseball game, _____ owned the ball.*

8 *_____ said they had caught the ball.*

9 *In the end, however, it wasn't a happy ending for _____ .*

see Reference page 127

9 **a** Find the mistakes in five of the sentences and correct them.

1 I like both buying expensive things or finding bargains.

2 I don't like neither borrowing or lending money.

3 Either of my two best friends likes going shopping at all.

4 I pay for things either by cheque nor by credit card – always in cash.

5 I usually leave a tip for both the waiter and the chef.

6 My best friend and I neither like doing the lottery.

b Now change the sentences from exercise 9a to make them true for you. In pairs, take turns to say your sentences.

Pronunciation | emphasising details

10 **a** ⬤ 2.40 Listen to a dialogue between two women. What four things have they got in common?

b We can give words extra stress when we want to emphasise details. Listen again and notice the extra stress on three of the words.

see Pronunciation bank page 148

Speaking

11 **a** Work in pairs and find four things you have got in common. Think about the topics from the box.

> borrowing money   doing the lottery
> going shopping   lending money
> owing money   paying for things
> saving money   spending money

b Tell the class what you found out.

12 Communication

Can do | ask survey questions and report the results

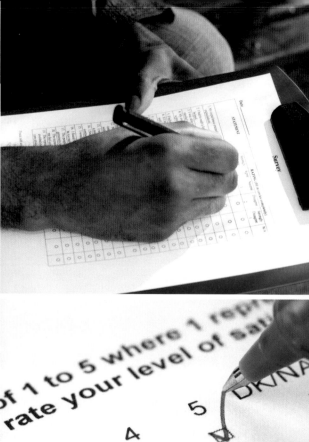

1 A large clothes shop has asked a market research company to do a survey about attitudes to money. In pairs, ask and answer the survey questions.

Market research by *MoneyMatters*

Attitudes to money

1 Would you describe yourself as basically:
(a) a 'spender' ☐   (b) a 'saver' ☐ ?

2 Would you lend £50 to a friend?   Yes ☐ No ☐
Would you be worried about the
possible effect on your friendship?   Yes ☐ No ☐

3 Do you use a credit card regularly?   Yes ☐ No ☐
How often do you pay your credit card bill? _____

2 🔊 2.41 Listen to someone from Money Matters reporting the results of their survey. What do the numbers/statistics refer to?

1 forty percent of people: _____
2 forty-five percent: _____
3 fifteen percent: _____
4 two-thirds of people: _____
5 the majority of those people:
_____
6 eight out of ten people: _____
7 a minority of those people: _____

3 **a** Work in pairs and prepare to do your own survey. Choose a topic from the box and write six questions. Use the prompts (1–6).

education   food/cooking   holidays/travel
jobs/work   learning English   music
sport   transport/traffic

1 How do you feel about ... ?
2 How often do you ... ?
3 When was the last time you ... ?
4 Have you ever ... ?
5 What would you do if ... ?
6 ... ?

b Walk around the class. Ask as many students as possible to do your survey. Make a note of their answers.

4 In pairs, collect your results. Write one or two sentences for each question. Use the language from exercise 2 and audioscript 2.41 on page 160 to help you.

5 Report your results back to the class.

Our first question was about sport and twenty-five percent of people said they did some sport every day ...

126

Second Conditional

We use the Second Conditional to talk about …

a) situations in the future which are possible, but unlikely to happen.

b) imaginary situations in the present.

Second Conditional: *If* + Past Simple, *would (not)* + verb

! The *'if'* clause can come first or second.

*If I **won** some money, **I'd go** on holiday.*

*I'd train to be a pilot if I **wasn't** afraid of flying.*

We use a comma only after the *'if'* clause.

! Compare with the First Conditional, which we use for talking about possible situations in the future.

*If I **pass** all my exams, I **will go** to university. (possible)*

*If I **passed** all my exams, I **would go** to university. (less possible)*

! When we are less certain, we can use *might*.

*If I **had** more money, I **might buy** some new clothes.*

Reported speech

When we change direct speech into reported speech, we usually change the tense/form of the verb, e.g. a verb in the Present Simple will usually change to the Past Simple.

Direct speech	Indirect reported speech
'I **have** £50.'	*He said (that) he **had** £50.*
'Janice **is living** in Spain.'	*She said (that) Janice **was living** in Spain.*
'She **went** home.'	*He said (that) she **had gone** home.*
'He **has worked** there since March.'	*He said (that) he **had worked** there since March.*
'I'm going to start guitar lessons.'	*She said (that) she **was going to start** guitar lessons.*
'I'm sure she**'ll pass** her exams.'	*He said (that) he was sure she **would pass** her exams.*
'I **can't come** to the party.'	*He said (that) he **couldn't come** to the party.*

To report what someone said, we use *say* or *tell*. With both verbs, we can use *that*, but it is not necessary. *Tell* is followed by an object. *Say* is not followed by an object.

*She **said** she saw Gordon on Friday.*

*She **told me** she saw Gordon on Friday.*

Sometimes we need to change the pronouns.

*'**We** don't like Tony.'*

*She said that **they** didn't like Tony.*

! If somebody said something that is still true when it is reported, tenses don't always change.

*'I **don't like** carrots.'*

*She said that she **doesn't like** carrots.*

both, either, neither

When we are talking about two people or two things, we can use *both*, *either* and *neither*.

We use *both* with a plural noun. It means 'one **and** the other'.

***Both** jackets are expensive.*

We can use *both … and …* : *He's **both** intelligent **and** good-looking.*

We use *either* with a singular noun. It means 'one **or** the other'.

*I don't like **either** jacket.*

We can use *either … or …* : *Why don't we get **either** the red one **or** the blue one?*

We use *neither* with a singular noun. It means '**not** one and **not** the other'.

***Neither** jacket fits me very well.*

We can use *neither … nor …* : *He speaks **neither** Russian **nor** Polish. (This is quite formal.)*

Both/either/neither can be followed by *of* + pronoun/ *the/these*, etc. ***Both of my sisters** are at university.*

*I haven't seen **either of them** for ages.*

***Neither of them** is married.*

! We usually use *neither* instead of *both … not*.

***Neither of them** came to the meeting.*

NOT ~~**Both of them** didn't come to the meeting.~~

Key vocabulary

Money

a bargain   a discount   a coin   a note   a cashpoint
a cash till   a credit card   cash   a currency
an exchange rate   a receipt   a bill   a wallet
a purse   be able to afford   borrow   earn   lend
owe   save   spend   win   withdraw
check your change in a shop
earn a salary for working a thirty-five hour week
get a pension when you retire   leave a tip in a restaurant
pay a bill by direct debit   pay a fare on a bus or train
pay interest on money that you borrow
pay tax to the government

Money in education

be in debt   get a grant   get a loan   get a prize
get a scholarship   pay back a loan
pay fees (for a course/school/university)
take part in a reward scheme

Verb + preposition (2)

agree with   apologise for   apply for   argue with
belong to   borrow (something) from   depend on
lend (something) to   listen to   play for   wait for

  Listen to these words.

ACTIVE BOOK

---

  see Writing bank page 146

12 Review and practice

1 Find the mistake in each sentence and correct it.

If I got stuck in a lift, I'd to be scared.

If I got stuck in a lift, I'd be scared.

1 I'd do things differently if I have my life again.
2 I'd buy a dog if I wouldn't live in a city.
3 What you do if you saw an accident in the street?
4 If Karla studied more, she would passed her exams.
5 If I would had Pete's address, I'd send him a birthday card.
6 People would understand me more easily if my English is better.
7 What would you take you went on a cycling holiday in France?
8 If you would had more time, would you read more?

2 Complete the sentences with the correct Second Conditional form of the verbs in brackets.

We _'d move_ (move) to the country if our jobs _weren't_ (not be) in the city.

1 If I _____ (have) some money, I _____ (buy) this CD.
2 My job _____ (be) much easier if I _____ (speak) Spanish.
3 If he _____ (get) up earlier, he _____ (not be) late for work.
4 I _____ (feel) happier if my daughter _____ (phone) more often.
5 If you _____ (not work) so hard, you _____ (not be) so tired.
6 I _____ (do) an art course if I _____ (have) more time.
7 If I _____ (find) a wallet in the street, I _____ (take) it to a local police station.
8 If I _____ (fail) my exams, I _____ (retake) them in October.

3 Choose the correct words in *italics*.

He *said/told* the police nothing.

1 They didn't *say/tell* Peter that I was at home.
2 She *said/told* him to go.
3 Why did you *say/tell* that you hated your job?
4 Nobody *said/told* that the station was closed for a month.
5 You shouldn't *say/tell* you want to leave school if you don't mean it.
6 Who *said/told* you that I was with Carmen?
7 She didn't *say/tell* them she was getting married.

4 Somebody says the opposite of what they said earlier. Complete the replies.

A: Tim likes chocolate.
B: I thought you said *Tim didn't like chocolate!*

1 A: I'm going home soon.
  B: I thought you said …
2 A: We'll see Steve and Jim tomorrow.
  B: I thought you said …
3 A: I don't have much time at the moment.
  B: I thought you said …
4 A: They borrowed my car for the weekend.
  B: I thought you said …
5 A: I've talked to Tara.
  B: I thought you said …

5 Find the mistakes in four of the sentences and correct them.

Neither of them wanted to do the washing-up. ✓

1 Both of men were wearing long black coats.
2 Neither hotels has a swimming pool.
3 I was invited to two parties at the weekend, but I didn't go to either of them.
4 I thought that both candidates for the job were very good.
5 I'm afraid the maths teacher has had problems with either of your sons.
6 I don't think I like neither of her brothers.
7 I can't believe it. She's asked both of her ex-boyfriends to the party!

6 Complete the sentences with the words from the box. There are three extra words.

apologise argue ~~belong~~ borrow depends
lend pension result reward tax

Who does this bag _belong_ to? There's no ID in it.

1 My father has just retired and is getting a good company _____ .
2 Why do you always _____ with your brother? Can't you agree on anything?
3 I'm taking the children swimming this afternoon as a _____ for being good.
4 Can I _____ your car for the afternoon? I'll bring it back around 6:00 p.m.
5 We might have the party outdoors. It _____ on the weather.
6 I think the government should increase the _____ on cigarettes. It might stop some people smoking.

Communication activities

Unit 1 Lesson 1.1 Exercise 10

Student B

How do you like spending your free time?

1 What are your main hobbies/interests?

2 Do you like guided walks or tours? Why/Why not?

3 What three things do you like doing on your summer holiday? Why?

4 What three kinds of sport or exercise do you like? Why?

5 What three things do you like doing with your friends? Why?

6 Do you like going clubbing? Why/Why not?

7 What three things don't you like doing? Why?

Unit 2 Lesson 2.2 Exercise 2a

Student A

Shakira Isabel Mebarak Ripoll was born on 2 February 1977. She grew up in Barranquilla in Colombia. Her father is American (of Lebanese origin), her mother is Colombian and, as a child, she learned to speak five languages. Her father was a jeweller and, at first, Shakira had a comfortable life. She knew at the age of four that she wanted to be a performer and at school, every Friday morning, Shakira danced and sang for the whole school. Nobody else, just her.

When she was eight, however, her father's business failed and he lost a lot of money. The family sold their two cars, their TV and most of their furniture. It was a shock for Shakira to experience this poverty. But her parents took her to see children living in really terrible poverty to show her that her life wasn't so bad. It gave her huge determination to get a good job and earn a lot of money to help these children.

At the age of thirteen, she made her first album, *Magia (Magic)*. A second album, *Peligro (Danger)*, followed two years later and she bought her parents a car with the money she earned. She then decided to take a break from recording and she concentrated on passing her exams at school.

1 Where do Shakira's parents come from?

2 How old was she when she decided to be a singer and dancer?

3 What happened when Shakira was eight?

4 Why did her parents take her to see poor children?

5 When did she make her first album?

6 What did she do with the first money she earned?

Unit 3 Lesson 3.3 Exercise 6

Student A

Explain the words to your partner. Your partner listens and guesses the word you are describing.

cooker   ice cream   knife   pilot   plate   salt   tea

Communication activities

Unit 4 Lesson 4.1 Exercise 4a

Sara <u>isn't afraid of anything</u>. Freediving is a very dangerous sport. *brave*

1   My aunt <u>gives her time and money to other people</u>. She gave me £200 at Christmas!
2   Jane <u>feels sure</u> that she will pass her end-of-year exams.
3   Mick <u>always makes people laugh</u>. He's very good at telling jokes.
4   Sarah <u>can understand things quickly</u>. She's got lots of qualifications.
5   Petra <u>always does what she says she will do</u>. She won't be late.
6   Flora <u>is very keen because she's interested in what she does</u>. She studies hard and gets good results.
7   My dad <u>never lets anyone/anything stop him</u>. He's decided to run a marathon and I'm sure he'll do it.
8   Penny <u>is very healthy and strong</u>. She exercises at least five times a week.
9   Sam <u>has a lot of natural ability</u> as a writer. She won a short story competition in June.

Unit 4 Lesson 4.1 Exercise 9

Student Bs

Match each question with an adjective from exercise 4a, page 41, and compare your answers with other students in group B.

1   How do you feel about running 10 km? Do you feel fine, or exhausted just thinking about it?
2   How many of these things are you good at: sports, art, music, languages, maths, drama or none of these?
3   For a friend's birthday, are you more likely to buy a nice present or buy nothing because it's too expensive?
4   How do you feel when something doesn't work out for you the first time you do it? Do you give up immediately, try again once or try again until you succeed?

Unit 7 Communication Exercise 4a

Total Stress Factor

10–15: You are one cool customer who is always calm under pressure. Well done!

16–25: Not bad … you're mostly stress-free – just a little hot sometimes!

26–35: Keep an eye on yourself. You are nearly at dangerous levels of stress … don't go there!

36–50 Watch out! You are getting too stressed, too often. You need to keep calm before you go completely crazy!

Unit 5 Lesson 5.1 Exercise 3a

Student B

Name: *Miguel Jiménez*

Nationality: *Spanish*

My name is Miguel and I turned eighteen about six months ago. I left school last month and now I am working in the family business – it's a food export business.

I live with my parents and my sister – she's fifteen. My brother, who is nearly twenty-seven, left home a month ago because he got a job in another city. This means I don't have to share my bedroom anymore. Our mother cooks and irons for us. She is quite busy because she also works in the family business – so I suppose I should help more at home really! We're all a bit spoiled – my mother shouldn't do everything for us, but she enjoys it!

I like working in the business. It's hard work, but I'm learning a lot and I like earning my own money. I haven't got enough money to move out into my own flat, but it's good to have extra cash for going out and doing things with my friends. I have to work long hours during the week, but my parents say I can have time off at the weekends, so life is mostly quite good. Generally, I'm happy with working – the only thing is that I'd like to do more travelling, but I can't go away for more than a few days at the moment as my father needs me at work.

Unit 8 Lead-in Exercise 2b

1 True
2 The speed limit on motorways in Spain is **120** kmph.
3 About **twenty-five percent** of British drivers are fined for speeding every year.
4 True

Unit 8 Lesson 8.1 Exercise 10b

1 Eighty-five percent of international phone calls are made in English.
2 In the US, more messages are carried by email than by post.
3 About seventy percent of emails are junk email.
4 Four million tons of junk mail are delivered by post every year in the US.
5 Seventy percent of websites aren't visited by anybody.
6 Over a billion people visit the website YouTube every day.
7 150 million people use Facebook and about fifty percent of them use it every day.
8 Messages on Facebook are written in thirty-five different languages.

Unit 9 Lesson 9.2 Exercise 11a

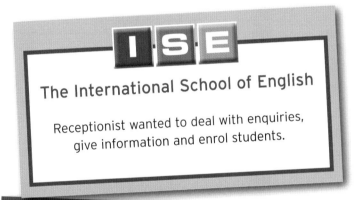

I·S·E

The International School of English

Receptionist wanted to deal with enquiries, give information and enrol students.

Wessex University

Department of Languages ...

... is looking for foreign students to provide one-to-one speaking practice to university students learning foreign languages.

Horizon

Children's Summer School ...

... requires enthusiastic helpers to supervise groups (ages 6–15) during afternoon activities (sports, drama, etc.) while in UK.

Unit 9 Lesson 9.3 Exercise 10a

Student A

A

Steve Taylor (1) _____ (arrest) for stealing some boots from a shoe shop in Kansas, USA. He (2) _____ (use) a knife to threaten the staff and then walked off with a pair of size 10 ½ brown walking boots. At his trial, the judge suddenly (3) _____ (notice) something: Taylor was wearing a pair of size 10 ½ brown walking boots.
He was immediately found guilty and he (4) _____ (send) to prison in his socks.

B

A home supplies shop in Barnsley, UK (5) _____ (break into) by David Goodhall and two other thieves. They (6) _____ (put) a pair of curtains into a plastic bag and (7) _____ (decide) to leave by separate exits. All three were surprised when they (8) _____ (catch) immediately by several security guards. What they didn't realise was that the shop was holding a security guard training course at the time.

Unit 9 Communication Exercise 5

Group A

You have worked for a small family company for two years. The company sells books over the internet. You have worked hard for a low salary. Now you and your eight co-workers feel that conditions need to improve.

You would like ...

- to get higher salaries.
- to increase the number of days' holiday per year (currently fifteen).
- to reduce the number of hours' work per week (currently thirty-six).
- to get benefits for staff (e.g. free lunch, free coffee and cheap books).

Work with your colleagues and decide ...

1 what you really want.
2 what you could compromise on.
3 what you could offer in return.

Communication activities

Unit 10 Lesson 10.1 Exercise 7

Student A

- book holiday ✔
- get dollars from bank ✗
- buy camera ✗
- plan which sights to see ✔
- ask for time off work ✔

Student B

- book holiday ✔
- rent car ✗
- buy shoes ✔
- arrange for someone to look after cat ✗
- ask for time off work ✗

Unit 10 Lesson 10.2 Exercises 3 and 4

Group B

3 Read the text. Which customs from exercise 2a, page 102, are mentioned in your text?

ADVICE FOR
UK BUSINESS TRAVELLERS

Forms of address

In most countries, business people use surnames when they talk to each other. In some countries (e.g. Germany and Switzerland) business people use surnames even when they know each other well. To be safe, continue using someone's surname until they offer you their first name as an alternative.

Personal space

People in South America and southern Europe tend to stand quite close to each other when talking – about sixty centimetres apart; while in the Middle East, they generally stand even closer – less than thirty centimetres apart. People from northern Europe and the US give each other more space and feel uncomfortable if you stand too close. Their preferred distance is seventy-five to ninety centimetres apart.

Physical greetings

In most countries, people shake hands when they meet in business situations. You should be careful that your handshake is not too strong or too weak. In Asia, the main form of greeting is the bow. When greeting Europeans, many Asians follow the bow with a handshake. Even in countries where it is common to kiss (e.g. Italy and Russia), you usually only kiss people you know well.

4 **a** Read the text again. What is the significance of the words/phrases from the box?

> bowing   first names   kissing   strong handshakes   surnames   thirty centimetres

b Work with a student from Group A. Answer your partner's questions about your text.

c Now ask your partner the questions about his/her text.

1 When should you give presents in Japan?
2 What kind of gift should you give in Japan?
3 Is it a good idea to give four flowers in Japan?
4 Should you give clocks as a gift in China?
5 Why should you be careful with leather products in South America?
6 Is it always acceptable to give red flowers in Europe?

Unit 10 Lesson 10.3 Exercise 7

Student A

1 How do you feel about motorbikes? Why?
2 What do you think of Gael García Bernal? Why?
3 How do you feel when you miss a bus or train? Why?
4 What do you think of musicals? Why?
5 How do you feel the night before you go on holiday? Why?
6 What do you think of beach holidays? Why?

Unit 11 Communication Exercise 2

Ronaldinho is world famous as one of the most talented footballers of his generation. He was born in Porto Alegre, Brazil in 1980. He came from a very poor background and is now one of the highest-paid footballers in the world. In club football, he has played for Paris St. Germain, then Barcelona and then Milan, transferring there on a three-year contract worth about €6.5 million a year. At an international level, he first played for Brazil in 1997. In 1999, he scored six goals in the final of the Copa America, helping Brazil to victory and establishing himself as a world-class player. In the 2002 World Cup in Japan and Korea, he was a key member of Brazil's team which went on to win their record fifth world title. In 2005, he was named both European Footballer of the Year and FIFAPro World Player of the Year.

Angelina Jolie was born in California, USA in 1975. She is an actress and Goodwill Ambassador for the UN Refugee Agency. She is also one of the most famous people in the world, and her life is often reported on in the media. She has starred in countless films – her international breakthrough came in 2001, when she starred as Lara Croft in the *Tomb Raider* series. Other more recent films include *Mr and Mrs Smith* and *The Changeling*. She has received three Golden Globe Awards, two Screen Actors Guild Awards, and an Academy Award for her acting. Jolie has promoted humanitarian causes throughout the world, and is noted for her work with refugees through UNHCR. In 2003, she received the Citizen of the World Award from the United Nations and in 2005, she received the Global Humanitarian Award.

J K Rowling is the author of the Harry Potter books and one of the richest women in the world. She was born near Bristol, UK in 1965. Joanne started writing stories at the age of six. In 1990, she started writing the first Harry Potter book, finishing it six years later, as a single mother living in Edinburgh. The book was rejected by several publishers before Bloomsbury agreed to publish it in 1996. The day she signed her contract, the publishing representative told her she would not make any money selling children's books. There are now seven Harry Potter books and together with the films, they have made her a fortune. Rowling is a best-selling author and the first to become a billionaire from writing books.

Sir James Dyson is an industrial designer, born in England in 1947. He is best known as the inventor of the Dual Cyclone bagless vacuum cleaner. After inventing one or two products in the 1970s, his breakthrough came when he invented his new type of vacuum cleaner in 1983. It was based on a new design which did not reduce in power as the vacuum cleaner was filled. Dyson couldn't get any companies to make or sell his product, so in 1993 he set up his own company. In the UK and US, Dyson cleaners are now one of the most popular brands and in 2008, Dyson was reported to be worth €1.2 billion. In 1997, Dyson was awarded the Prince Philip Designers Prize and in 2006, he was made a Knight Bachelor and became 'Sir James Dyson'.

Unit 2 Lesson 2.2 Exercise 2a

Student B

After she left school in 1995, Shakira released more albums: *Pies Descalzos (Barefoot)* and *Laundry Service*. Many of her songs were hits and went to the top of the charts and she became more and more famous around the world. In the last decade, she has earned nearly $40 million and, in 2008, she won a star on the Hollywood Walk of Fame – the first Colombian to win this award.

As well as her music, Shakira has done a huge amount of work for charity. She gives speeches about her work and she regularly performs on stage at charity concerts, including for Live Earth and Latin American charities. She has also given large amounts of money to disaster appeals and, in 2003, she became a UNICEF Goodwill Ambassador. Her own charity, the Pies Descalzos Foundation, has now paid for five schools in Colombia, helping over 30,000 families to have a better life.

So, what is more important to her: her music or her charity? 'One thing feeds the other one,' she says. 'If there's no more music, I'm sure I won't have one more penny to go into the foundation.' She has big ambitions for her charity and her next step is to go worldwide. She wants the Barefoot Foundation to reach the 300 million children in the world who don't go to school.

1 What did she do when she left school?

2 What happened in 2008?

3 Which international charity concert did she perform at?

4 How many schools has her charity paid for?

5 What is more important for her: her music or her charity?

6 What is her plan for the future of her Barefoot Foundation?

Communication activities

Unit 3 Lesson 3.3 Exercise 6

Student B

Explain the words to your partner. Your partner listens and guesses the word you are describing.

bowl   doctor   fork   fridge   mineral water   pepper   soup

Unit 5 Lesson 5.1 Exercise 3a

Student C

Name: *Wong Fei*

Nationality: *Chinese*

My name is Fei. I am an only child and I live with my parents in Shanghai. I am eighteen and I'm studying law at Shanghai University.

I'm studying very hard at the moment, so I think eighteen is a difficult age in some ways. I am quite ambitious – I mean, my goals for the future are to graduate from university, to go to England to study marketing and then to come back and get a good job. China is changing and it's possible to earn a good salary here now.

In other ways, being eighteen is not bad. I am living with my parents at the moment because I'm at university. I don't have to work, but my parents are quite strict and I can't just sit around and do nothing in the house! I have to help with things like the washing-up and cleaning. Traditionally in China, when your parents get older and retire, you should look after them. My parents are very generous and they say I can do what I want. In the future, I will look after them, but I also want to have a good job at the same time. In my opinion, people shouldn't give up their jobs completely when they get married or look after their relatives.

Unit 10 Lesson 10.3 Exercise 7

Student B

1   What do you think of travel books? Why?
2   How do you feel about going on a plane? Why?
3   What do you think of camping holidays? Why?
4   How do you feel about being a commuter? Why?
5   What do you think of horror films? Why?
6   How do you feel about public transport? Why?

Unit 9 Lesson 9.3 Exercise 10a

Student B

A

A woman who lived in Baltimore, USA, got a shock when her house (1) _____ (break into) by a thief one night. The thief asked the woman for money. But when he (2) _____ (discover) that she only had $11.50 in cash, he asked for a cheque made out to himself: Charles A. Meriweather. The woman then (3) _____ (phone) the police, told them his name and Meriweather (4) _____ (arrest) a few hours later.

B

The staff in a jewellery shop in Liverpool, UK (5) _____ (threaten) by a man in a mask holding a gun. Edward McAlea pointed the gun at the shop assistants and (6) _____ (demand) money and jewellery. The shop assistants (7) _____ (notice) that the gun was, in fact, a toy and they pulled his mask off. McAlea (8) _____ (arrest) quickly when the shop assistants recognised him as a customer from the previous day.

Unit 9 Communication Exercise 5

Group B

You own and run a small family company which sells books over the internet. You employ nine people. You started the company two years ago. After a difficult start, things are beginning to look more positive, but the future is still very uncertain.

You would like ...
• to avoid giving higher salaries.
• to avoid increasing the number of days' holiday per year (currently fifteen).
• to increase the number of hours' work per week (currently thirty-six).
• to avoid giving benefits to staff (e.g. free lunch, free coffee and cheap books).

Work with your colleagues and decide ...
1   what you really want.
2   what you could compromise on.
3   what you could offer in return.

1 | A personal profile

Can do write about yourself and your interests

1 Read the text quickly and match the headings (a–d) with the paragraphs (1–4).

  a Personal description

  b About us

  c My interests

  d My aims

2 Read the text again and answer the questions.

  1 What are the two aims of 'couch surfing'?

  2 Why does Massimo want to speak English?

  3 What is Massimo's job?

  4 What are two of Massimo's hobbies?

3 **a** Look at the sentences around each <u>underlined</u> word in the text from exercise 1. Then complete the How to... box with the words below.

> and   because   but   or   so   when

  b Find one more example of each word in the text.

How to... join ideas and sentences (1)

Linkers are used to join two ideas or two parts of a sentence.

1 We use _____ to add similar information.

2 We use _____ to add different/ contrasting information.

3 We use _____ to introduce a reason (why we do something/why something happens).

4 We use _____ to introduce a consequence (what happens because of something else).

5 We use _____ to give another choice.

6 We use _____ to say the time that something happens.

4 Choose the correct words in *italics*.

  1 I'm really keen on football *and/but* tennis.

  2 Do you have coffee *but/or* tea for breakfast?

  3 I've got an exam tomorrow, *because/so* I'm staying in tonight.

  4 I understand a lot of French, *but/and* I can't speak it very well.

  5 I like meeting local people *so/when* I'm on holiday.

  6 I go to the gym a lot *because/so* I want to get fit.

5 **a** Prepare to write your own CouchSurfing profile. Make notes for three paragraphs: (1) your aims, (2) a personal description and (3) your interests.

  b Now write your profile. Use linkers to join ideas and sentences.

Login   Surf/Host   Community   Messages   Share   About

1 _____

We are a global organisation, connecting travellers with local people. Through CouchSurfing, you can find local people to stay with – for free! And it's a way you can meet people in the place where you are travelling.

Massimo Toniolo, Rome, Italy

2 _____

I want to make friends, have a good time and improve my English. I speak English, <u>but</u> I'm not very good at it. I need to use English at work, <u>so</u> I'd like to practise with you.

3 _____

I live in Rome with two other flatmates. It's a really exciting city <u>and</u> I love living here. We are very keen on having people to stay and there's plenty of space for visitors <u>because</u> we live in a large flat. I'm an architect and I usually work long hours from Monday to Friday, but at the weekends, <u>when</u> I'm not working, I like going out.

4 _____

I've got a lot of hobbies and interests. I really enjoy taking people to famous places, restaurants and nightclubs in Rome. I really like going clubbing because I love dancing all night! And I quite like having lazy days when I stay at home <u>or</u> go to a friend's house. I absolutely love keeping fit, so I do a lot of sport. I usually go running or cycling at the weekends and I go to the gym about three or four times a week.

2 | A biography

1 **a** Number the topics in the order you think they will appear in a biography about someone's life.

a details of career ☐
b childhood and family ☐
c when and how he/she died ☐
d main achievements ☐
e early career/how it all started ☐

b Read the biography of Bob Marley and check your ideas.

Bob Marley was born on 6 February 1945 in Jamaica. Marley's mother was black and her family was from Jamaica. His father was white and his family was from England. He was a captain in the British Navy and Marley didn't see him much because he often worked away. He then died when Marley was just ten years old.

At the age of fourteen, Marley left school to play music and he met many influential musicians, including Bunny Wailer and Peter Tosh. Five years later, the three of them formed a band called The Wailers. Marley was the lead singer, songwriter and guitarist and the band played mostly reggae music. In 1974, Marley became a solo singer and he had some huge international hits, like *I Shot the Sheriff* and *No Woman No Cry*. In the 1970s, he did many tours, promoting peace as well as his music. In 1977, Marley found he had cancer. He died on 11 May 1981 at the age of thirty-six.

During his short life, Marley made a huge impact in the world of music. In 1976, he won an award for 'Band of the Year' from *Rolling Stone* magazine. Many of his awards, however, came after his death. In 2000, the BBC named Marley's song *One Love* as 'Song of the Millennium' and in 2001, he received a Grammy Lifetime Achievement Award.

2 Read the text again and complete each sentence with one or two words.

1 Bob Marley was born in _____ .
2 His father's family came from _____ .
3 When Marley was ten, his _____ .
4 Marley started The Wailers when he was _____ years old.
5 He left the band and started as a _____ in 1974.
6 Marley was _____ when he died of cancer in 1981.
7 He received the 'Song of the Millennium' award for his song _____ .

3 **a** Complete the How to... box with the headings (a–c).

a Make notes – e.g. what vocabulary will you need.
b Plan what to write in each paragraph
c Select the most important facts

How to... plan your writing

1 _____	internationally famous, solo career ...
2 _____	Born: 18 June 1942, Liverpool, England
3 _____	Para 1 – childhood and family Para 2 – career Para 3 – achievements

b Organise the information about Paul McCartney into the three paragraphs from part 3 of the How to... box.

a Born: 18 June 1942, Liverpool, England
b During the 1960s: became internationally famous with The Beatles
c Age twelve: met George Harrison at school
d Sixteen Grammy awards, eight Brit awards and numerous others
e 1970: The Beatles broke up
f Song *Yesterday*: most played song on American TV/radio with over seven million plays
g Age fifteen: met John Lennon and soon after formed The Beatles
h Continued solo career and worked with many other musicians
i In Guinness Book of Records as 'most successful musician in pop music history'

4 **a** Prepare to write a biography about another famous person or a member of your family. Use the How to... box and make notes.

b Now write your biography.

3 | Notes and messages

Can do write a note or message to a friend

1 Read the written notes (A and B) and the text messages (C and D). Then match them with the reasons for writing (1–4).

1 arrange to do something with a friend ☐
2 offer to do something for a friend ☐
3 accept an invitation from a friend to do something ☐
4 accept an offer from a friend to do something ☐

A

Hi Mel
Want to meet for lunch on Saturday?
Going shopping a.m. but could meet
1:30ish at The Blue Café. Be in meeting
all afternoon now so can you leave me
note? Really hope you're free – haven't
met for lunch for ages.
Laura x

B

Laura - yes, great. See you at The Blue
Café 1:30p.m. on Sat. Look forward to it!
Mel xx

C

Trains 2 Manchester leave at 8:15 & 10:45 a.m. Friday. Which one better 4 u? Want me 2 book ticket 4 u? Let me know by 6:00 cos going out soon.

D

Hi. Yes pls book 8:15 train. Let me know cost. Pay u back Fri. Thanx. C u later.

2 Read the notes and messages again and write true (T) or false (F).

1 We usually write full sentences in notes and messages. ☐
2 We often use abbreviations (short forms of words) in notes and messages. ☐
3 The abbreviations in text messages are sometimes different from abbreviations in written notes. ☐

3 **a** Complete part A of the How to... box with the headings (a–c).

a articles   c subjects
b auxiliary verbs and subjects

b Look at part B of the How to... box and write the abbreviations (1–6).

c Look at the notes and messages from exercise 1 and find four more abbreviations.

How to... use short forms in notes and messages

We often miss out words and use abbreviations to make notes and messages shorter and quicker to write.

A Missing out words

Miss out ...

1 _____ : (**We**) Could meet 1:30ish.

: (**Do you**) Want to meet for lunch
2 _____ : on Saturday?

: Will be in (**a**) meeting all
3 _____ : afternoon.

B Using abbreviations

1 _____ = Friday
2 _____ = morning
3 _____ = because
4 _____ = for
5 _____ = see
6 _____ = please

---

4 **a** Rewrite the notes using appropriate language.

1 Do you want to meet for breakfast at the café on the corner on Sunday? We could meet at 10:00.
2 Yes. I would like you to drive me to the airport this afternoon. I will see you at 4:30. Thanks.
3 I could get you a magazine after work today because I go past the shop. Do you want me to get you one?

b Rewrite the text messages using appropriate language.

1 I will meet you at the station. Can you buy a sandwich for me? I will see you later.
2 Do you want to come for dinner on Friday? I haven't seen you for ages. Please come.
3 Thanks for inviting me to your party. I'd love to come.

5 **a** Prepare to write a note or text message to a friend. Choose one of the reasons for writing from exercise 1 and think about what you want to say.

b Now write your note or text message using appropriate language.

4 A 'thank you' email

Can do | write a 'thank you' email

1 **a** Think of four reasons for writing a 'thank you' email. Which one(s) have you written recently?

b Read the 'thank you' emails. What is the reason for each one?

To: Kate; Ben
From: Beth
Subject: Thank you

Dear Kate and Ben,

I'm writing to thank you for the beautiful cushions. They look perfect with our new sofa and really add a splash of colour. It was so lovely to see you at our wedding and I hope you enjoyed yourselves. Our honeymoon in Florida was really brilliant – probably the most relaxing holiday I've ever had. We had great weather and lots of delicious meals.

John sends his love and says that we'll have to get together for a meal very soon! Look forward to seeing you both soon.

Best wishes,

Beth

To: Giovanna
From: Lorraine
Subject: Thanks

Hi Giovanna,

Just a quick note to say thanks so much for having me to stay. It was lovely to see you again and I had the most fantastic time in Milan. Thank you for spending time with me and taking me to see so many interesting places. It was much better than being on my own and not knowing where to go! And it was really good to meet some of your friends.

Hope to see you again really soon. And don't forget when you're in London – come and stay. Say hi to Mia and Luisa from me!

Lots of love,

Lorraine

---

2 Read the emails again and answer the questions.

1 Did Beth and John have a good time on their honeymoon?
2 What did Lorraine do when she was in Milan?

3 **a** Look at the How to... box and complete the sentences from the second email.

How to... structure a 'thank you' email

Open the email	Dear Kate and Ben, (1) _____ Giovanna,
Say thank you	I'm writing to thank you for the beautiful cushions. Just a quick note (2) _____ so much for having me to stay. (3) _____ spending time with me.
Give details	They look perfect with our new sofa. It was (4) _____ meet some of your friends.
End the email	John sends his love. Look forward to seeing you both soon. Hope to (5) _____ really soon.
Close the email	Best wishes, (6) _____ love,

b Complete the sentences with the words from the box. There are three extra words.

> have   having   much   see   seeing   sends
> soon   thanks   very

1 Hope to see you all again very _____ .
2 I'm writing to thank you for _____ us all to stay last weekend.
3 Just a quick note to say _____ so much for the chocolates.
4 I'm really looking forward to _____ you on the 20th.
5 Sarah _____ her love and says she'll phone you soon.
6 Thank you very _____ for the lovely dinner party last week.

4 **a** Prepare to write a 'thank you' email. Make notes for the questions.

1 Who are you going to write to?
2 What are you going to thank him/her for?
3 What details are you going to give?
4 How are you going to end your email?

b Now write your 'thank you' email. Use your notes to help you.

5 | A form

Can do | complete a simple form

1 Look at the different types of form. Then read forms A and B. What type of form is each one?
- a bank account application form
- a homestay application form
- a job application form
- a landing card
- a request for personal information from a shop

2 Read the forms again and answer the questions.
1 Do you have to complete all the information in both forms?
2 What special instructions does each form have?
3 Who makes a mistake on the form?

3 Look at the How to... box. Match the words/phrases from A with the words/phrases from B.

A

Please write in BLOCK CAPITALS
It is ESSENTIAL you complete the whole form

Title: *Miss*   Surname: *Jenkins*   Forename: *Jayne*

Date of birth (dd/mm/yyyy): *09/02/1987*

Gender (male or female): *female*   Marital status: *single*

Nationality: *American*   Occupation: *Teacher*

Contact address in the UK (in full): *16 Maryland Road, London, NW3 4TY*

Passport number: *238751933*

Length of stay in the UK: *2 months*

Arrival flight number: *BA 2331*

Signature: *Jayne Jenkins*

How to... understand the language on forms

Different forms have different ways of asking for the same information.

A	B
1 Surname	a) Job
2 Forename	b) DOB
3 Gender	c) Postal address inc. postcode
4 Title	d) M/F
5 Marital status	e) First name
6 Date of birth	f) Family name
7 Contact address in full	g) Signed
8 Occupation	h) Mr/Mrs/Miss/Ms/Dr
9 Signature	i) single/married/separated/divorced

B

Please TYPE or use BLACK INK to complete the form

Family name: *Tanaka*   First name: *Junko*

Mr/Mrs/Miss/Ms/Dr: *Mr*   M/F: *M*

single/married/separated/divorced: *Single*

DOB: *12.11.91*

Postal address inc. postcode: *5-2-1 Ginza, Chuo-ku, Tokyo, 170-3293, Japan*

Email address: *juntan@dion.ne.jp*

Job: *student*   Nationality: *Japanese*

What languages do you speak? *Japanese and English*

Do you have any allergies? *no*

Are you a vegetarian? *no*

Are you a smoker? *no*

Do you mind if someone in your host family smokes? *yes* *

Do you want a single or shared room? _____ *

Signed: *Junko Tanaka*

* = optional

4 Complete the form. Make sure you follow any special instructions.

FIRST IN FASHION – CUSTOMER INFORMATION

Please complete the WHOLE form using BLOCK CAPITALS

Family name: _____   First name: _____

Mr/Mrs/Miss/Ms/Dr/other: _____

single/married/separated/divorced: _____

M/F: _____   DOB: _____

Nationality: _____   Job: _____

Postal address inc. postcode: _____

Mobile phone number: _____

Email address: _____

How often do you shop at First in Fashion? _____

How much do you usually spend on clothes every month? _____

How do you want to receive information about our sales and special offers? by post/by phone/by email

Signed: _____

6 A competition entry

Can do write a description of a favourite place

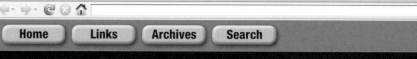

Home **Links** **Archives** **Search**

My English Magazine - the magazine for learners of
English all over the world
Enter our writing competition and win one of five great prizes!
The winning entries will also be printed in next month's magazine!
Click here for more information and terms and conditions

Writing competition – official entry form
Name: José Romero **Category:** Description
Title: One of my favourite places

1 One of my favourite places is a few kilometres from where I live in Spain. It's an area in the north of Spain which is mostly covered in forest. The part of the forest which I like best is about ten kilometres long, with tall trees stretching up to the sky. You can get impressive views across the valley towards the north coast because it's the highest land in the area.

2 In any season, the forest is a peaceful and wild place to be. It isn't very far from noisy urban areas, but it is always quiet. I'm often amazed that there aren't many people there. At first, you can't hear anything at all, but as you start walking you can hear the noises of the forest. Dry leaves under your feet and little animals running around in the trees are always louder than you think. One day I was there, I was really pleased to see some deer only a few metres away from me.

3 The main reason that the forest is one of my favourite places is that it always makes me feel calm. It's a very good place to go to get away from my stressful daily life. I really hope that I will enjoy it for many more years.

1 Read the text and answer the questions.

1 What is the purpose of the text?

2 Why does José like the place which he is describing?

3 Do you think you would like to go to this place? Why/Why not?

2 **a** Read the text again and match the headings (a–c) with the paragraphs (1–3).

a What you like best about it ☐

b The atmosphere and other details ☐

c The location and geographical features ☐

b Which topics are included in the text? Give details about each topic that is mentioned.

1 things you can see

2 things you can hear

3 things you can smell

4 how the place makes you feel

3 **a** Complete the How to... box with phrases from the text.

How to... use a range of introductory phrases

We often start sentences with subject + verb.

It's an area in the north of Spain. **You can get** impressive views across the valley.

You can make your writing more interesting by starting your sentences in different ways.

(1) _____ , the forest is a peaceful and wild place to be.

(2) _____ , you can't hear anything at all.

(3) _____ , I was really pleased to see some deer.

(4) _____ is a few kilometres from where I live.

(5) _____ which I like best is about ten kilometres long.

(6) _____ is that it always makes me feel calm.

b Rewrite the paragraph by writing five sentences. Start each sentence with a phrase in **bold**.

I like my grandmother's house. It is **one of my favourite places**. I like the garden. That is **the part of the house which I like the best**. There are lots of really big trees there. That is **the main reason** I like it there. It is a relaxing place to be **in any season,** but I especially like it in the summer. We had a lovely picnic sitting under the trees. That was **the last time I was there**.

4 **a** Prepare to write a description of one of your favourite places. Make notes for each of the paragraph headings from exercise 2a.

b Now write your description. Use your notes to help you.

Can do | write an apology with an explanation

1 Read the two emails and answer the questions.

1 What is each person apologising for?
2 Who is each person apologising to?
3 What explanation does each person give?

2 Read the emails again and number the topics in the order they appear.

a make an offer ☐
b apologise again ☐
c apologise ☐
d give an explanation ☐

3 **a** Complete the How to... box with the parts of punctuation from the box.

> apostrophe (')   comma (,)   exclamation mark (!)
> full stop (.)   question mark (?)   quotation marks (" ")

How to... use punctuation

Use ...
1 _____ to finish a sentence.
2 _____ to finish a sentence and show emotions like surprise, excitement, etc.
3 _____ to finish a sentence and show you are asking a question.
4 _____ to show a pause in speech or to separate clauses in a sentence. Also used to separate items in a list.
5 _____ to show the words someone speaks.
6 _____ to show where letters are missed out of a word (a contraction) or to show possession.

b Add the correct punctuation to the sentences.

1 Why dont we go out for dinner next week
2 Im sorry I didnt go to Bens party
3 Jenny David and Kevin all said sorry
4 What a fantastic surprise
5 When I last spoke to Jane she wasnt feeling well
6 If you finish your essay will you come out with us after work

4 **a** Prepare to write an email apologising for not going to something. Make notes for each question.

1 What did you not go to?
2 What is your explanation for not going?
3 What will you offer to do to make things better?

b Now write your email. Use your notes to help you and check punctuation is used correctly.

To: Kate
From: Michael
Subject: Sorry!

Dear Kate,

I apologise for not coming to class last week. It was raining really heavily when I left the house and when I got to the bus stop, I was completely soaked. I waited for about ten minutes for a bus, but when it arrived, it was full and I couldn't get on. After waiting for another fifteen minutes, I was really wet and cold, so I went home.

Is there any homework I need to do? I'll make sure I do it before next week's class. Once again, I'm sorry that I couldn't come to class.

All the best,

Michael

To: Emily
From: Selena
Subject: Sorry

Hello Emily,

I'm very sorry I couldn't come to your party last Saturday. That morning, I woke up feeling terrible. I had a splitting headache, a really high temperature and I felt sick. I went straight back to bed and I thought that I would be better by the evening, but I felt worse and worse! In the end, I stayed in bed for three days and now I finally feel better.

I'm so upset that I missed the party. I was really looking forward to seeing you all. I hope you had a good time. Why don't we get together very soon? I'll phone you! Sorry again! By the way, Gary says "hi".

Love,

Selena

Can do | write a short story describing a sequence of events

1 Read the text and answer the questions.

1 Where have Jack and Dinah been? Why?
2 What four things went wrong?
3 How does Dinah feel now?

2 a Read the email again and tick (✓) the correct answers.

1 The main purpose of Dinah's email is …
a to tell a story. ☐
b to describe a place. ☐

2 A short story is mainly about …
a a series of events. ☐
b someone's opinion. ☐

3 In a short story, we usually focus on …
a the events only. ☐
b the events and the order they happened. ☐

4 We use the Past Simple for …
a the main events of the story. ☐
b the background events/scene setting. ☐

5 We use the Past Continuous for …
a the main events of the story. ☐
b the background events/scene setting. ☐

b Which of the three paragraphs (1–3) could you divide into two parts? Where could you divide it?

1 Introduce the story in an interesting way
2 Give details of the events of the story
3 Say how the story ends

3 a Complete the How to… box with the <u>underlined</u> phrases from the text from exercise 1.

How to… use time linkers

To refer to the beginning of a situation	***At first*** (1) _____
To refer to actions happening at the same time	***When*** (2) _____
To refer to something happening after a long time or a lot of effort	***Finally*** (3) _____
To show the order of events in a story	(4) _____ ***After waiting*** (5) _____

To: Susie
From: Dinah
Subject: Disaster!!

Hi Susie,

1 Jack and I have just got back from our skiing holiday in Austria. You'll never believe all the disasters we had!

2 At first, everything went well. The journey was OK. We had a delay at the airport – nothing too serious, but quite annoying. <u>After we arrived</u> at the hotel, things started to go really wrong! It was about 11 p.m. when we got there and we were both exhausted. When the receptionist told us that someone else was in our room, we couldn't believe it. After waiting about two hours, they found us another room and finally we went to bed. The next morning, when we looked out of the window, the sun was shining and the snow was melting. For the next three days, <u>while</u> we were waiting for better skiing weather, we tried to entertain ourselves in the village and, <u>to begin with</u>, we were quite optimistic. <u>Then</u>, on the fourth morning, we went bowling and things went from bad to worse. I slipped on the floor and when I tried to stand up, I couldn't. Basically, my leg was broken – without putting on any skis!!

3 <u>Eventually</u>, the weather improved and Jack had two days of skiing – which was better than nothing, I suppose! We're back home now and my leg is in plaster for the next six weeks. Please come round and see me! I'm so bored!

Love, Dinah

b Choose the correct words in *italics*.

1 I had a terrible evening! Someone stole my bag. *Then/When* I left my phone in a café.

2 *After/At first* hearing a strange noise, I decided to phone the police.

3 *While/To begin with*, the traffic was fine, but it got busier and busier.

4 *Finally/After*, three hours later, we found the hotel we were looking for.

5 *Then/While* I was buying a magazine, I noticed someone standing near me.

6 *At first/Then*, I was really nervous, but I got more confident as the interview went on.

7 *Eventually/When*, I found her, after looking for over four hours.

8 *At first/After* I got on the bus, I realised everyone was looking at me.

4 a Prepare to write an email telling a friend about something that happened to you. Choose an idea from the box and make notes. Use the paragraph headings from exercise 2b.

> a change in someone's life   an achievement
> meeting someone important
> something that went wrong

b Now write your email. Use your notes and think about how to use time linkers correctly.

9 | A professional profile

Can do | write a professional profile

ProConnect

Home Profile Contacts Groups Jobs Inbox More...

Name: Nadia Johnson

Looking for a position as: a Customer Services Officer

1 _____: I am committed to my career in Customer Services and to increasing my skills and experience.

2 _____: I have worked in Customers Services, in the restaurant/catering industry, for five years. I have specific experience of working in small companies in the UK, Spain and Portugal.

3 _____: I am good at working with people, both in person and on the phone. I am efficient and have good time-management skills. I can deal with pressure and I am always enthusiastic about solving problems. I am a native English speaker and I can speak Spanish and Portuguese fluently. I also have some understanding of French and Italian.

4 _____: I am now keen on developing my experience and working in the hotel/tourism industry. I am also interested in the idea of living abroad for my job.

---

1 Read the text quickly and match the headings (a–d) with the paragraphs (1–4).

a Skills and abilities
b Experience
c Interests for future career
d Introduction

2 Read the text again and answer the questions.

1 Where could you read this kind of text?
2 Why did Nadia write this profile about herself?

3 a Complete the How to... box with adjectives from the text.

How to... use positive language in professional writing

When writing about yourself for professional reasons, you need to be clear and use positive adjectives. All these adjectives are followed by a preposition + noun/-ing form.

(1) I am _____ **to my career** in Customer Services.
(2) I am _____ **at working** with people.
(3) I am always _____ **about solving** problems.
(4) I am now _____ **on developing** my experience.
(5) I am also _____ **in the idea** of living abroad for my job.

b Underline any other words and phrases in the text which show a positive attitude.

c Choose the correct words in *italics*.

1 I am very *good/keen* at dealing with angry customers.
2 I am *committed/interested* in doing some further training.
3 I am always *keen/enthusiastic* about learning new skills in my job.
4 I am completely *committed/interested* to this company.
5 I am *enthusiastic/keen* on getting as much experience as I can.

4 a Prepare to write a professional profile for you. Use the headings from exercise 1 and make notes.

b Now write your professional profile. Use your notes and make sure you use words and phrases which make your profile sound clear and positive.

1 Read the travel blog and answer the questions.

1 Which two places did James and Alice visit in India?

2 Was their experience positive, negative or both?

2 Read the text again and complete each sentence with one adjective.

1 The writer describes Fatephur Sikri palace as _____ .

2 She felt _____ because of the sandstorm and the car journey.

3 They were _____ about seeing the Taj Mahal the following day.

4 She says the Taj Mahal wasn't _____ – there were only six other people there.

5 The writer describes the Taj Mahal as _____ and grand.

6 She was _____ because it was bigger than she imagined.

3 **a** Look at the How to... box and answer the questions.

1 Part A: what do the underlined pronouns in the text refer to? Write your answers in the box.

2 Part B: which words from the text have a similar meaning to the adjectives?

> ### How to... avoid repetition
>
> You can make your writing more interesting by avoiding repetition: by using pronouns and a range of vocabulary.
>
> | Use pronouns | 1 *it* (line 6) = <u>the sandstorm</u> |
> | | 2 *that* (line 8) = _____ |
> | | 3 *one* (line 10) = _____ |
> | | 4 *he* (line 11) = _____ |
> | | 5 *it* (line 26) = _____ |
> | Use a range of vocabulary | 1 *beautiful* – _____ |
> | | 2 *good* – _____ |
> | | 3 *surprised* – _____ |

b Rewrite the paragraph by replacing the words/phrases in **bold** with pronouns and more interesting vocabulary.

We're on holiday in Faro in Portugal. **Faro** is a **nice** town and the weather is **nice**. Our hotel is called Hotel Bellavista. **The hotel** is **nice** and the people are very **nice**. **The people** do everything they can to help us. I was surprised – I really didn't expect **people to be so nice**. There are two beaches near our hotel. We've just come back from the smaller **beach**. I was **surprised** how clean the sea is. **The sea** is completely clear.

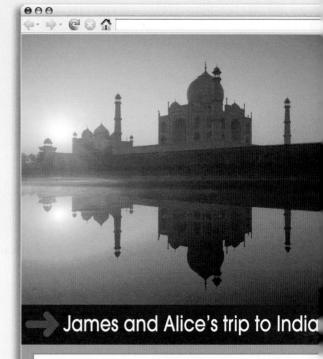

→ James and Alice's trip to India

11 June

On our way to Agra, James and I stopped at a palace called Fatephur Sikri. It was beautiful,
5 but there was a sandstorm while we were there. Sand was blowing up into our faces. <u>It</u> wasn't very pleasant! The sandstorm and the long car drive made us feel a bit miserable. But <u>that</u> didn't last long because we soon met two young boys.
10 The older <u>one</u>, who was about fifteen, agreed to be our tour guide. <u>He</u> was very friendly and he showed us around. In the end, we had a good time there. We're really excited about tomorrow. We haven't seen the Taj Mahal yet ... and we
15 can't wait!

12 June

We've just got back from an amazing morning at the Taj Mahal! We woke up early to get there at 5:30 a.m. We wanted to see the sunrise and
20 to avoid the heat of the day. When we arrived, I was surprised to see only six other people there. I thought it would be really crowded and we might be disappointed. But it was really great – especially to be so close! It's a stunning building
25 and very grand! I was really amazed to see how big <u>it</u> is! By 7:00 a.m., lots of tourists started arriving. They were really noisy, so we went back to the hotel to have our breakfast!

4 **a** Prepare to write two paragraphs for a travel blog/diary. Write about a different place in each paragraph. Think about which adjectives to use to describe (a) the place and (b) your feelings.

b Now write your travel blog/diary. Make sure you avoid repetition by using pronouns and a range of vocabulary.

Can do write about your opinions of a film

1 Read the text and answer the questions.

1 Why do people write and read this kind of text?

2 Do the people have the same or different opinions about the film?

2 Read the text again and answer the questions.

1 Which person/people mention the topics from the box?

> the acting/main stars
> the differences between the book and film
> the plot/story   their overall opinion of the film

2 Can you find three ways of giving opinions and three ways of agreeing or disagreeing?

3 a Read the sentences. Then look at the How to... box and choose the correct underlined words.

- Overall I enjoyed this film. I was sometimes confused about the story.
- I was sometimes confused about the story, **although** overall I enjoyed this film.
- **Although** overall I enjoyed this film, I was sometimes confused about the story.
- Overall I enjoyed this film. **However,** I was sometimes confused about the story.
- Overall I enjoyed this film. I was sometimes confused about the story, **however.**

How to... join ideas and sentences (2): *although* and *however*

We use *although* and *however* to link two opposite or contrasting ideas.

Although

1 *Although* is used to contrast two ideas in _the same sentence_/_two different sentences_.

2 *Although* can be used _before_/_after_ or between the two ideas.

3 We separate the two ideas with a comma.

However

4 *However* is used to contrast two ideas in _the same sentence_/_two different sentences_.

5 *However* is used in the _first_/_second_ sentence.

6 It can be used at the beginning or end of the sentence.

7 We separate *however* from the rest of the sentence with a comma.

The Time Traveler's Wife

Anna47 yesterday 11:48 a.m.

The review says that the film *The Time Traveler's Wife* is a perfect adaptation of the book by Audrey Niffenegger. Although the story is similar to the book, I think the film is disappointing. I loved the book and some important scenes are missed out in the film. If a film is really good, the differences don't matter. However, in my opinion the acting isn't very good and the story is confusing.

SimonP yesterday 4:01 p.m.

I completely disagree with Anna47! It seems to me that you are worrying too much about the differences between the film and the book. I think the acting is very good – especially Eric Bana, who is brilliant. It's certainly not a boring film. Some scenes are a bit silly, I suppose. It's one of the best films I've seen for a long time, however.

Sunny yesterday 5:15 p.m.

It's interesting how many different opinions there are about this film! I mostly agree with SimonP. I think it's an entertaining film and Eric Bana and Rachel McAdams are both very good. However, I agree with Anna47 in some ways, too – some scenes are missing. I was sometimes confused about the story, although overall I really enjoyed this film.

b Complete the sentences with *although* or *however*.

1 _____ I like Brad Pitt, I didn't enjoy the film *Troy*.

2 I don't usually like cartoon films. _____ , I loved the film *Up*.

3 The acting was really fantastic. I thought the plot was very weak, _____ .

4 In my opinion, the *Harry Potter* films are very entertaining, _____ I prefer the books.

5 Generally, I love science fiction films. _____ , *Wolverine* was disappointing.

6 _____ the film was interesting, in my opinion it was too long.

4 a Prepare to write some comments on a film review message board. Choose a film and make notes about what you liked/didn't like about it. Use the ideas from exercise 2 to help you.

b Now write your comments. Use your notes to help you.

To: admin@madridcollege.org.es
From: Davis, Matt [mattdavis@topmail.uk]
Subject: Summer Intensive Courses

Dear Sir/Madam,

I recently saw your advertisement in *The Times* for Spanish language Summer Intensive Courses at your school and I would be grateful if you could give me some more information.

A Firstly, I would like to know the dates of the courses during July and August. Can you tell me if it is possible to start the course on any date, or only at the beginning of a month? Would it be possible to study for about three hours a day?

B Secondly, I am interested in finding out about the other students. Do you know how many students there will be in the classes? Also, could you tell me what other nationalities will be in your school? I am an English speaker and I would prefer not to have too many other English speakers in the same class.

C Finally, can you tell me about accommodation? Does your school give help with arranging accommodation with local families or is that something I have to do myself?

Yours faithfully,

Matt Davis

1 Read the email and answer the questions.

1 Who is Matt writing to? Why?
2 Which topics from the box does he want to know about?

> accommodation   social activities
> dates/times of courses
> other students   prices

2 Read the email again and answer the questions.

1 Does Matt know the name of the person he's writing to?
2 How does he finish the email?
3 How many of the topics from exercise 1 does he write about in each paragraph (A–C)?
4 Does he use contractions, e.g. *I'd*, *I'm*?
5 Does he use mostly direct or indirect questions?

3 **a** Complete the How to... box with the headings (a–d).

a Start a formal email/letter
b Finish a formal email/letter
c Ask for the exact information you need
d Say your main reason for writing

How to... structure a formal email/letter

1 _____	***Dear Mr Smith*** (if you know their name) ***Dear Sir/Madam*** (if you don't know their name)
2 _____	*I recently saw your advertisement in The Times and **I would be grateful if you could** give me some more information.*
3 _____	*Does your school give help with arranging accommodation with local families?*
4 _____	***Yours sincerely*** (if you know their name) ***Yours faithfully*** (if you don't know their name)

b Complete each sentence from the text with three words.

1 I would _____ you could give me some more information.
2 I would _____ the dates of the courses.
3 Can you _____ it is possible to start the course on any date?
4 Would it _____ study for about three hours a day?
5 I _____ finding out about the other students.
6 I _____ to have too many other English speakers in the same class.

4 **a** Prepare to write a formal email/letter asking for information. Read the advert and think about (a) how to start and finish your email and (b) three things to ask about.

Learn English magazine offer!

Come and study at Clayhill College!

The college is in a beautiful part of England. Some courses are now at discount prices. We have small classes and friendly teachers.

For further enquiries, email us at:
clayhillcollege@hotmail.co.uk

b Now write your email/letter.

Pronunciation bank

English phonemes

Consonants

p	b	t	d	k	g	tʃ	dʒ
park	**b**ath	**t**ie	**d**ie	**c**at	**g**ive	**ch**urch	**j**udge

f	v	θ	ð	s	z	ʃ	ʒ
few	**v**isit	**th**row	**th**ey	**s**ell	**z**oo	fre**sh**	mea**s**ure

h	m	n	ŋ	l	r	j	w
hot	**m**ine	**n**ot	si**ng**	**l**ot	**r**oad	**y**ellow	**w**arm

Vowels and diphthongs

iː	ɪ	e	æ	ɑː	ɒ	ɔː	ʊ	uː	ʌ
f**ee**t	f**i**t	b**e**d	b**a**d	b**a**th	b**o**ttle	b**ou**ght	b**oo**k	b**oo**t	b**u**t

ɜː	ə	eɪ	əʊ	aɪ	aʊ	ɔɪ	ɪə	eə	ʊə
b**ir**d	b**ro**ther	gr**ey**	g**o**ld	b**y**	br**ow**n	b**oy**	h**ere**	h**air**	t**our**

Sound–spelling correspondences

Sound	Spelling	Examples
/ɪ/	i y ui e	this listen gym typical build guitar pretty
/iː/	ee ie ea e ey ei i	green sleep niece believe read teacher these complete key money receipt receive police
/æ/	a	can pasta
/ɑː/	a ar al au ea	can't dance* scarf bargain half aunt laugh heart
/ʌ/	u o ou	fun husband some mother cousin double
/ɒ/	o a	hot pocket watch want

Sound	Spelling	Examples
/ɔː/	or ou au al aw ar oo	short sport your bought daughter taught small always draw jigsaw warden warm floor indoor
/aɪ/	i y ie igh ei ey uy	like time dry cycle fries tie light high height eyes buy
/eɪ/	a ai ay ey ei ea	lake hate wait train play say they grey eight weight break
/əʊ/	o ow oa ol	home open show own coat road cold told

Silent letters

Some words in English have silent letters which are not pronounced. Some common silent letters are:

Silent letter	Examples	Pronunciation
b	thumb debt	/θʌm/ /det/
g	design foreign	/dɪˈzaɪn/ /ˈfɒrɪn/
h	honest white	/ˈɒnɪst/ /waɪt/
k	knee know	/niː/ /nəʊ/
l	talk would	/tɔːk/ /wʊd/
p	cupboard psychology	/ˈkʌbəd/ /saɪˈkɒlədʒi/
t	listen castle	/ˈlɪsən/ /ˈkɑːsəl/
w	write who	/raɪt/ /huː/

* In American English the sound in words like *can't* and *dance* is the shorter /æ/ sound, like *can* and *man*.

Weak forms

Word	Strong form	Weak form	Examples of weak forms in sentences
a, an	/æ/, /æn/	/ə/, /ən/	I've got **a** new car. Did you bring **an** umbrella?
at	/æt/	/ət/	Let's meet **at** six o'clock.
and	/ænd/	/ən/	I'd like a burger **and** fries.
are	/ɑː/	/ə/ (or /ər/ before vowels)	What **are** your phone numbers?
been	/biːn/	/bɪn/	I've **been** to San Francisco.
can	/kæn/	/kən/	She **can** sing very well.
do	/duː/	/də/	**Do** you like skiing?
does	/dʌz/	/dəz/	**Does** she work hard?
has	/hæz/	/həz/, /əz/	**Has** he left? Where **has** she been?
have	/hæv/	/həv/, /əv/	**Have** you seen the film? What **have** you got?
than	/ðæn/	/ðən/	She's taller **than** Juan.
them	/ðem/	/ðəm/	Let's take **them** to the cinema.
to	/tuː/	/tə/ (before consonants)	I want **to** go home now.
was	/wɒz/	/wəz/	He **was** an architect.

Weak and strong forms

do/does (Lesson 1.2); *have/has* (Lesson 2.2); *was/were* (Lesson 8.3)

Auxiliary verbs like *do/does*, *have/has* and *was/were* can be pronounced in two different ways. We usually use weak pronunciation in affirmative sentences and questions and strong pronunciation in short answers.

She was watching TV when I arrived.
   /wəz/

Were they all watching TV? Yes, they were.
/wə/   /wɜː/

Stress

Sentence stress (Lesson 1.1)

When we speak, we stress 'content' words like nouns and main verbs, which give us important information. 'Non-content' words (e.g. pronouns, auxiliary verbs, articles) are often unstressed.

When we <u>arrived</u> at the <u>station</u>, the <u>train</u> was <u>leaving</u>.

Emphasising important words (Lesson 4.1)

We can put extra stress on certain words which we want the listener to focus on.

My sister is <u>much</u> taller than me. (We want to emphasise the big difference.)

Emphasising details (Lesson 12.3)

I went to an Italian restaurant last night … an <u>expensive</u> Italian restaurant. (The new, important information is that the restaurant was expensive.)

Schwa on unstressed syllables (Lesson 7.2)

Unstressed syllables are often pronounced with a schwa /ə/.

a<u>void</u> /əvɔːd/; *re<u>member</u>* /rɪmembə/; *re<u>liable</u>* /rɪlaɪəbəl/

Phrasal verbs (Lesson 8.2)

We usually stress the particle in phrasal verbs.

look <u>after</u>; look <u>up</u> to; come <u>across</u>; put <u>up</u> with

Changing word stress (Lesson 9.2)

We sometimes change the main stress on different words in the same word family.

em<u>ploy</u>er / employ<u>ee</u>; <u>na</u>tional / natio<u>na</u>lity

Connected speech

Consonant to vowel (Lesson 3.1)

We usually link words that end in a consonant sound with words that begin with a vowel sound.

My parents are coming for dinner at eight.

Consonant to consonant (Lesson 5.1)

When two consonants are next to each other, one of the consonants is often not pronounced.

You shouldn't smoke. You can't come in here.
    /ʃʊdn̩ smoʊk/   /kɑːn kʌm/

Contractions

will (Lesson 6.1)

When we speak, we often make contractions with subject + *will* in affirmative sentences (but not in negative sentences, questions or short answers).

Will it be sunny tomorrow? No, I think it'll rain.
/wɪl//ɪt/   /ɪtəl/

Intonation

Questions (Lesson 2.3)

There are two intonation patterns for direct questions. Our voice usually goes up at the end of *Yes/No* questions.

Are you from Australia?

Our voice usually goes down at the end of *Wh-* questions.

Where are you from?

Indirect questions (Lesson 4.3)

We use polite intonation with indirect questions. Our voice starts high, then falls a lot and rises a little at the end.

Could you tell me where the post office is please?

Conditional sentences (Lesson 7.1)

In conditional sentences, our voice goes up at the end of the first clause and down at the end of the sentence.

If you work hard, you'll pass your exam.

Showing interest (Lesson 10.1)

We vary our intonation to show interest in what someone is saying. Our intonation is flat when we are less interested.

Fantastic! (interested)   *Fantastic!* (not interested)

Really? (interested)   *Really?* (not interested)

Fillers

anyway (Lesson 10.3)

When we tell a story, we often use *anyway* to show we are returning to the main story after giving some extra, background information.

John arrived really late at work yesterday … John is the one who started at our office about three months ago.

… Anyway, he walked in at about 9:45 and seemed very upset about something.

well, so, erm (Lesson 11.2)

In conversations, we often use *well*, *so* and *erm* when we want time to think about what we are saying (and we don't want someone else to start speaking). We often make these words a bit longer to stop someone from interrupting.

A: *Where shall we go for lunch?*

B: *Erm … , well … , we could go to the café on the hill.*

Irregular verbs

Verb	Past Simple	Past Participle
be	was/were	been
beat	beat	beaten
become	became	become
begin	began	begun
bend	bent	bent
bite	bit	bitten
blow	blew	blown
break	broke	broken
bring	brought	brought
build	built	built
burn	burned/burnt	burned/burnt
burst	burst	burst
buy	bought	bought
can	could	been able
catch	caught	caught
choose	chose	chosen
come	came	come
cost	cost	cost
cut	cut	cut
dig	dug	dug
do	did	done
draw	drew	drawn
dream	dreamed/dreamt	dreamed/dreamt
drink	drank	drunk
drive	drove	driven
eat	ate	eaten
fall	fell	fallen
feed	fed	fed
feel	felt	felt
fight	fought	fought
find	found	found
fly	flew	flown
forget	forgot	forgotten
forgive	forgave	forgiven
freeze	froze	frozen
get	got	got
give	gave	given
go	went	gone/been
grow	grew	grown
hang	hung	hanged/hung
have	had	had
hear	heard	heard
hide	hid	hidden
hit	hit	hit
hold	held	held
hurt	hurt	hurt
keep	kept	kept
kneel	knelt	knelt
know	knew	known
lay	laid	laid
lead	led	led
learn	learned/learnt	learned/learnt

Verb	Past Simple	Past Participle
leave	left	left
lend	lent	lent
let	let	let
lie	lay	lain
light	lit	lit
lose	lost	lost
make	made	made
mean	meant	meant
meet	met	met
must	had to	had to
pay	paid	paid
put	put	put
read/riːd/	read/red/	read/red/
ride	rode	ridden
ring	rang	rung
rise	rose	risen
run	ran	run
say	said	said
see	saw	seen
sell	sold	sold
send	sent	sent
set	set	set
shake	shook	shaken
shine	shone	shone
shoot	shot	shot
show	showed	shown
shut	shut	shut
sing	sang	sung
sink	sank	sunk
sit	sat	sat
sleep	slept	slept
slide	slid	slid
smell	smelled/smelt	smelled/smelt
speak	spoke	spoken
spend	spent	spent
spill	spilled/spilt	spilled/spilt
spoil	spoiled/spoilt	spoiled/spoilt
stand	stood	stood
steal	stole	stolen
stick	stuck	stuck
swim	swam	swum
take	took	taken
teach	taught	taught
tear	tore	torn
tell	told	told
think	thought	thought
throw	threw	thrown
understand	understood	understood
wake	woke	woken
wear	wore	worn
win	won	won
write	wrote	written

Audioscripts

Track 1.3

M = Man, W = Woman.

W: Hey, Jerry, I'm making some coffee … would you like some?

M: Mmmm … ?

W: Coffee? … Would you like some coffee?

M: Mmm? Oh, yes.

W: What are you reading that's so interesting … ?

M: It's an article about Valentino Rossi. You know – the motorbike racer. It's fascinating!

W: He's from Italy, isn't he?

M: That's right – and he's very successful – one of the best motorbike racers ever.

W: Is he the world champion, then?

M: He's actually won nine world championships. It says here that he's won nearly half of all his races in his career …

W: Really? That's amazing!

Track 1.4

M = Man, W = Woman.

M: Yes … The article is about his typical day – it's quite surprising actually!

W: Really? Why's that?

M: Well, his race days are very busy and stressful … and he works very hard. You know, he gets up early – at about six or seven o'clock and prepares for the race in the morning. Then he races in the afternoon.

W: Yes, I'm sure it's really busy … What's surprising, then?

M: Well, most sportspeople work really hard every day, and spend all their time training … but Rossi's 'normal' days – when he doesn't go to a race – are very relaxing. He has quite a lazy lifestyle actually! He says that his normal life is like being on holiday!

W: What does he do?

M: Well, he gets up late … He says he isn't a morning person.

W: What time does he get up?

M: He gets up at eleven o'clock …

W: Eleven o'clock!

M: Yes, and he's always quiet in the mornings. He doesn't talk to his family for the first hour!

W: Oh, same as me! I don't chat to anyone in the morning. Sorry, anyway, what about Rossi's training? Does he go to the gym or something?

M: Yes, he needs to stay fit for his racing, so he goes to the gym between twelve and two in the afternoon.

W: Really? Only two hours in the gym.

M: Mmm … it's not much, is it? I think it's quite an unusual routine for a top sportsperson.

W: Yeah, I sometimes go to the gym for two or three hours.

M: Do you?! Really? How often do you go to the gym?

W: Well, I go about once a week, I suppose!

M: No, you don't! You go about twice a year!!

W: Oh, ok … Anyway, back to Rossi … What does he do for the rest of the day?

M: Umm … it says that in the afternoon, he often listens to music and plays computer games. And he sometimes watches a film.

W: What about the evening? Does he go out late?

M: Yes, he does!! He hardly ever goes to bed early. His evenings are fun and he usually has a plan to go out with friends. He likes going out to parties and clubs. He's a real party animal apparently … He usually goes to bed about three or four in the morning!!

W: That's late!!

M: Yes, he says he's got a lot of energy after 2:00 a.m.

W: What about before a race day? What time does he go to bed then?

M: Before race days, too … he goes to bed at two or three in the morning … and then he usually wins the race!!

W: Wow! Rossi's life is very exciting! My life is really boring! I'd like to have his lifestyle!

M: Me too.

Track 1.6

M = Man, W = Woman.

M: So, let's see … what time do you get up … you know, on a work day?

W: Well, um … I suppose I usually get up at about six o'clock during the week.

M: Six o'clock!!

W: Yes … it's usually about six o'clock.

M: Are you serious?! Why do you get up so early?

W: Um … I often go running in the mornings before work … for about half an hour in the park.

M: Do you?!

W: Well, yes … I mean, I like starting the day with some exercise.

M: Really? I don't!

W: I find it wakes me up … What about you? How often do you do exercise or sport during the week?

M: Oh, probably about four or five times a week.

W: Really? Me too. What kind of exercise do you do?

M: Well … I don't really like going to the gym. It's really boring.

W: Yes, that's the same as me.

M: So, I usually go for a swim after work – you know, Monday to Thursday … I don't usually go on Fridays.

W: What do you do on Fridays then? Do you go out?

M: Yes, of course. It's the end of the week … I always go out with friends.

W: Yes, definitely … It's the start of the weekend.

Track 1.7

Stig

I'm learning Japanese at the moment which is quite a hard language. I want to speak it erh because my wife's parents don't speak English they speak only Japanese. Erh I'm quite good at speaking now and my listening's not bad. The most difficult thing about learning Japanese is learning to read and write. There are so many letters in the Japanese alphabet, so I really want to improve my reading and writing.

Tessie

Erm right well erm I am learning Spanish at the moment erm erm I'm I have decided to learn Spanish because I I I would I'm dreaming of going and living in erm Latin America erh and erm I'm quite good at understanding erm what people say in Spanish because I already speak good French, so there are a lot of similarities erm and I'm I'm also pretty good at reading but I'm finding it rather difficult to express myself and erm I would really like to improve my speaking skills. I'd really like to to erh be a little bit more fluent, not perfect but just enough to get by when we go to Argentina. Erm communication is is the most important thing.

Track 1.9

I = Interviewer

Hello and welcome to *Friday Film Festival* – the programme where we look at films – old and new. Today, we're talking about James Bond films and the incredibly successful music associated with them. The English writer, Ian Fleming created the character of James Bond in 1952. Bond is a spy – also known as double oh seven – who works for the British Secret Service and saves the world from various enemies or 'baddies'. The first Bond film was in 1962 and there are now twenty-two films of the Bond books. Different actors star in the role of Bond, including Daniel Craig, Pierce Brosnan and, of course, the first one, Sean Connery – my personal favourite. The films are probably one of the most successful series of films ever, earning over twelve billion dollars. It's not only the films, however, which are popular but also the theme songs connected with the films … including one of the most recent, *Another way to die* by Jack White and Alicia Keys for the film *Quantum of Solace*. Today, we have Tony Andrews, film critic from *WeLoveFilm* magazine and a fan of everything James Bond, to tell us more about the music for double oh seven. Welcome, Tony …

Track 1.10

I = Interviewer T = Tony

I: Welcome, Tony.

T: Hello. Great to be here.

I: So, we know that the James Bond films are incredibly successful … but as I said, the theme songs are hugely popular, too. I mentioned *Another way to die* … Can you tell us a bit about that one?

T: Yeah, that's right … *Another way to die* is from the film *Quantum of Solace* … It came out in 2008 and was really popular.

I: It's a duet, isn't it?

T: Yes, it's a duet by Alicia Keys and Jack White – the lead singer of The White Stripes. Actually, it's the first duet used for a Bond theme song – all the others are solos, with just one singer. I think it appealed to young people … although some people didn't like it at first. The words of the song are great. Personally, I loved it.

I: Yes, the lyrics are really good and have a strong message. And I think Alicia Keys is very cool. I love that song. Let's hear a bit of it … Mmm … great song! So, when was the first famous Bond theme song?

T: Well, the first Bond film, *Dr No*, and the second one actually, *From Russia with Love*, had great soundtracks. They had music, obviously. But they didn't have a theme song connected with them. *Goldfinger* was the first big song.

I: Mmmm. That's right … *Goldfinger*.

T: When *Goldfinger* came out, in 1964, the real connection between film and theme song started. After that, I suppose the public expected a great theme song in every film.

I: Yes, that was a great film. And Shirley Bassey made *Goldfinger* into a classic song, too.

T: Yes, she's an amazing singer. That song started her career and she became an international star immediately. It wasn't Bassey's only Bond song either.

I: Oh, yes – that's true. How many did she sing?

T: She sang three Bond songs altogether – the only singer to do more than one.

I: Really?

T: Yes, she sang another classic song, *Diamonds are forever* in 1971. And then, eight years later, *Moonraker* although that one wasn't very successful. But it's not just Shirley Bassey. What's good about Bond is that there are different singers and different styles for each film. Many of the songs really are classics …

I: Tell us about some of the other successful ones.

T: Well, yes, many Bond songs got to the top of the charts in different countries, but *A View to a Kill* by Duran Duran is the only Bond song actually to be Number One on the Billboard Hot 100 chart.

I: The only Number One? *A View to a kill* – really? That's interesting.

T: Mmm … there are other real classics which did really well. In the 1970s, there were two great Bond songs … first *Live and let die* by Paul McCartney and Wings, in 1973. Then, *Nobody does it better* by Carly Simon, in 1977.

I: And *Another way to die* of course that we talked about earlier … Jack White and Alicia Keys had huge success with that one.

T: Yes, that was one of my personal favourites.

I: Not all Bond songs were hits though, were they? There have been some flops, too.

T: Yes, there was a very mixed reaction to Madonna's *Die another day*, when it came out in 2002. It wasn't a complete flop … but strangely, it got awards for being the best song, but also the worst!

I: I liked that one actually. It had a really catchy chorus.

T: Did you? Yes, I thought so, too.

Track 1.13

M = Man W = Woman

M: I've got an article here about the *Mozart Effect* … It says music can affect your mood. You know, different music makes you feel happy or relaxed or something. I don't know about that … Can music change how you feel? Ermm … What do you think?

W: Erm I don't know, I think maybe when you're in a bad mood or upset about something, and you put happy music on, it makes you feel better. Yeah, I think music can change your mood … but maybe also, it depends what kind of person you are I suppose … and what kind of music you like.

M: Mmm …

W: Sometimes I like listening to music that reminds me of old times. You know, I put on a song the other day and it really reminded me of my summer holidays a few years ago. I remember listening to it when I went to Italy with my family. It's got great memories I suppose and it made me feel really good, you know, listening to it again.

M: Yeah, I know what you mean … How often do you listen to music, then?

W: I listen to music every single day … erm … all day, sometimes! From the moment I wake up, the radio is on … or the MP3 player … I never go anywhere without my MP3 player – even when I'm out on my bike.

M: So, do you listen to music when you're travelling? You know, when you're going to work or something?

W: Yes … that's a really good time for listening to music. I have the radio on in the car, and it makes the journey go quicker. You know, you can sing along … and have fun when you're sitting in a traffic jam!

M: What's your favourite type of music?

W: Erm I love all kinds of music … anything that's good. I love old stuff, I love new stuff. My favourite type is probably rock, but lots of other stuff too. I think that it's quite difficult to say your favourite, especially because I listen to so much music.

M: What about live music? When did you last see live music?

W: Oh, it was ages ago. The last concert I saw was years ago. Erm … I don't know

why, I suppose it's really expensive usually and sometimes the place is so big, you can't really see the person properly. I'm not really bothered about live music so much …

Track 1.15

I = Interviewer ML = Mark Leyton:

I: On *My top three* today, we're talking to actor Mark Leyton. What are his top three records? Imagine he is alone on a desert island for ten weeks. Which music would he want? Which three pieces of music would he take with him to this desert island? Let's talk to him and find out. Hello Mark – welcome to *My top three*.

ML: Hello.

I: So, imagine – you're going to be alone on a desert island. You can only take three pieces of music. Which three do you want? First … tell us about number three.

Track 1.16

I = Interviewer ML = Mark Leyton:

ML: Well, it's very difficult to choose – but I think number three for me is *Feelin' so good* by Jennifer Lopez. I love it!

I: Yes. So do I!

ML: It reminds me of when I was at school. We finished our exams and then this song was on the radio all summer. It makes me feel so happy. I always want to dance when I hear it!

I: Well, let's hear it … … Great! So number three is Jennifer Lopez, what about number two?

ML: Number two for me is something completely different … it's a piece of classical music. It's got great memories for me. I heard it first when I was about ten years old and I didn't know anything about classical music at that time. It's the fourth movement of Mahler's *Symphony number 5*. When I first heard it, it made me cry because it was so beautiful!! And I still love it.

I: OK … so here it is … the fourth movement of *Symphony number 5* by Mahler … … That really is lovely, isn't it?

ML: Yes …

I: So, number one … what's your all-time number one favourite piece of music?

ML: Well, I think my favourite song ever is *Imagine* by John Lennon. I think he's got a fantastic voice. It reminds me of a great holiday I had. I remember listening to it when I was on the beach in Spain. It's so relaxing – I could listen to it every day!

I: Mmm … here it is … … A great choice! Thank you for coming in today to tell us about your top three, Mark.

Track 1.17

1 It reminds me of when I was at school.
2 It makes me feel so happy.
3 It's got great memories for me!
4 When I first heard it, it made me cry!
5 It reminds me of a great holiday I had.
6 I remember listening to it when I was on the beach.

Track 1.18

A: I prefer meat. I never choose fish when I go out to a restaurant.

B: Not really. I think a lot of them are a waste of time. They don't really work.

C: Yes, I have. It was when I was a teenager. I didn't think it was right to eat animals.

D: Yes, I can't eat nuts or seafood. They make me really ill.

E: I like to have a lot of choice in a

restaurant. Then you always know there's something you like.

F: I really love apple pie – it's very traditional where I come from.

G: Yes, there are lots. I really like Jamie Oliver. He makes cooking seem simple and fun.

H: Yes, I do. I use them to help me get new ideas.

Track 1.20

1 What are you going to do this year?
2 I want to work in a restaurant as a chef.
3 I'm going to get a job as a waiter in October.
4 I'd like to speak English better because I want to work abroad.
5 I'm going to get a place at college to learn about hotel management.

Track 1.21

T = Tarin M = Marcos

T: Hi Marcos, what are you doing next Thursday? And your brother too … is he around?

M: Erm … next Thursday? Ermm … my brother is staying with friends next week … but I'm not doing anything … Why?

T: Well, I'm having a meal at my house to celebrate Thanksgiving and I'd really like you to come.

M: Oh, thanks, I'd love to! That's very kind of you! I've never been to a Thanksgiving meal before. It's an important festival here, isn't it?

T: Yes … and I'm going to cook roast turkey! Thanksgiving is all about the food … well … really just getting together with family and friends and having a lovely meal. Sometimes, after the meal, people go out for a walk or something, but mostly, they just sit around and watch TV together.

M: Mmm … And what about presents and things? Is it a time when you give presents to people, like at Christmas or … ?

T: Ermm … no, not really … it's a really big and important celebration but it isn't commercial. People don't usually buy lots of presents or anything. There are some big public celebrations like the Macy's parade in New York … but, for most people, it's just a time for giving thanks, and getting together with family and friends and eating turkey!

M: Mmm … I love roast turkey!

T: Yes, me too. Traditionally, we have roast turkey as the main part of the meal … and then there are lots of other dishes. I mean, basically, there are four other essential parts to the meal … sometimes more than four …

M: Really …?

T: Mm … There are lots of variations, too. It depends on where you come from in the States. I'm from the north east and one of the things we have is sweet potatoes with maple syrup … it's very sweet, and some people don't like it, but I love it!

M: Mm … I think it sounds delicious … sweet potatoes and maple syrup … mmm.

T: Yeah … some people have sweet potatoes baked in the oven … in a sort of pie … but we usually have them boiled … and then mashed up and … then with maple syrup on top. Not everyone has maple syrup – in some parts of the States they have sweet potatoes with fresh fruit – things like apples, oranges and pears.

M: Really? Mmm … Interesting!

Audioscripts

T: The second thing we always have is cranberry sauce. Have you ever had that?

M: Cranberry sauce? No, I don't think so.

T: It goes really well with turkey – it's made of small red berries – it's also very sweet actually … Not everything we have is sweet though. There are some savoury dishes!

M: What else then?

T: Well, stuffing is really important. I love it … it's one of my favourite parts of the meal.

M: Stuffing … ? What's that?

T: It's made of bread and meat … sausages usually – all mixed up together … and it's often very spicy.

M: Mmm … . So, … there are basically four other dishes. What was it? … Sweet potatoes, … cranberry sauce … and stuffing … What's the fourth one?

T: Well, apple pie of course!

M: Aah yes … I've heard about traditional American apple pie.

T: Actually, some people don't have apple pie. In some places, they have pumpkin pie … or pie made of pecan nuts, which is very popular … But in our house, we have apple pie – baked in the oven. It's fantastic!

M: Mmm … I'm getting hungry just thinking about it all. So, is there anything I can bring?

T: Oh, no! Don't worry about that. Just come and enjoy yourself. We're eating at about two o'clock in the afternoon – so why don't you come at about midday for some drinks first?

M: Perfect! See you then. I'm really looking forward to it.

Track 1.23

T = Tarin M = Marcos

T: Hi Marcos, what are you doing next Thursday? And your brother, too … is he around?

M: Erm … next Thursday? Ermm … my brother is staying with friends next week … but I'm not doing anything … Why?

T: Well, I'm having a meal at my house to celebrate Thanksgiving and I'd really like you to come.

M: Oh, thanks, I'd love to! That's very kind of you!

…

M: So, is there anything I can bring?

T: Oh, no! Don't worry about that. Just come and enjoy yourself. We're eating at about two o'clock in the afternoon – so why don't you come at about midday for some drinks first?

M: Perfect! See you then. I'm really looking forward to it.

Track 1.26

W = Woman M = Man

M: So, come on then, Anita, tell me all about it! Have you found a place for your new restaurant?

W: Yes! I'm really excited about it actually. I'm renting a fantastic space … it's on the ground floor of a big building … in the centre of town … near the school.

M: Oh great … That's a really good place for a restaurant. What are you going to call it?

W: Well, I think I'm going to call it 'Anita's' … after me!

M: Why not? Yes … , 'Anita's' … That's good … And, what type of food are you going to serve?

W: Well, traditional English food, mostly … but with some food from Europe … some Italian and modern French food, too – European food, I suppose.

M: That sounds good …

W: The thing is, I want the food to be simple, but delicious …

M: Yes …

W: … and I think it's really important that the prices are reasonable. You know, I don't want it to be really expensive … I want ordinary people to come and to get affordable, good food … I've decided that we're going to keep the menu simple, but change it every two weeks.

M: That's a good idea.

W: So, we're going to have three starters, three main courses and three desserts.

M: Mmm, yes … what kind of things, then?

W: In our opening weeks, we're going to have, as starters: fresh mussels in a garlic sauce, Italian salad and … tomato soup.

M: Lovely!

W: For the main course: cheese and lemon pasta, grilled fish of the day with green beans and roast chicken with potatoes.

M: Mmm …

W: And finally, for dessert: chocolate mousse, homemade ice cream and apple pie with cream.

M: Fantastic! You really have got it all planned out! It sounds delicious! And what about the service? Is it going to be waiter service at the table or self-service?

W: Ermm … waiter service … I think it's really important to have friendly waiters who are really efficient. There's nothing worse than bad service in a restaurant … the customers just won't come back!

M: And what are your plans for the décor? I mean, you must have an idea about the kind of atmosphere you want.

W: Yes, like the food, I want the place to be quite simple, but modern at the same time. And we're going to have music to create a young, lively atmosphere. I'd also like to have paintings on the walls … art by local artists.

M: Yes, that's a nice feature.

W: It's an extra thing really – to attract more customers … Anyway, that's the plan. We'll have to see how it goes …

M: Well, good luck with it all. I can't wait to come and try it out.

Track 1.27

1 It was a few months ago … I was really nervous … really scared. It was for a good promotion and I wanted it so much! I decided to use a kind of meditation – and I repeated positive things to myself to try and stay focused and to control my fear. I think it worked … because the interview went well and I got the job!

2 My brother had a serious illness last year … he had problems with his heart. He's much better now, thankfully, but because of his illness, I decided to do something positive, something to help … I ran one marathon every day for a week to raise money. It was a huge challenge … really difficult … but I did it … and I raised nearly £2,000 for charity.

3 Next year, I'm going to South America with a friend of mine … We want to see the world a bit before we go to university. I'm going to have Spanish lessons and try to learn as much as I can before we go. The thing is that my friend speaks very good Spanish, but I don't speak any … and I don't want to rely on her all the time.

4 When you go on a long trek somewhere – like the Arctic – where it's very cold, or across a desert – where it's very hot – it's obviously hard to survive. You know, … you need a lot of physical strength.

You also need a lot of mental strength. You need to be prepared to face difficult things without giving up.

5 I've wanted to be a doctor since I was really young … for as long as I can remember, really. I know that you have to study for years and years, and do very long hours, all through the night sometimes. But I am definitely prepared to do the hard work … I'm determined to achieve my goal and be a doctor.

Track 1.28

1 Carla is much more motivated than Louisa. Louisa isn't as motivated as Carla.

2 Louisa is a bit fitter than Carla. Carla isn't as fit as Louisa.

3 Louisa is a bit more determined than Carla. Carla isn't as determined as Louisa.

4 Carla is much braver than Louisa. Louisa isn't as brave as Carla.

Track 1.30

Good evening and thank you for coming to find out about the Hillside Survival School. My name's David Johnson. I started the school and I'm the school's chief instructor. I learned my survival skills while I was in the army and before starting the Hillside Survival School, I worked in other well-known survival schools. So, first, why do people come on our courses? What are our aims? Well, firstly, we aim to help people to discover nature and the outdoor life … and to remind people that there is more to life than city living. Secondly, and perhaps more importantly, we want people to work well as a team and to have fun together … and a lot of people come to do just that!

Who comes on our courses? Who are our courses for? Well, the answer is anybody and everybody. We get a lot of groups of colleagues – people who work together, like you. The weekend courses are a fantastic way of team-building, and having fun together, as I said. The courses are also popular with groups of friends who want to do something a bit more challenging than lying on a beach!

So, let me tell you about what happens on some of our courses … The most popular course we run is our basic survival course which lasts a weekend and takes place throughout the year. This course teaches you the basic skills that you need to survive in the wilderness and costs a hundred and seventy-five pounds per person. Choose this one and you will have the best weekend you've ever had! If you want an even bigger challenge, our extreme survival course takes place between November and February, when the conditions are more difficult. These courses also last for a weekend and cost a hundred and ninety-five pounds per person. The extreme survival course teaches you to survive in a wet and cold environment. In fact, we aim to give you the wettest, coldest weekend ever! The course offers you the chance to push yourself, both physically and mentally. No tents, no gas cookers; just you and the wilderness. You learn to find food and cook it over an open fire. You learn to build a shelter and then you actually sleep in it. It could be the hardest thing you've ever done by far … You won't have the most comfortable weekend of your life, but you will probably be surprised how well you can cope with difficult conditions.

Well … thank you very much for inviting me here to your company to tell you about Hillside Survival School. If you're interested in doing any of our courses with a group of colleagues, speak to your manager. You can also pick up a booklet before you go ... it includes information about all the courses, prices, dates and application forms. Push yourself. It really could be the best thing you've ever done! ... And, yes, I think we've got time for a few questions ... before you all get back to work. Erm ... yes ... the man at the back ...

Track 1.31

1

A = Assistant P = Train passenger

A: Can I help you?
P: I'd like a return to Edinburgh, please.
A: Yes ... when would you like to travel?
P: On Friday afternoon ... and coming back on Sunday evening.
A: OK ... uh ... there's a train at five forty-five p.m. on Friday.
P: Yes, that's fine. Oh, and can you tell me how long the train takes?
A: Erm, yes ... it takes about five hours.
P: Thank you.

2

P1 = Passenger 1 P2 = Passenger 2

P1: Err ... do you know if this is the train to Cardiff please?
P2: Yes, it is.
P1: Oh ... good. Is this seat free? ... I mean, is it OK with you if I sit here?
P2: Yes, of course. No problem.
...
P1: Excuse me, is this your newspaper? Do you mind if I read it ... ?
P2: No, that's fine. Go ahead.

3

S = Shop assistant C = Customer

S: Hello. How are you?
C: I'm good thanks. How are you?
S: Good thanks ... Do you need any help?
C: Oh, yes, please. Can you tell me if you have this jacket in medium?
S: Yes, certainly ... I'll just have a look for you. ... Here you are.
C: Thanks. Oh, and could you tell me how much it is, please?
S: Yes, of course. It's fifty-five dollars.
C: Is it OK if I pay by credit card?
S: Yes, that's fine.

Track 1.34

1

A: Can you tell me if you have this jacket in medium?
B: Yes, certainly ... I'll just have a look for you.

2

A: Could you tell me how much it is please?
B: Yes, of course. ... It's fifty-five dollars.

3

A: Is it OK if I pay by credit card?
B: Yes, that's fine.

4

A: Do you mind if I read it ... ?
B: No, that's fine. Go ahead.

Track 1.35

W = Woman M = Man

M: I'm really excited about this weekend ... I think it's going to be difficult, but I'm sure we're all going to have a great time.
W: Yes ... I'm really looking forward to it as well. I've always wanted to go on one of these survival courses. It might be a bit strange going with a group of people who you don't know very well. But I suppose it's good to get to know our colleagues better!
M: Yes, I think that's the idea ... I'm sure it'll be fun.
W: Anyway, we can take five things, can't we? Shall we think about it now ... and try and decide which things to take?
M: Yeah ... good idea.

W: Erm ... Which of them do you think is the most important?
M: Well, it's quite cold ... erm ... I don't want to be cold at night! I think we should take the blankets to keep us warm.
W: OK ... so, do you think they're more important than the penknife?
M: No, no ... not more important. We can have the penknife as well ... We are allowed five things after all.
W: That's true. So what else?
M: Well, in my opinion, we should take the matches, so we can make a fire from all the wood you can chop up with the penknife!
W: Good idea ... and ... how about the tent?
M: Hmmm ... I'm not sure. That sounds like cheating a bit. Couldn't we make a shelter from the trees and leaves and things?
W: Well maybe you could!
M: OK ... we'll have the tent ... and why don't we have the chocolate as number five as a bit of luxury?
W: Yes, great idea ... I think we're going to need it!

Track 1.37

M = Man W = Woman

1

W: One of the daughters of a friend of mine has got married and she's eighteen. Now I think that's too young to get married. What do you think?
M: I agree, I think eighteen is far too young to get married because you haven't got any experience of life. I ... I think if you get married at eighteen, you have so many responsibilities. At ... ah that age, you need to be able to travel and try different jobs and um ...
W: Yes, I ... I think you're right and um ... also, I think at that age you, you really haven't become the person that you you're going to be. You haven't developed, um, so I think you change between eighteen and, say, twenty-five. You change so much and young people who get married at eighteen, by the time they reach twenty-five, they might not be interested at all in their, their husband or wife.
M: I agree, I ... I think um it's, it's too, ah it's too early to get married. If you make a mistake and um you marry the wrong person then, marriage is for life but ... ah the ... you should be able to wait just another few years and maybe get married at twenty-five or thirty ... um there's still plenty of time.
W: It's better, yes that's definitely better ...

2

M: I agree, I think it would be very good if young people these days did military service, because it teaches them responsibility and it also um ... teaches them how ... ah to cooperate in a group. I think it's a very good idea.
W: Um ... I'm not so sure about that. Um, OK, it teaches them cooperation. It teaches them to work in groups, but on the other hand it teaches them how to be aggressive. It teaches them to go out and kill people.
M: Um, yeah well, I ... I don't agree. I've spoken to young people in countries where they still have military service and ... ah maybe they have military service for a year or eighteen months, and apart from being very pleasant, polite, young people, many of them also say that they enjoyed their military service.
W: Mmm ...in
M: And um, met some very good friends and ...
W: Yeah, in my opinion, it doesn't have to be military service. Erm, in some countries you have the, the possibility of ... um a

kind of civil service where they work in hospitals or on farms and generally do good things for their country, but it's not to do with the military and I think you have to give young people the choice because some young people don't want to be in the military service – they don't want to be involved in that kind of thing and I can understand that. So why can't they do something else which helps their country?

3

W: I don't know, teenagers these days, they only ever think about their girlfriends, their boyfriends, about money, about what they want to do in the evening – they're just terrible! They really are, don't you think so?
M: I ... I don't agree. Um, I mean, I think that teenagers have all sorts of problems and things that they have to deal with these days. I'm ... I'm always amazed by the amount of schoolwork they have to do for example, far more homework than I did when I was at school.
W: Well maybe ...
M: Don't you think so?
W: Maybe some ... no, I don't. Um, I think some teenagers are very irresponsible. They, they should be more responsible about their lives ... they ... I think a lot of teenagers don't study ... don't study very much at all ... um. They come out of school with no qualifications. They don't get jobs ... um. They cause problems in the streets. I don't know, I think that um the parents are to blame really. The, the main reason is their parents um aren't strict enough with them.
M: Well, I ... I agree that there are lots of teenagers who do cause problems, but I think most teenagers now are much more responsible than they used to be and ah, there's a lot of pressure on them to do well at school, so that they can go to university and ah and get a good career.

Track 1.38

M = Martin T = Tina

M: It's great to be back ... We've got so much catching up to do!
T: Yeah, there's so much to tell you! I know, I'll show you some photos from my birthday party.
M: Oh, that's a good idea ... I can see who your friends are.
T: Yes, I had a bit of a party with some of my best ... you know, my closest friends. We had a lovely time. Let's see ... where are they? OK ... here we are ... this is a good one. So, well, first, this is Alison.
M: Mmm ... yes, I think I remember her ...
T: Yes, I've known Alison for years. I mean, we're old school friends – from primary school – so, I suppose I've known her nearly all my life really. We first met when we were in the same class at school from the age of four and a half.
M: Four and a half? Really?
T: Yeah, even when we were at school together, we never fell out with each other about anything. She's a very easy-going person and still a really great friend. I'm very glad we've kept in touch. I suppose we see each other about once a month and we still get on really well.
M: Mmm, that's really nice. And who's that? He looks like a bit of a character!
T: Yes! He's great ... That's my friend Jake. Basically, I go to the gym with him! Actually, he was a colleague first. I got to know him at work and we've worked together for about five years now. Then,

about a year ago, we started going to the gym together. It's really good because we help each other to keep motivated.

M: I need a friend like that!

T: Well, that's right. It's hard to keep going to the gym and exercising on your own, isn't it? Because I've got someone to go with, it's much easier. He's always encouraging me, and motivating me. I think he feels the same, too. So, yes, we see each other at work, and we go to the gym together … and I would definitely say he's a really good friend.

M: Yes …

T: Oh, … and Melanie. That's her … She's a lovely friend – always there for me. I met her at a party, actually – about ten years ago … but then we lost touch for a while.

M: Oh, really?

T: Well, yes, but a couple of years ago, we met again and we've been really close since then. I call her my 'three o'clock in the morning' friend because she really is the kind of person who you can phone up at three o'clock in the morning if you need to, and she really wouldn't mind.

M: That's great …

T: In fact, I have phoned her at that time on a couple of occasions. You know, when I've been really down about something and really needed someone to talk to. I see her at least once a week … She's my best friend … she really is … She's a very special person – she doesn't give you advice, you know. She just listens. It's a great quality in a friend, I think.

M: Yes, definitely … Oh, who's that? I think I recognise him …

Track 1.39

M = Man W = Woman

M: OK … so three things about my childhood. Well, firstly, I used to … well, every summer, I used to go to the same place for my holidays. We used to go camping near a lovely beach in Wales.

W: OK … Did you use to drive there?

M: Yes … it took about three hours from where we lived.

W: Mmm … next one?

M: Next one … we used to have a dog …

W: Right … when did you get it? I mean, how old were you?

M: Well, I wanted a dog so much … I was really upset and I used to ask my mum all the time … And then my parents gave me a dog on my eleventh birthday! I couldn't believe it. I was so pleased.

W: OK … and … erm … the last one?

M: And number three, … well, about school. I used to love playing out on the street with my friends.

W: What did you use to play mostly?

M: Ermm … We used to play football in the middle of the road … you know, there weren't many cars, so it was OK.

W: OK … so … so which one is false? Let's see … Erm … about the dog … What was your dog's name?

M: Ermm … she was called Meg.

W: Meg? What colour was she?

M: Oh, sort of black and white.

W: Did you use to take her out for walks?

M: Yes, but mostly my dad took her out.

W: Oh, but she was your dog…

M: Err … yes, but …

W: It's not true, is it? You didn't have a dog … that one's false …

M: Ermm … no I didn't actually! You're right. It's false. I really wanted a dog – but we never got one! OK … your turn…

W: OK, first one …

Track 1.40

Today on *This is your life*, we are talking about a woman who is probably one of the most famous and influential women in the world. Going back to her early life, she was born on January the seventeenth, 1964, and grew up in Chicago, USA. She did well at school and then went on to get a law degree from Harvard University in 1988.

After graduating, she worked at a law company in Chicago. This is where she met her future husband, who was working for the same company. They got married on October the eighteenth, 1992. She has had an impressive career; with senior positions in several large companies and universities. Looking at family matters, in July 1998, she had her first child; a daughter called Malia. And a second daughter, Natasha – known as Sasha – followed in June 2001. After her husband was elected to the U.S. Senate, she and her husband decided to keep their children in Chicago. She wanted to continue with her career, as well as keeping a stable family life for the children.

Currently, she is the First Lady of the United States, and manages to juggle being a mother, a career woman and the wife of the President. She usually goes to bed by nine thirty and gets up each morning at four thirty, to go running. It is this discipline that helps her keep calm and organised in her busy, stressful life.

Track 1.41

I = Interviewer W = Woman

I: Welcome to *Tourism Today* – the programme that looks at aspects of tourism throughout the world. Today, we're talking about a tourist destination in Europe. With its fantastic summer weather and beautiful islands, Greece is extremely popular with holiday makers. An expert on the Greek islands, Alanna Papadakis, is here to talk about some changes – both positive and negative – that are happening there. … Hello, Alanna.

W: Hello, Mike.

I: Greece is a major tourist destination. And many of the islands – like Crete, Mykonos and Santorini – are familiar to us from the tourist guides … most of us know these names.

W: Yes, that's right. Many Greek islands are well-prepared for the hordes of tourists who come every summer. These islands expect to see thousands of visitors every year. Other islands remain quiet and undiscovered by tourists though … and many of them will stay that way.

I: One island, however, may soon change dramatically. Tell us about that …

W: Well … Skopelos is an island in the Aegean Sea to the east of Athens. It's very small – there are only 4,696 residents there … and yes, they might need to prepare for a huge increase in tourists.

I: 4,696 residents – that is small! So, what's going on there?

W: There are reports that some tourists want to get married there. Others want to have parties in their own private bay. Others just want to dance on the beach. It's called the *Mamma Mia!* effect – and it seems everyone wants to go to Skopelos now. It all started when the film *Mamma Mia!* was released. You know … the film version of the musical … the hit Abba musical, starring Meryl Streep, Colin Firth and Pierce Brosnan.

I: It's proving to be hugely popular, isn't it?

W: Yes, not only the film … but also the island! Until they started filming *Mamma Mia!*, Skopelos was famous for plums, pears and pine forests. It was a surprise to everyone that the island itself became one of the biggest stars of the film!

I: Why did they choose this particular island?

W: Well, producers looked at about twenty-five Greek islands before they decided on Skopelos. In the end, they chose this one because it has many different places which fitted with the story.

I: Can you tell us exactly where some of those places are?

W: Yes … some of the film takes place around Kastani Bay and the beaches there. Other parts were filmed at the top of the cliffs, above Glisteri Beach. That's where the main character – played by Meryl Streep – has a house.

I: And what about the famous wedding scene at the end of the film?

W: Yes, the wedding scene is filmed on the mountain on the peninsula near Glisteri. It's beautiful … unforgettable really.

I: So, this beautiful location provided the backdrop for an extremely successful film. But will the film bring success for the island of Skopelos? Or will the changes have a negative effect?

W: Well, things will change there. Sometimes films like this have a huge effect on the location … Skopelos won't stay the same …. it won't be the same unknown place that it used to be. There's a positive side and a negative side, I suppose… On the negative side, things may be less peaceful. The local people may not keep the peaceful atmosphere of the island completely. But on the positive side, they are pleased to get more business, at least during the summer months.

I: Yes, the film might be very good for business …

W: Mmm … and I'm sure the *Mamma Mia!* effect will increase tourism on other islands.

I: Yes, it might increase tourism for the whole of Greece, but … at the moment, nobody really knows if these changes will be positive or not … in the long run, I mean …

Track 1.42

1

A: Will tourism change the island of Skopelos?

B: Yes, I think it'll change it a lot.

2

A: Where will you live when you're older?

B: I think I'll live by the coast.

3

A: Where are they going on holiday next year?

B: I think they'll go to Greece.

4

A: Do you think you'll pass the exam?

B: Yes, I think I will.

Track 1.43

Gavin

OK, um, growing up, I used to go on holiday to a place in Northumberland called Seahouses, um, and the most **impressive** thing about Seahouses is the miles and miles of **unspoilt**, **idyllic** beaches. You can walk for miles and miles and only see a man and his dog and it's fantastic. The biggest feeling you get when you're there is being entirely relaxed. Um, it's such a, a good um contrast with the city, um, and generations of my family have been going there. Erm, I think it was my great great grandfather ah discovered this small seaside town ah many years ago and ever since my ahm family's been going there and ah yeah it's fantastic.

Heather

One of the most beautiful places I've ever been to is in Southern Thailand and it's a peninsula called Railay. It's a **beautiful**, **unspoilt** lush scenery. It takes five minutes to walk from one side of the peninsula to the other. Erm, one of the beaches that I used to visit I had to walk through caves to get to it, ahm, and it was a hidden beach … um um … and when I went swimming um you can see to the bottom in about ten feet of water. There's tropical fish everywhere, the sun is shining and in the distance all you can see is dots of other islands in the distance. It's very **relaxing**, ahm very calm very serene. It's a very tranquil place to spend, spend the afternoon.

Track 2.2

M = Man W = Woman

W: Hi, Jack. … What are you doing?

M: Oh, it's SimCity … have you ever played it?

W: SimCity? No, I haven't … and I can't believe you're still playing that! Aren't you bored of it? It's been around for over twenty years, hasn't it?

M: Well, yes … but it's a fantastic game … really – one of the most popular computer games ever made. And, they bring out new versions all the time. It's a great game …

W: What's does it involve, then? What do you have to do?

M: Well, your basic task is to build a city. You make choices about what things you want in your city, how to keep the people in your city happy and how much to spend.

W: What kind of things are you talking about?

M: Well, you plan the whole city. You decide what different areas there are, for example, a residential area – where people live – or a commercial area, with shops and things. You can also decide where to put things like parks, cinemas, swimming pools and other facilities.

W: Is it only leisure facilities?

M: No, your city shouldn't have too many leisure facilities. There isn't enough space to have whatever you want – and you need to have the basic things, too. So, you decide how much to spend on basic things like roads, bus stations, hospitals and libraries.

W: What about money? Can you spend as much as you want on these things?

M: No … that's a big part of the game – you can't spend too much money. Most of your money comes from tax, but the people don't want to pay too much tax.

W: No, of course not!

M: But, they want enough facilities. You know, if you don't spend enough money on things like schools and hospitals, the workers might stop working … they might go on strike. And if the workers stop working, your city begins to break down. And with each new version, they've added new things; like having areas of the city which become too crowded for people to live in, and so they begin to leave. They're too noisy – you know, they're not quiet enough for some people to live in anymore.

W: So, it's basically about designing your city?

M: Not only … I mean, there are various bad things that happen, like earthquakes and other natural disasters, and you can see how your city survives, or not …

W: So, why do you think it is so popular? I mean, twenty years … that's a long time …

M: Ermm … I think it's about choice and control … and the fact that it's an open-ended game. I mean, I think SimCity is popular because it's not about killing or destroying things. Too many computer games are about killing, I think.

W: Yes, I agree.

M: But, in SimCity, you make decisions and choices which help you in a positive way and you create your own city. The game is really well designed. They've designed it well enough to appeal to a lot of people … and … it really holds people's attention for a long time. I think people like being in control of their own city. It is a virtual city, but the technology is very good, it feels very real …

Track 2.3

H = Harry L = Linda

H: Well, what do you think? We're going in March, so we need to get the tickets soon. Where would you like to go?

L: Umm … I think Barcelona sounds really good, or maybe Edinburgh … I'm not sure. There are lots of great things to see and do in both places. What do you think?

H: Umm … I think Edinburgh is too cold for me … I mean, cold weather isn't my idea of fun! I like warmer weather … four degrees is too cold! Barcelona is a bit warmer. Is it warm enough?

L: Yes, I think so … it's warm enough for me … I don't like it too hot.

H: Oh really? I'd prefer somewhere very warm … like Rio. I like the idea of going to the beach.

L: Yes, but Rio is too far away. I'm not keen on sitting on a plane for twelve hours or something … And it's too expensive to get there …

H: I suppose you're right … But, look … Edinburgh is expensive, too… the accommodation, I mean.

L: Well, what about Barcelona? I'd like to go somewhere on the coast.

H: OK … it sounds really fun there. And it isn't too far away, is it?

L: OK, then … Shall I book the tickets this afternoon?

Track 2.7

1 Are you ambitious?
2 Are you usually hard-working or lazy?
3 Are you more open or more reserved?
4 Are you an organised kind of person or disorganised?
5 Are you chatty or are you the quiet type?
6 Are you an easy-going person?

Track 2.8

H = Helen D = Daniel

H: Hi Daniel. Have you finished doing your essay? I want to show you something … just five minutes … it won't take long.

D: Yes, sure. I've decided not to do my essay now, actually … It's really difficult and Michael has offered to help me later … What do you want to do?

H: Well, erm … I want to look at the shape of your fingers.

D: What? … Why?

H: I'm going to tell you about your personality.

D: Oh … hmm … I'm not sure about that. What are you going to say about me?! You have to promise to be nice!

H: Well, we'll see what your fingers say!

D: Oh, OK … why not? I enjoy doing this kind of thing actually. So, where do we start?

H: OK, well, erm … there are three main things to look at.

D: Mmm …

H: First, there's the length of your fingers. People with long, slim fingers are quite sensitive. People with shorter, thicker fingers, like yours, are more open. They talk about their feelings more. So, you're quite an open person …

D: No, I'm not sure about that … Actually, I don't think I'm very open. I think I avoid telling people about my feelings most of the time … In fact, I don't think I talk about my feelings much at all.

H: Yes, you do …

D: I don't think so, really … only to really close family and friends. I mean, I'd never even consider showing my feelings to someone I didn't know.

H: No, well, obviously not … But you seem to be quite open with people you know – that's what I mean.

D: Well … I'm really not sure … But let's move on … What else then?

H: Well, secondly, there's the shape of your fingers. Are you fingers straight?

D: Erm … yes … I think they are quite straight.

H: Ermm … that means you're organised. Is that true?

D: Yes. I think that's true about me. I mean, especially with writing essays and things … I'm very organised. You can't afford to be disorganised really. There's so much work at university … it all piles up if you're not organised about it.

H: Yes …

D: So, you said I'm open, organised … OK … what else?

H: Well, finally, the thumb is very important … Let's see how long your thumb is …

D: Hmm … I think it's quite long.

H: Well, a long thumb means you're ambitious. You know, you really want to be successful in what you do. You've got quite a long thumb, so I guess you're quite ambitious.

D: That's absolutely right! I think I am ambitious … yes. Hmmm … not bad … you said I'm ambitious, yes, organised, yes … and open, well, I'm still not sure about that one … but not bad, I suppose.

H: Mmm … I think that's quite accurate, actually.

D: OK, now it's your turn! Let me look at your hands …

Track 2.9

1
A: You look terrible. What's the matter?
B: I feel sick and I've got stomachache.

2
A: Are you better today?
B: No … I've got flu. I've got a high temperature and a headache.

3
A: How you are? You don't look well.
B: I've got a cough and sore eyes. I don't think it's serious – I've got a cold. That's all.

4
A: Is your back feeling better?
B: No. I've got terrible backache and my leg hurts. I've got toothache today, as well.

5
A: How are you feeling?
B: Terrible! I've got a sore throat and earache. I've got a rash as well.

Track 2.10

1

G = Georgia J = Jenny

G: Hello?
J: Oh, Georgia …This is Jenny … I'm so sorry … Did I wake you up?
G: Ermm … no, well … not really …

Audioscripts

J: Oh dear ... you sound terrible. How are you?
G: Not very well, really. I've got an awful sore throat and I can't stop coughing ...
J: Poor you! Have you taken anything for it?
G: Ermm ... well, no ...
J: I remember having a sore throat a lot when I was a child ... and my mother always gave me hot water with honey and lemon. Why don't you try drinking some of that? It really helps.
G: Thanks. That's a good idea.
J: Have you got any honey or lemon at home?
G: Erm ... well ... I don't think I've got any honey, no.
J: Well, listen – on the way to college, I'll stop to get some honey at the supermarket and bring it round.
G: Oh, no ... don't worry about ...
J: ... It's not a problem – don't worry ... And try not to cough too much ... You should go back to bed now ...
G: Yes, I think I'll do that ...
J: I'll come round in about half an hour.
G: OK ... Thanks, Jenny. Oh ... will you remember to get the homework for me?
J: That's fine ... See you later.
G: Bye.

2
G = Georgia I = Ivan
G: Hello?
I: Hello? Georgia, is that you?
G: Yes ...
I: Oh dear ... I hope I didn't wake you up. It's Ivan here. I got your email and I wanted to check you were OK ... Do you need anything?
G: It's really kind of you to phone, Ivan ... Erm, I think I just need to sleep really ... and Jenny is going to bring me some honey and lemon for my sore throat.
I: Honey and lemon? Oh really, that's an English remedy, isn't it?
G: Yes ... I suppose it is.
I: Well, have you tried having honey and butter in hot milk? In Russia, my grandmother always gave us that. I remember having it a lot when I was a child.
G: Erm, ...I haven't tried that. Did you say it's a Russian remedy?
I: Yes ... it's really good. I used to love it and it makes your throat feel much better. Would you like me to come and see you? I could bring some round for you to try.
G: Oh, no ... really. It's fine ... I mean, Jenny will be here soon.
I: It's no bother really. I'll just come in on my way to college. Try to get some sleep now ...
G: Ermm ... OK – see you in about half an hour ...

3
G = Georgia M = Madison
G: Hello?
M: Georgia? Hi, it's Madison here.
G: Oh, hi ...
M: You don't sound very well. How are you?
G: I'm not feeling very well ...
M: Were you asleep? Sorry – I probably woke you up, didn't I?
G: Well ... it's really nice of everyone to phone me. I mean, Jenny and Ivan just phoned ... and ... well, it's lovely really ...
M: But you can't sleep ...
G: Well, yes ... I suppose ...
M: Oh dear ... you have got a bad cough. You should have honey and vinegar in hot water.
G: Honey and *vinegar*?! Oh, I don't fancy that!
M: It's good ... You use apple vinegar. It's an old American remedy. My mom used to give to us children when we were ill. It smells bad, but it's really delicious and ... it makes your throat feel better.

G: Really? Jenny said the English remedy is hot water with honey and lemon. Ivan said the Russian remedy is hot milk with honey and butter, and ...
M: Oh! I'm so sorry. You've got all the advice you need, haven't you? Well, OK ... I know what you really need – you need some rest ... and some peace and quiet. You need people to stop phoning you! Why don't you try turning your phone off?
G: Yes, that's a good idea. Oh! That's Jenny, I think ... with the honey and lemon ... or it could be Ivan. Sorry Madison, I'd better go and answer the door.
M: OK ... look after yourself – and try to get some rest ...
G: Bye .

Track 2.12

1
A: Why don't you try hot water with honey and lemon?
B: Thanks. That's a good idea.

2
A: You should go back to bed.
B: Yes, I think I'll do that.

3
A: Have you tried honey and butter in hot milk?
B: No, I haven't tried that.

4
A: You should have honey and vinegar in hot water.
B: Oh, I don't fancy that!

Track 2.13
P = Polly A = Amber
P: Um, waiting too long for a bus is definitely a major stress alert for me. Um, it happens quite often and it's really really annoying.
A: Especially if you're late for work.
P: Yep, definitely if it makes you late for work or anything else, and there's nothing you can do about it – it's out of your control.
A: Um, I get quite stressed out when I'm um on the phone to customer services and, um, I don't actually manage to speak to a human.
P: Oh yeah, that's really really annoying as well.
A: Especially when they ah they play the annoying music, makes me get a little bit tense ...
P: I'd say I get more than tense, I get really really stressed out about that.
A: Would that be a major stress alert for you?
P: I think so yeah, especially if I was having to pay for ah the phone call while I was waiting in line.
A: Yeah ...
P: Definitely. But maybe, ah ... yeah, it's definitely more stressful than, um, than losing a game of tennis or something.
A: I was just thinking that ...
P: I wouldn't really be that worried about that.
A: ... be no problem for me.
P: Naw, it's just a bit of fun, and I'm not really comp, very competitive ... so it wouldn't be a bit of a ...
A: Yeah, especially if you're playing with a friend.
P: Yeah, it'd be just for fun ... umm ... are there any other ones?
A: Um, not being able to sleep, um, doesn't make me very happy um
P: Yeah, but you could always put in earplugs or you could ...
A: You can, but ah, it's not ah a major stress alert but ah if you're tired and you can't sleep and there's a lot of noise going on outside, dogs barking, etc. then yeah that's a, that's pretty stressful.

P: I ... I don't agree that much. I'm er, a quite a heavy sleeper, so I don't think it would be that much of a problem

Track 2.14
I = Interviewer W = Woman
I: Welcome to *Changing World*. Almost everything in the modern world is speeding up. The pace of life is getting faster and faster and most people, it seems, think that 'fast is good'. My guest today, however, is someone who thinks that 'fast is bad' and 'slow is good'. Petra van Stroud is a member of the Slow Movement and she's here to tell us why. Petra, welcome to the programme.
W: Hello, thank you.
I: So, in a fast world, you have chosen to join the Slow Movement. Why's that? I mean, don't you think that there are benefits from being able to do things faster – like faster communication using computers and mobile phones and things?
W: Ermm ... well, it can be good ... there are some benefits from a lot of new technology. In my opinion, however, the problem is that people get addicted to doing things fast and then they forget about important things in our lives – like, communicating in real time with a 'real' person. People start living in a virtual world ...
I: They just communicate through a computer or something ...
W: That's right. We need to remember to see each other in the real world ... And that's really what the Slow Movement is all about – having some of the good things about the old, slower life.
I: OK. The Slow Movement – tell us about that. How did it all start?
W: Well, it actually started as the Slow Food organisation in 1986.
I: Slow Food?
W: Yes, in 1986, in Italy – in Rome – a group of people protested about a fast food restaurant – McDonald's – opening there.
I: They didn't want a McDonald's in Rome.
W: That's right. They were against fast food and they wanted people to continue to eat home-cooked 'slow' food. It wasn't just about the food, though. Of course food is better if you cook it yourself – but it was also about the social side of food. You know, when people eat fast food, they are often in a hurry and they often don't talk to each other.
I: So, the Slow Food organisation wanted people to slow down – and take their time to eat and socialise together.
W: Exactly. Then, as more people got interested in the idea, the Slow Food organisation grew into the Slow Movement, including communication, for example, and many other aspects of people's lives. You know ... the aim remains the same: to encourage people to slow down and enjoy spending time with each other – whatever they're doing.
I: I mean, I agree with that philosophy – it is important to spend time with people. I'm just not sure that we can slow down the pace of life now, or even that most people really want to. Fast technology is everywhere and for many of us, the benefits are huge. We live busy fast lives and enjoy them.
W: Many people enjoy their busy lives, yes. But many people don't. I suppose the Slow Movement wants to remind people that in your fast life, sometimes, it's good to slow down. And maybe turn your computer

off, or leave your mobile phone at home – at least sometimes. People might be surprised how much they enjoy slowing down sometimes.

Track 2.15

1 In what language are most international phone calls made?
2 In the US, are more messages carried by email or by post?
3 What percentage of emails are junk email?
4 How much junk mail is delivered by post every year in the US?
5 What percentage of websites are not visited by anybody?
6 How many people visit the website YouTube every day?
7 How many people use the social networking site Facebook every day?
8 In how many different languages do people write messages on Facebook?

Track 2.18

D = Deepa F = Fiona

D: Hi Fiona. What's the matter?
F: I don't know. I'd like to meet someone nice … you know, a nice boyfriend. I feel that I've totally got over Daniel now … You know, we just grew apart really … and then we finally split up with each other at Thanksgiving. Ermm … well, it was in November. Oh, actually – I remember now, we split up on my birthday – on the eighteenth of November!
D: Oh dear …
F: I'm fine now, but … I haven't found anyone nice to go out with since then, and I don't know where to meet anyone. There's nobody at work, that's for sure! … How did you meet your husband?
D: Oh, I was lucky, I suppose … My parents helped me.
F: Your parents? Really?
D: Yes, it's the Indian tradition; you know, arranged marriage. It's different now, though. Nobody forces you to get married to someone you don't like. Your parents help you find someone, but you can say 'no' if you don't like him. You certainly don't have to put up with someone you don't like for the rest of your life!
F: So, what did you do?
D: Well, like a lot of young Asians from Britain, I went to India for a couple of months in the winter. The winter is 'wedding season' – lots of people get married at that time. Indian weddings last about a week, and they are a really good place to meet other young single people.
F: Really?
D: Yes, so my parents came with me and they arranged for me to go to lots of social events. I spent most of the time going to weddings and parties, and visiting lots of friends and family. I met loads of single men there and some of them took me out on dates.
F: So, you meet people properly and talk to them in a social situation?
D: Yes, it's all very normal really. The thing that's different is that it's all speeded up. I mean, most parents would like everything done in about one or maybe two months.
F: One or two months?
D: Yes, I arrived in India in December … at the beginning of December … and I got married at the end of January – on the twenty-eighth of January actually. When I came back to Britain, I was a married woman!
F: Really?! That is quick!
D: Yes. The whole process is really fast – meeting people, going out with different boyfriends and then getting married. Job done!
F: It's a bit like speed-dating!
D: Speed-dating? Have you ever done that?
F: Yes, I did it once. It was OK, but you only have three minutes to talk to each person and it feels very unreal. It really is like a job interview and you don't get enough time.
D: Mmm … The arranged marriage thing is different because although it's quick, you have time to get to know someone in a real social situation.
F: Yes, with speed dating you meet twenty people in one hour! And I was there for two hours!
D: Sounds quite fun though – did you meet anyone you liked?
F: Well, there was one who was quite nice …

Track 2.19

So, erm … Valentine's Day started hundreds of years ago. There was an emperor in Italy … and, well, … the emperor didn't want his soldiers to get married … because he wanted the soldiers only to fight. But, a priest called Valentine helped soldiers to get married secretly. The emperor was angry about that and … he killed Valentine … on the fourteenth of February. So, now people celebrate love and romance … on that day … in memory of Valentine.
So, Valentine's Day is on the fourteenth of February and people celebrate all over the world. Traditionally, people send cards to each other. And they give presents – flowers and chocolates, usually. And of course, it is traditional for a boyfriend to take his girlfriend out for a romantic dinner in a restaurant. It's also a popular date for getting married.
Some people think that Valentine's Day is too commercial. They think that people buy too many cards and presents … but I don't agree. I mean, people buy things of course, but I think it's really good to celebrate love and romance.

Track 2.20

eight thousand, eight hundred and eighty centimetres
three million, two hundred and thirty-five thousand, eight hundred and ninety-nine metres
six and a quarter kilograms
nine and three-quarter hours
seventy-five and a half minutes
nought point one five seconds
forty-four point nine kilometres per hour

Track 2.22

1

I really think that my life is too busy, I'm always on the go … and I don't sit down and rest very much… so, that's what my presentation is about today. I do everything in my life very quickly. Every day, I've got too much to do and I spend my time in a hurry. I'm always rushing around and I'm always late for everything because I don't have time to fit everything in. It makes me really stressed because I feel I can't do anything properly. My mobile phone rings all the time and it interrupts me when I'm working. It would be a good idea to turn it off, but I like people contacting me. I think that it might be something really important – but it isn't usually! The other reason why I'm always rushing around is that my work is very far away from where I live. That means I have to travel for about an hour each way … at least. I mean, usually I spend about two hours or maybe more travelling … and I'm usually late. I use the time when I'm sitting on the train and I send emails and go on Facebook and things

on my laptop. But it's very tiring because I don't get home until quite late. So, yes, all in all, my life is very fast and busy.

2

The topic of my presentation is 'The benefits of technology in my life'. The main points I will talk about are: firstly, how technology benefits my work life and secondly, how technology benefits my personal life. Let's begin with my work life. I am a doctor and there are huge benefits to my professional life from technology. In the past, I wrote all my patient's notes on paper and sometimes things got lost. It is much easier for me to look at my patients' notes now because they are all on computer. I can also look for symptoms, illnesses and medicines online if I need to. Also, my patients can book their appointments with a computer system which makes it quicker and more efficient. Now we're going to look at my personal life. My mobile phone is very important to me; I don't go anywhere without it. I have a very busy life so it is good to have a mobile. I use it on the train to keep in touch with friends or to make arrangements. My laptop is also very important; I can use it anywhere to shop online or book cinema tickets and other things. I'd like to finish by saying that some people think that there are disadvantages to modern technology, but I think that if you use it thoughtfully, there can be huge benefits.

Track 2.25

1

My worst interview experience was about three years ago. I had a group interview for a sales rep job with a big media company. There were about ten or twelve interviewees … and about three interviewers, I think. At first, I was quite confident … I mean, I had good experience and the right qualifications and I felt I was right for the job. But, erm … I don't know why… but when they asked me the first question … I began to feel very nervous. My throat went dry and I couldn't speak. Then, I started coughing and … erm, it was really awful because I just couldn't speak. One of the interviewers gave me a jug of water. I was really nervous and I couldn't really think clearly by that time … Anyway, he gave me the jug, and … slowly, I took it from him … you know, the jug was really heavy and my hands were shaking. I really didn't want to spill it. So, erm … I poured it very carefully … but all fifteen or so people in the room stopped and looked at me … and my hands were shaking so much that the water went everywhere … all over me … and all over the floor. It was terrible … I was really embarrassed! At that point, I grabbed my bag and left the room. I still go cold all over when I think about it.

2

Well, I think my worst experience was about two months ago. I had an interview for a good job as a marketing director. I really wanted the job. I remember that it was raining that day … so I decided to drive. But the traffic was really bad and when I arrived, I didn't have much time. I didn't want to be late for the interview. So, … I drove into the company car park and quickly parked my car in the nearest place. Well, it turned out that it was the Managing Director's parking place. That was bad … but it got worse because … erm … just as I was getting out of my car, the Managing Director himself arrived in his car – a great big BMW or something. Well, as you can imagine, he wasn't very happy at all. In fact, he shouted at me angrily … and told me to park somewhere else. By that time, I was really worried about

Audioscripts

being late ... so, I ignored him and ran off to the interview. I know I behaved really rudely ... but I was desperate to get to the interview. Well, it got worse ... because he was one of the interviewers and he was really angry about it all and he refused to give me an interview in the end.

3

My first interview after leaving college was for a job as a receptionist for a large company. I prepared myself for the interview really well. You know – I found out about the company and prepared my answers and everything – but, when it came to the actual interview, the whole thing was a bit strange really. Erm ... I arrived on time and I confidently walked into the interview room. But then I got a real shock ... because as soon as I stepped into the room, the interviewer threw a tennis ball at me! I quickly moved to one side and it didn't hit me. Well, unfortunately, I didn't get the job ... I was quite upset about that. They told me afterwards that the tennis ball was to test people's reactions. They wanted to see what people did with it. The person who caught the ball and threw it back got the job! The people who moved to one side or caught it and put it back on the desk, didn't! I wasn't very happy about the whole thing really ... I felt really cheated, to be honest. The whole interview went really badly for me – I just don't think they took it seriously at all and I didn't get a chance to talk about myself or show them what I could do.

Track 2.26

E = Employee B = Boss
E: Oh, hi, can I talk to you a minute, please?
B: I'm a bit busy right now, actually.
E: Well, it's really important because I want to take Friday off. Is that OK?
B: As I said, I'm rather busy. If you come back later, I'll be able to talk to you properly.
E: I need to know now, though. I mean, my brother has got tickets for something. And I need to let him know now.
B: Well, I really don't think you're listening to me. I'm busy now and if it's really urgent, I will talk to you after my meeting this afternoon.
E: But ... I need an answer now ...
B: No, actually, I've changed my mind. I don't like your attitude. The answer is 'no'. You can't take Friday off.

Track 2.27

E = Employee B = Boss
B: Good morning, James. Come in. Now, you wanted to talk to me about taking the day off on Friday?
E: Yes, that's right. The thing is ... if possible, I'd like to have the day off because my brother is over here from Australia for two weeks ... and he's got tickets for a show. It's really special and I'd really like to go.
B: I understand what you're saying, yes. I know that you don't see your brother much and this sounds like a chance you don't want to miss. Ermm ... what about the report? Will you able to finish it by the end of Thursday?
E: Yes ... no problem. Obviously, I'll make sure that the report is finished before I go and I'll work late this week if necessary.
B: Yes, I know that you work long hours and I'm very pleased with your work. Ermm ... I think it sounds fine. Go ahead and have a good day.
E: Thank you very much for your understanding.

B: Not at all. And I hope you have a good time.
E: Thank you.

Track 2.28

L = Lucy A = Andy
L: Andy, umm ... we need to talk ...
A: Yes?
L: Well, I was thinking ... I think we need to travel separately now ...
A: Oh! Really? I'm enjoying being with you so much ... I think that would be a real shame ...
L: Well ... yes ... I like travelling with you, too ... but ... I want to practise my Portuguese and when I'm with you, we just speak English all the time.
A: Oh ... I promise I'll speak Portuguese to you ...
L: No ... I don't think that would work, do you?
A: No ... you're probably right.

Track 2.29

L = Lucy M = Man
M: Hi, Lucy ... you're back! I wasn't sure when your flight was.
L: Yes ... well, I've just got back actually. I arrived last night, so I'm really tired... you know, I haven't got used to the time difference yet.
M: Did you have a good time?
L: Yes! It was great. I mean, there were some difficult moments ... but mostly it was really good. When I was in Rio, I met an old school friend of mine – Andy. I didn't know he was there, but we bumped into each other in an internet café.
M: That's amazing!
L: Mmm ... well, we travelled together for a bit, but actually he was really annoying, so in the end, I told him I wanted to travel on my own. It was a bit difficult, but after that I had a fantastic time.
M: Where did you go?
L: Well, after Rio, I went up the coast to Salvador – it was really lovely. Then I went further north to Fortaleza and to lots of amazing beaches near there. It's completely idyllic actually – miles and miles of beautiful beaches.
M: Wow! Were you on your own all the time?
L: No, actually – there were lots of other people travelling, so most of time I wasn't on my own at all. In fact, I met a really nice woman called Emily – she was Australian. We got on really well and travelled together for the rest of my time in Brazil.
M: That's great!
L: Yes, it was very good.
M: Have you got any photos yet?
L: Well, yes, I've put some up on Facebook already ... and I'm going to put some more up today.

Track 2.31

P = Presenter G = Guest
P: Hello and welcome to this week's edition of *Travellers' Tales*. Later in the programme, we're talking to a group of young people who have just finished a sponsored cycle ride across Europe. But, before that, we're going to start with today's look at 'My travel inspiration' with our special guest, TV reporter, Ben Gardner. Hello, Ben.
G: Hello.
P: So, your travel inspiration ... is it a book, or a film or a piece of music, Ben? Tell us about something inspiring ... which has made you want to travel.

G: Yes, well, 'My travel inspiration' is a film – *The Motorcycle Diaries*. It's set in South America and it's about the early life of Che Guevara when he was a young man.
P: Mmm ... *The Motorcycle Diaries* ... Yes, so, who plays Che Guevara?
G: Well, Guevara is played by Gael García Bernal – he's very good. I really think he is the perfect choice for this role actually.
P: Had he starred in any other films, before he made this one?
G: Yes, yeah, a few ... but this was a turning point in his career I think ...
P: And the film is set in the 1950s, isn't it?
G: Yes, 1952, in fact. Before Che Guevara arrived in Cuba and got into politics, he had lived in Argentina with his family. He and a friend, Alberto, decided they wanted to travel and see South America.
P: Mmm ...
G: Anyway, at the beginning of the film, we see them preparing for their trip in Buenos Aires. They buy an old motorbike ... and the rest of the film then follows them on their amazing 8-month-long trip through Argentina, Chile, Peru, Columbia and Venezuela ... Basically, it's about two young men seeing a bit more of the world and learning about life. They have some really exciting adventures. There are some dangerous moments, too ... you know, on the motorbike!
P: So, what was most inspiring for you about this film?
G: Well, three things I think. Firstly, I was inspired by the two main characters – they are very believable. García Bernal is brilliant as Guevara, and Rodrigo de la Serna, as his friend Alberto, is also excellent. Anyway, as the film goes on, I was fascinated to see how their personalities grow and change. All their adventures were really inspiring ... and it's great how they learned so much from all the people they met along the way. At the beginning of the trip, they were young men – just interested in having fun – and they had become much more grown up ... and mature, by the time they reached the end.
P: Mmm ...
G: There's a particular scene when they were in a sort of hospital in a poor part of the countryside in Peru ... It was a depressing place and very sad, but Guevara got very close to the people in the hospital. It was inspiring to see that.
P: And the second thing ...?
G: The South American people that these young men met on their travels ... Almost all the people they met were kind and helpful – they went out of their way to help Guevara and Alberto, even though they didn't have much themselves. The supporting cast is excellent at showing that aspect. And the South American people also like a good party ... so they have a lot of fun!
P: Yes, I'm sure! And thirdly?
G: Well, ... the scenery. In fact, I think I'd say that the scenery of South America is possibly the main star of the film!
P: Really?
G: Well, yes. Before I saw this film, I hadn't thought about visiting South America ... but it inspired me to go there almost immediately. I was surprised by the incredible beauty of this continent. I was really amazed by the huge diversity there. I followed the route of the film – more or less. I mean, first, I started in the

southern parts of Argentina and Chile where it's really cold. And then, I went up to the hotter desert parts of Chile. Then, I travelled further north into Peru – Machu Picchu in Peru was really incredible. Then, finally, I got to the beautiful jungle areas of Colombia and Venezuela.

P: Well, you've certainly inspired me – and I hope our listeners – to want to go to South America. It sounds fantastic …

G: Yes, … well, I'm sure you won't be disappointed.

P: OK … so Ben, I hope you'll stay with us for the rest of the programme and take some calls from listeners later.

Track 2.33

M = Man

M: Well … something really frightening happened to me the other day. I had a really unusual – and frightening journey – going from London to Paris. I'd got a really good last-minute deal and I was going for the weekend with my wife. Anyway, it started off badly when our flight was suddenly cancelled and so obviously we were quite annoyed about that. It was really annoying because we were only going for a short time. But then they said there was another flight we could go on … which was only twenty minutes after our cancelled flight. So, we all got on the flight and nothing happened really until we got to Paris. And then, just as we were coming in to land, … it's hard to believe, but suddenly we started climbing again. The wheels were almost touching the ground I think … and the engines came on very, very … very, very loud and we started climbing violently. There was no announcement from the captain. And then the engines went quiet again and then we climbed again violently and then we went sideways and then we went another way and then we climbed again and … believe it or not, this went on for about five minutes – maybe longer. Actually, it felt like about half an hour, but it was probably about five minutes. After a while, the plane started flying normally again and then the captain made an announcement and apologised. It's incredible, I know, but a lorry had been on the runway. He said that a lorry had been in the middle of the runway … and he had had to take off again in order to avoid it. Well, what a journey! Thankfully, we had a really good weekend in Paris, and the flight back was fine!

Track 2.34

1

E = Emma M = Man

M: So, Emma, who was the person who most influenced you when you were growing up? I mean, like a role model … or something?

E: Well erm my parents both worked a lot when I was young, erm especially my dad, and well, he worked abroad a lot of the time so … I would see him three times a year or something. He used to have a job which took him to different countries all the time – mostly Japan and China – so I only saw him in the school holidays really. I lived with my mum, but I was always really close to my grandmother, too. I got on really well with my mum, but I think the person who most influenced me was my grandmother.

M: Mmm … Did you see her a lot?

E: Yes. My mum and my grandmother brought me up really. I mean, she didn't

live with us, but she would look after me a lot when my mum was working. I think I would see her almost every day. Erm I really looked up to my grandmother. She's she was a wonderful person. I mean, she was incredibly kind and generous. And she would always spend time with me. You know, she always seemed interested in what I had to say.

2

G = George W = Woman

W: George, who do you think was the most influential person in your life when you were a child?

G: Erm well, I was really into ice skating – particularly ice hockey – when I was young. I loved playing ice hockey … I used to be really good! I picked it up really quickly and … and did it all the time, you know. I started playing when I was about five and … well, went on until … eighteen, or something – when I left school. And my coach was an amazing man called Frank. He was a really good trainer. He, he taught me so much about the sport and was very good at motivating me and keeping me focused. He was a really inspiring person. He was a really good mentor … and role model … in many ways.

W: How often did you see him?

G: Well, I would see him all the time! … You know, … I used to wear my skates more than my shoes probably! I mean I really played a lot. I would play six or seven times a week and he was always there. It wasn't just the training though. I think I really looked up to him. When you asked him something, he wouldn't say much, you know, but what he did say always seemed to be the right thing to say. I remember thinking … I want to be like him!

Track 2.35

P = Presenter W = Woman

P: Today, we're talking about advertising. The aim of any company is to sell; and to continue to sell, more than other companies. And to keep ahead of the competition, companies need to advertise their product better and better in order to influence potential customers. Top advertising executive, Sarah Delaney, is with us today to talk about new developments in advertising and the amazing technological developments which make them possible. Good morning, Sarah.

W: Hello.

P: So … , before we talk about these new developments, Sarah, can you tell us … what kinds of adverts have the most influence on people?

W: Well … , that's an interesting question. Erm, I think that all advertising has some kind of influence on people. I mean, we may think, perhaps, that we make free choices about which products to buy … but actually, the adverts that you've seen will certainly influence what you think about different products … even though you may not think about that consciously.

P: Yes, adverts put ideas in your head, even if you don't want them there! So … , what do you think makes an advert effective? What are the most effective types of adverts?

W: Erm, … the most effective types of adverts … well, I think it depends really. Some people respond to humour; some people like an advert to have a lot of information; other people are very influenced by their favourite celebrity in an advert. I think, in the end, adverts are effective because

they are very clearly aimed at certain groups of people … and a lot of research goes into which group of people your advert is aimed at.

P: And it's not just who the adverts are aimed at – there is also a lot of research into how and where to advertise, isn't there?

W: Yes, and with new technological developments, things are changing all the time.

P: So…, what's new in the advertising world, then?

W: Well …, there's one new innovation which means that television viewers may soon see adverts during their favourite documentary or drama series.

P: Oh, really?

W: Yes. Some developers for television companies are planning pop-up advertisements. That means logos or messages can be flashed up on the screen during a programme so the company doesn't have to wait until the commercial break to advertise. Basically, erm … the new technology is used to find a blank space on the screen to put the logo on – like some blue sky or a blank wall – you know, not covering someone's face in your favourite soap opera.

P: Even on a blank space, it sounds annoying!

W: Well, yes – some people would say very annoying! Some people are worried that these pop-up adverts will destroy their enjoyment of a programme. The developers are convinced, however, that consumers will like them.

P: I'm not sure they're right about that! …

W: Well… there are other developers who agree with you. In Japan, they are developing an approach which is very different… almost the opposite really.

P: Mmm…?

W: Yes … Nintendo has created a new internet video site for games consoles, and it uses a new system for advertising. The company did some research about the way customers are influenced by adverts and they decided they didn't want to force viewers to watch adverts. With the new system, no adverts are shown on the screen at all. Consumers choose to watch adverts only if they want to.

P: Ah! That sounds better!

W: Mmm … and if they do choose one, they get a very informative kind of advert … with more detailed and interesting information about the product. And as well as the advert itself, consumers can do other useful things, like receive vouchers to get discounts or even order some free samples of the product. The company hopes that adverts will change from something we avoid watching, to something we want to watch. They may even become one of the most popular things on TV, you never know; … these entertaining adverts may actually become a form of entertainment in themselves, in fact.

P: Yes – that would really turn things around, wouldn't it? Adverts either spoil your favourite show or they become your favourite show!

W: That's right! But you know, in whichever way companies choose to get their message across, one thing is for sure: advertising, in some form, is here to stay …

Audioscripts

Track 2.37

1

W1 = Woman W2 = Woman 2 A = Announcer

W1: Hey Lisa ... Are you coming out with us tonight?

W2: No, I can't. My hair looks terrible!

A: Are you worried about your hair? Is your hair boring and lifeless? Does it stop you going out? You need ShinePower from Studio-X. With ShinePower, even the most boring hair suddenly comes to life. ShinePower will make your hair shine like never before. After one wash with ShinePower from Studio-X, your hair will look amazing!

W1: Hey Lisa ... Are you coming out with us tonight?

W2: Of course I am.

W1: Hey, your hair looks amazing!

A: ShinePower from Studio-X. Your hair will look amazing!

2

The new G5 by Kurama is the car you've wanted all your life ... Designed by an expert car designer ... Engineered by an expert car engineer ... Made by an expert car maker ... Now, ... driven by an expert driver. You. The new G5 by Kurama: a car by experts – for experts.

Track 2.38

W = Woman M = Man

W: OK ... we're going to play the 'Yes-No' game. Do you know how to play?

M: No, I've never played that. How do you play?

W: Well, basically, I ask you questions and you must not answer with either 'Yes' or 'No'.

M: What can I say, then?

W: You can say anything else ... like ... 'I'm not sure', or 'Maybe', or 'I'll think about it' or 'Definitely'. You know, anything else, but not 'Yes' or 'No'.

M: OK. That sounds easy!

W: OK. Let's start. Ready?

M: Y ... umm ... I am!

W: OK. Have you seen any good films recently?

M: I have.

W: Have you ever seen a film that changed your life?

M: Maybe.

W: Did you say 'Maybe'?

M: Err ... I'm not sure.

W: What about 'Yes Man'? Have you seen that?

M: I have.

W: You have? Really?

M: Yes! Ohhhh! You tricked me ...

W: That's the idea!

M: OK ... now I'll ask you. Ready?

W: Definitely.

M: Right. Are you going to go on holiday this summer?

W: I've told you that.

M: Are you going to the seaside?

W: Sure.

M: Are you looking forward to it?

W: I certainly am.

M: Oh. What can I ask you? Do you believe in fate?

W: Fate?

M: Yes, do you believe in fate? You know, that our lives are planned already somehow, and you can't change them?

W: Not at all. I believe that you can change a lot about your life.

M: So you don't believe in fate?

W: No, I don't!

M: Got you! You said 'No'.

Track 2.39

P = Presenter M = Michael Dennis
C = Caroline Clarke PA = Parent H = Holly

P: A quick summary, now, of the main *Money in Education* stories this week ... Firstly, as any parent knows, the cost of education can be huge, especially as children get older and want to go to university. You will be faced with huge fees – and the problem of how to pay for them. Earlier this week, I spoke to financial adviser, Michael Dennis, and he told me about this month's figures and the almost unbelievable cost of going to university these days.

M: University has always been expensive and there are schemes in which you can get a grant to help pay the fees, or for the top students, you can sometimes get a scholarship. But these aren't always available, and in most cases, when you're at university, you may need to get a loan from the bank to pay for everything. Of course, you're not earning money when you're studying, so you can't even begin to pay the loan back until you leave university and, hopefully, get a job. It's not much fun starting your working life in debt ... and owing the bank a lot of money. Official figures out this month show that the average student debt is around fifteen thousand pounds. For medical students, the figure rises to around twenty-five thousand pounds.

P: Twenty-five thousand pounds ... that's a lot of money. And that could take at least twelve years to pay back – if you manage to get a well-paid job ... That was financial adviser, Michael Dennis. The news is not all bad for students, however. Some schools have taken part in reward schemes in which they actually pay their students. St. Luke's School in Bristol has given eleven thousand pounds to its A-level students for getting good exam results. Before their exams, the school gave each student target grades to try and achieve. Now the results have arrived, St. Luke's sixth form college has given five hundred pounds to every student who got into university and students get prizes of twenty pounds for achieving each target grade. Caroline Clarke, Head of Sixth-form Education, had to say ...

C: The results this year show the success of the scheme. Unlike many schemes, this one rewards every student for doing well, not just the best students in the year.

P: I asked various people what they thought of the scheme. Yesterday, I spoke to a parent of a student at the school and asked her how she felt about the reward scheme.

PA: Well ... I'm not sure really. I don't think they should pay students ... I mean, young people should work hard for exams because they want to do well ... not because they'll earn some money! I think people think about money too much.

P: Later, I spoke to Mike Bell, Head Teacher at St. Luke's. He told me that more students had got places at university this year than ever before. He also said the students were working much harder than before and his school would continue with the scheme next year. Holly, a student at St. Luke's, said she was really pleased that her school had taken part in the scheme. She told me it was a great idea ... and that it had made her work much harder. She also said that she was really excited because she had earned over five hundred pounds. When I asked what she was going to do with the money,

she told me she was going to buy a new laptop computer, which now she could afford to buy.

H: Yeah, with the five hundred pounds, I can afford a new computer ... which is great news ... as I really need one for my studies. At my school, most of us thought the reward scheme was really good. Some of us weren't sure at first, but in the end, certainly we all agreed that the scheme had made us work harder.

P: Finally, we heard this week about another reward scheme ... this time in the US. With holidays coming up soon, one school in Florida has set up a homework scheme using the internet. Students who do more than twelve hours of practice exercises on the specially-designed internet site during the school holidays, will get prizes: children aged six to ten get a bicycle, those aged eleven to fourteen get a hundred dollars and those aged fifteen to eighteen get MP3 players. Some people feel that reward schemes like this are controversial but with prizes like those, I'm sure the students will study as hard as they can! ... Well, that's it for today. I hope you can tune in for next week's *Money in Education* summary. And now ... over to Fiona in the weather studio ...

Track 2.40

W1 = Woman W2 = Woman 2

W1: So, let's find four things we've got in common ... erm ... what about going shopping? Do you like going shopping?

W2: Ermm ... well, I'm not very keen on shopping in general, but ... I like clothes shopping.

W1: Yes, me too. I really like looking for interesting clothes ... you know, something a bit unusual ...

W2: Mmmm ... I like looking for interesting, cheap clothes. Lots of clothes are so expensive, but if you look hard enough, you can usually find some bargains.

W1: Yes, it's always good to find bargains! OK ... well, I think that's two things we've got in common: We both like shopping ... clothes shopping, I mean. And both of us like looking for bargains.

W2: How do you usually pay for things when you go shopping? I pay in cash. Actually, I always pay in cash because I haven't got a credit card or anything.

W1: Yes, that's the same for me. I haven't got a credit card either.

W2: OK ... So, neither of us has got a credit card – that's number three ... ermm ...

W1: And ... number four is ... we both pay in cash when we go shopping. Yeah ... that's four things we've got in common.

Track 2.41

We asked fifty students various questions about their attitudes to money and the results are as follows:
Firstly, forty percent of people said they would basically describe themselves as a 'saver'. Forty-five percent said they were a 'spender' and fifteen percent weren't sure or said they were a bit of both.
For the second question, we asked about lending and borrowing money. Two-thirds of people said they would lend fifty pounds to a friend. However, the majority of those people said they would be worried about doing so, in case it spoilt their friendship.
The third question was about credit cards. Eight out of ten people said they used a credit card regularly. And only a minority of those people paid off their bill completely at the end of each month.
Question four was about shopping habits ...